On the Edge of the Global Economy

On the Edge of the Global Economy

Edited by

Jacques Poot

Professor and Director, Population Studies Centre, University of Waikato, New Zealand

Edward Elgar
Cheltenham, UK • Northampton, MA, USA

Published by
Edward Elgar Publishing Limited
Glensanda House
Montpellier Parade
Cheltenham
Glos GL50 1UA
UK

Edward Elgar Publishing, Inc.
136 West Street
Suite 202
Northampton
Massachusetts 01060
USA

A catalogue record for this book
is available from the British Library

ISBN 1 84376 185 8

Printed and bound in Great Britain by MPG Books Ltd, Bodmin, Cornwall

Contents

PART A: LOCATION, INFORMATION AND TRANSACTIONS

PART B: CONNECTIVITY AND SPATIAL INTERACTION

Figures

Tables

Contributors

Harvey W. Armstrong
Department of Geography, University of Sheffield
Winter Street, Sheffield S10 2TN, United Kingdom
h.armstrong@sheffield.ac.uk

Geoffrey Bertram
School of Economics and Finance, Victoria University of Wellington
P.O. Box 600, Wellington, New Zealand
geoff.bertram@vuw.ac.nz

Nils Bjorksten
Economics Department, Reserve Bank of New Zealand
P.O. Box 2498, Wellington, New Zealand
bjorkstenn@rbnz.govt.nz

Henri L.F. de Groot
Department of Spatial Economics, Free University Amsterdam
De Boelelaan 1105, 1081 HV Amsterdam, The Netherlands
hgroot@feweb.vu.nl

Tim Hazledine
Department of Economics, University of Auckland
Private Bag 92019, Auckland, New Zealand
t.hazledine@auckland.ac.nz

Bronwyn Howell
New Zealand Institute for the Study of Competition and Regulation
Victoria University of Wellington
P.O. Box 600, Wellington, New Zealand
bronwyn.howell@vuw.ac.nz

Lee Huskey
Department of Economics, University of Alaska at Anchorage
3211 Providence Drive, Anchorage, Ak. 99508, USA
aflh@uaa.alaska.edu

Özer Karagedikli
Economics Department, Reserve Bank of New Zealand
P.O. Box 2498, Wellington, New Zealand
karagediklio@rbnz.govt.nz

Rajendra Kulkarni
School of Public Policy, George Mason University
4400 University Drive, Fairfax, VA 22030, USA
rkulkarn@gmu.edu

Gert-Jan M. Linders
Department of Spatial Economics, Free University Amsterdam
De Boelelaan 1105, 1081 HV Amsterdam, The Netherlands
glinders@feweb.vu.nl

Sara Lipanovic
Ministry of Economic Development
P.O. Box 1473, Wellington, New Zealand
sara.lipanovic@med.govt.nz

Lisa Marriott
c/- New Zealand Institute for the Study of Competition and Regulation
Victoria University of Wellington
P.O. Box 600, Wellington, New Zealand
lisa.marriott@xtra.co.nz

Philip McCann
Department of Economics, University of Reading
Reading RG6 6AW, United Kingdom
p.mccann@reading.ac.uk

Laura Meriluoto
Department of Economics, University of Canterbury
Private Bag 4800, Christchurch, New Zealand
laura.meriluoto@canterbury.ac.nz

Peter Nijkamp
Department of Spatial Economics, Free University Amsterdam
De Boelelaan 1105, 1081 HV Amsterdam, The Netherlands
pnijkamp@feweb.vu.nl

Jacques Poot
Population Studies Centre, University of Waikato
Private Bag 3105, Hamilton, New Zealand
jpoot@waikato.ac.nz

Robert Read
Department of Economics, University of Lancaster
Lancaster, LA1 4YW, United Kingdom
r.read@lancaster.ac.uk

Laurie Schintler
School of Public Policy, George Mason University
4400 University Drive, Fairfax, VA 22030, USA
lschintl@osf1.gmu.edu

Geoff Simmons
UK Home Office
126 Craven Road, Rugby, Warwickshire CV21 3JZ, United Kingdom
geoff.simmons@nzoomail.com

Christie Smith
Economics Department, Reserve Bank of New Zealand
150 Terrace Road
R.D. 1, Waikanae, New Zealand
smithc@rbnz.govt.nz

Brendan Walsh
Department of Economics, University College, Dublin
Dublin 4, Ireland
brendan.m.walsh@ucd.ie

Upali Wickramasinghe
Department of Economics, University of Jayewardenepura
11/2 Wijerama Lane, Sri Dewananda Road,
Nawinna, Maharagama, Sri Lanka
upaliw@sjp.ac.lk

Preface

The causes and consequences of globalisation have been in recent years the focus of a huge volume of literature. For example, the electronic database *EconLit* recorded at the end of 2003 more than two hundred books with globalisation (or globalization) in the title. Yet, surprisingly, none of these books are specifically concerned with the prospects of small, or island, nations at relatively remote locations. This book aims to fill that gap.

Global trends offer both exciting opportunities and major challenges for small economies in rather distant corners of the globe. Exciting, because the decline in the costs of transportation and communication have made distant locations more accessible and information about such places (and, vice versa, the diffusion of knowledge to such places) merely a mouse-click away. On the other hand, agglomeration forces have also strengthened and have led to increased spatial inequality and divergence that may pose major challenges for small peripheral states to attract footloose firms and mobile workers.

Most of the chapters originated, after a review process, from a selection of papers presented at a symposium entitled 'Off the Map in the Global Economy?' that was held at Victoria University of Wellington in New Zealand on 20–21 November 2001.

The financial sponsorship of the symposium by the New Zealand Treasury and the School of Economics and Finance at Victoria University is gratefully acknowledged. I would also like to thank particularly Lesley Haines, Bob Buckle and Geoff Lewis for their enthusiasm and support in co-organising the symposium and Suzanne Freear for managing the conference logistics.

The University of Tsukuba in Japan kindly provided hospitality for a period of research and study leave during which much of the book took shape. The editing was done back at Victoria University of Wellington, my home institution until a recent move to the University of Waikato. I would like to thank my Victoria University colleagues for their friendship and support over many years.

At the University of Waikato, Katie McLean patiently prepared the final camera ready copy.

Finally, I am grateful to all chapter contributors for their insights, energy and cooperation, without which this book could not have been written.

JACQUES POOT
Editor

PART A

Location, Information and Transactions

1. Peripherality in the Global Economy

Jacques Poot

1.1 INTRODUCTION

It is perhaps a somewhat tired cliché to refer to our world as a 'global village' but there is no doubt that modern information and communication technology (ICT) has created a perception of greater closeness between individuals and nations that are physically far apart. The Internet, e-mail, wireless communication, and so on, have had a profound impact on the nature and cost of information exchange and communication. Deregulation, increased competition and technological changes have reduced the cost of transportation of information, goods and people. Trade barriers have been reduced. The reduction in the cost of bridging locations that are far apart has contributed to the greater integration among countries in the world economy, in terms of information exchange, technology diffusion, trade, foreign direct investment (FDI), finance, migration, travel, and so on. While there are large long-run gains from this process of globalisation, there are also costs. These have led to growing resistance to the globalisation phenomenon in some quarters, particularly among those who fear irreversible environmental damage, growing inequality across people and space in terms of income, wealth and power, and the increasing pervasiveness of global mass culture shaped by American and multinational corporations (e.g., Streeten, 2001).

This book is concerned with just one of these issues, namely the impact of globalisation on the uneven distribution of economic activity across the world and the role of economic geography in explaining differences in the standard of living across countries and regions. Specifically, the focus of the book is on small economies at relatively remote locations. Such economies can be sovereign nations or sub-national regions.

The issue that the book endeavours to address is the changing economic prospects for small and distant economies in the current 'age of

3

globalisation' (see also Kohno et al., 2000). Such countries or regions on the 'edge' of the global economy may suffer from 'peripherality': economic disadvantage due to a remote location and a relatively small scale and density of economic activity. The impact of globalisation may be greater on small economies than large ones (Van Den Bulcke and Verbeke, 2001). Does the reduction in communication and transportation costs, which – as some commentators have argued – have led to a 'death of distance' (Cairncross, 2001), improve the prospects of peripheral economies or are, instead, the agglomeration advantages of core economies strengthened by globalisation?

An interesting case, the focus of several chapters of this book, is that of New Zealand. Using a 'gravity model'-related index based on the size of countries measured by Gross Domestic Product (GDP), and the distance between the capital cities of these countries, Evans and Hughes (2003) calculated that New Zealand is the most remote of the Organisation for Economic Cooperation and Development (OECD) countries.[1] Yet from the 1870s until the 1950s this nation had one of the highest standards of living in the world (e.g., Gould, 1982).[2] However, following a number of detrimental internal and external influences, such as 'motherland' Britain's entry into the European Union (EU), unfavourable changes in the terms of trade, and growing protection and regulation of the domestic economy, the standard of living had declined to about three-quarters of the OECD average by the early 1980s. To counteract this trend, a far-reaching programme of economic liberalisation and reform commenced in 1984. Although significant adjustment costs led to a further decline in economic well being for some time thereafter, by 1996 the conclusion was reached that the reforms had been largely successful and that the country had moved on to a higher sustainable growth path (Evans et al., 1996). Subsequent economic growth has indeed been quite reasonable, but pales in comparison with, for example, the Irish economic boom. By 2001, progress in catching up with the OECD average had only been modest. At that time, New Zealand's real GDP per capita was in purchasing power parity terms about 87 percent of the OECD average, about the same as in Spain and about 70 percent of GDP per capita in Ireland (OECD, 2003).

Is peripherality an important reason for New Zealand's slow progress in catching up? In addition to New Zealand being the most remote developed country in the world, it may also have other disadvantages of physical geography, such as a long and narrow shape of the landmass and a predominance of mountainous regions.[3] These geographical features, referred to as 'first nature' by Krugman (1993), may discourage an inflow of capital and labour to this nation on the edge of the world and preclude the greater productivity resulting from a concentration of economic activity. But even without a locational disadvantage, New Zealand's small population (just over 4 million) and low population density (14 persons per km^2) also reduce the potential for agglomeration economies. Krugman refers to such scale and density features as 'second nature'.

The absence of agglomeration economies due to first and second nature disadvantages is by no means a problem unique to New Zealand. There are three geographical features that together can generate the type of economic disadvantage that will be referred to as 'peripherality'. First of these is low connectivity; that is, a large average distance between the peripheral economy and the core agglomerations. A second feature is a small population, which makes it difficult to reap economies of scale and scope in the domestic market. The third feature is a low population density measured across the entire country or region.[4]

Taking these three features together, countries such as Iceland, Finland and Eastern European countries – and to a lesser extent Ireland – can be considered as peripheral within Europe. Thus, an interesting question is: do the recent economic successes of particularly Finland and Ireland provide insight into economic strategies that can help to overcome peripherality? This question is addressed in Chapters 11 and 13 respectively.

There is of course a big difference between these European countries and the case of New Zealand. For example, while the population size and density of New Zealand and Finland are quite similar (population: 4 million and 5 million, density: 14 and 15 persons per km^2 respectively), New Zealand is far more distant from potential markets. The area within a circle with a radius of 2200 km drawn around Finland's capital Helsinki captures a population of more than 300 million people. The same circle drawn around New Zealand's capital Wellington captures only 4 million people, as even the nearest neighbours – on the Australian east coast seaboard – are still a little further away (Bushnell and Choy, 2001, p.18). The comparison is shown in Figure 1.1.[5]

Outside Europe, peripheral countries include Chile and Argentina in South America, middle-American countries, central Asian countries and many small African countries. Many relatively remote small economies are island economies. For example, islands account for two-thirds of a database of small states and island states discussed in Chapter 10. Many of these are in the Pacific Ocean (considered in Chapter 6). Even Australia, given the distance from its eastern seaboard cities to large metropolitan areas in North America and Asia, and a total population of less than 20 million, is in some sense also a small peripheral economy.

A core–periphery distinction can of course also be made with respect to regions within most countries. Agglomeration is a process that takes place at different levels: international, sub-national and even within metropolitan areas. As Fujita and Thisse (2002, p.2) note, there is no single theory to explain agglomeration at all spatial levels. In this book, the focus will be on both remote nations and remote sub-national regions, such as Alaska (referred to in Chapter 11), eastern Russia, and northern and western parts of Brazil, and so on.

The economies of small peripheral countries and regions tend to be quite vulnerable. Many of these are small states and micro-states with populations of 1.5 million or less and these can be particularly vulnerable (e.g., Peretz 2001; see also Chapter 10 of this book). Such economies are often very open and therefore subject to external trade shocks. The vulnerability is increased due to a lack of diversification in economic structure. This means that both terms of trade shocks and natural disasters in economies specialising in primary sector activity increase economic volatility. Such volatility can discourage investment and economic growth.

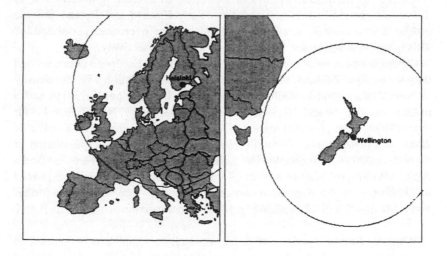

Figure 1.1 The remoteness of Finland and New Zealand compared

The problems and prospects of small open economies at remote locations are the central focus of this book. The book consists of three parts. Part A, including this chapter, provides a broad overview of the reasons why geography matters in the spatial configuration of economic activity; and why geography may matter even more in the ICT-driven and services-oriented 'New Economy' than in the Fordist industrial economy of the past (see also Higano et al., 2002). Part B of the book is concerned with the measurement of spatial interaction between nations, and the economic, social, political and cultural barriers to interaction. Having identified such barriers and their implications for economic performance, Part C turns to the various strategies that can be adopted to overcome peripherality. Throughout the book, the emphasis is on surveying important issues facing small remote economies and the related empirical evidence. No formal analytical models are presented here, but a wide range of models have been developed in recent years that are referred to as the 'New Economic Geography', to which Krugman's (1991) core–periphery model was the seminal contribution. For collections of detailed theoretical models of the spatial economy, agglomeration and policy, the reader is referred to Fujita et al. (1999), Neary (2001), Fujita and Thisse (2002) and Baldwin et al. (2003).

Each part of the book is introduced in the next three sections of this chapter. Some broad conclusions are drawn in Section 1.5.

1.2 LOCATION, INFORMATION AND TRANSACTIONS

Economic activity is not evenly distributed around the world. A small number of countries (e.g., the G7 countries) generate much of the world's output. Within countries, one or a few metropolitan areas represent most of the countries' output, employment and consumption. Both history and geography play important roles in generating the current distribution of economic activity. Human settlement has been determined by accessibility, climate, topology and fertility of the land, and strategic considerations. Borders between nations resulted from natural features, ethnic divisions, wars, political strategies, and so on. Borders themselves have acted as barriers to economic activity and can marginalise nearby regions on either side (e.g., van der Velde and van Houtum, 2000).

Nonetheless, agglomeration of economic activity would even emerge in a featureless landscape. The reason for this is that the spatial distribution of economic activities is the outcome of a process involving two opposing forces: agglomeration forces and dispersion forces. Agglomeration forces are economic advantages reaped from the spatial concentration of economic activity due to knowledge and information spillovers, specialisation in production, labour market economies, the viability of a greater variety in intermediate and final output, and economies of scope and scale. Dispersion forces are due to the cost of bridging distances in order to acquire inputs, deliver outputs, exchange information and coordinate economic activity. Dispersion can also be due to negative spillover effects resulting from population concentration, such as congestion and pollution. The balance of the opposing agglomeration and dispersion forces determines the theoretical distribution of economic activity on a featureless plane. This outcome is then modified in reality by the actual geographical features (referred to as 'first nature' in the previous section) and social, institutional and political influences (see also Landes, 1998).

An interesting question is then the extent to which geography matters. Gallup et al. (1999) study how income levels, income growth and population density of countries around the world are related to geographical features. They find, by means of regression models with data from all countries with more than 1 million inhabitants, that economic growth is explained better when the country's location, the spatial distribution of population and the prevalence of malaria are taken into account. Of these three factors, only location is truly exogenous but distances to the coast and waterways, and measures of topology, soil quality, the availability of water and climate – all exogenous aspects of geography – are important in explaining the cross-country variation in population density.

The importance of geographical features in the spatial variation of economic activity is an interesting but complex issue. Using US state-level data, Ellison and Glaeser (1999) find that 'at least half of the observed geographic concentration is due to natural advantages'. Roos (2002) argues that natural advantages are often defined too broadly in this context. For example, capital and labour endowments are not a natural advantage but the result of factor flows of the past, which may have responded to agglomeration advantages. Even so, Roos (2002) estimates that one-third of agglomeration in Germany can be attributed to geography. At the international level, this type of quantification is less fruitful due to the heterogeneity of any sample of countries in terms of other factors (historical, cultural, institutional) that could also explain agglomeration. Still, good institutions that are conducive to growth (such as political stability, well-defined property rights, legal systems, etc.) could themselves be a function of geography. Acemoglu et al. (2001) argue that good geography (e.g., a mild climate, low mortality) led during colonial times to colonists implanting good institutions, while bad geography (in parts of sub-Saharan Africa, Latin America and Asia) discouraged permanent settlement and the adoption of 'Western' institutions.

Although it may not be very meaningful, or easy, to estimate the contribution of geographical factors to the variation in economic performance across countries, the question of whether the modern ICT revolution has reduced the role of geographical factors is a valid and important one. Chapters 2 and 3 of this book provide a number of theoretical arguments as to why location and distance continue to matter in this respect.

Gert-Jan Linders, Henri de Groot and Peter Nijkamp provide in Chapter 2 a broad survey of the changing role of locality in the new global configuration of economic activity that is commonly referred to as the New Economy. This term was introduced during the buoyant 1990s to convey the message that the ICT revolution had fundamentally changed organisation of economic activity and generated continuing productivity gains. It has now become clear that a conventional speculative boom instead drove much of what was associated with the New Economy. There is nonetheless no doubt that there have been in recent years major changes in industrial organisation, which have important implications for countries, regions and policy (e.g., Higano et al., 2002).

Depending on which aspects of the ICT-driven economic changes are emphasised, the new global economic configuration is variously referred to as the 'information age', the 'global network society', the 'e-society', the 'internet economy', the 'knowledge economy', and so on. Linders et al. point to an interesting paradox about the changes that are taking place: transaction costs (which include trading and coordination costs) are declining in many cases, but the transactions themselves are becoming more complex. This is due to a trend towards highly customised goods and services on the output side and a growth of outsourcing, and less hierarchical organisational structures, on the input side. New theoretical paradigms have also emerged, such as the 'new growth theories' (e.g., Aghion and Howitt, 1998) and the (related) 'new trade theories' (Krugman, 1990). The importance of the 'right' policies has come to the forefront in these theories (as already pointed out by Lucas (1988) in an influential early contribution to the endogenous growth literature).

How does location matter in this context? Linders et al. point out that routine tasks have become footloose. With the right cost advance (e.g., cheap labour and infrastructure), this type of production activity can move to peripheral areas when transaction costs decline. For example, American companies outsource routine processing of financial transactions to companies in Ireland or India. Call centres for marketing and customer support can also be located in the periphery. However, 'know-how' plays a central role in the services-driven economy and the limits to codification of knowledge imply that not all production activity can become footloose (Nonaka and Takeuchi, 1995).

Innovation and managerial activity benefit from agglomeration because they rely on tacit knowledge that is only transferable through face-to-face contact. Trust between economic agents is also easier to develop by means of face-to-face contact. Storper and Venables (2002) argue that face-to-face contact, abbreviated to F2F in the current Internet jargon, has many advantages. First, it is an efficient form of communication that overcomes certain moral hazard and confidence problems. Second, it may raise effort levels. Third, it allows efficient matching of business partners.

Given such advantages, Linders et al. conclude that globalisation and localisation occur simultaneously. Having the right human capital, infrastructure and institutional environment are necessary but not sufficient conditions for e-commerce to take off, as distance from the major markets continues to matter.

Philip McCann reinforces these points in Chapter 3. McCann emphasises that the declining costs of transportation and communication impact differentially on the various sectors. Given the growing complexity of transactions, the customisation of output and the increased opportunity cost of time, distance matters more in some sectors and less in others. The shipment costs of goods are declining, but given that these account for only a small percentage of total unit cost, this is likely to have little effect on firms' location decisions. More important are the growing inventory costs and the resulting shift to just-in-time (JIT) delivery, which leads to greater coordination costs and trip frequencies. McCann shows in a simple model that when firms optimise trip frequency, they trade off the cost of a greater trip frequency against the loss of profit resulting from less face-to-face contact, or greater inventory holding. A standard convex bid rent curve emerges in this case even without the usual consideration of substitution between land and non-land costs in production.

Why does face-to-face contact remain essential for maximum profit? Like Linders et al. in Chapter 2, McCann emphasises in Chapter 3 the importance of building trust in business relationships and the importance of tacit knowledge exchange. Besides the social network type of cluster, a high density of economic activity can also result from pure Marshallian agglomeration externalities within cities. Finally, clusters of activity can result from industrial complexes that extend over a greater regional scale.

1.3 CONNECTIVITY AND SPATIAL INTERACTION

In recent decades, international trade has been growing faster than domestic absorption of output in many countries. This can be seen from Table 1.1. Trade in goods (exports plus imports) as a percentage of world GDP increased over the 1990–2000 decade by 23 percent to 40.0 percent in 2000. Table 1.1 shows that merchandise trade became more important in all regions of the world during the 1990s but, interestingly, the growth international trade relative to output is inversely related to the level of income.

Table 1.1 Integration with the global economy

Region	Trade in goods as % of GDP [a]		Gross private capital flows as % of GDP [b]		Gross foreign direct investment as % of GDP [b]	
	2000	1990–2000 % change	2000	1990–2000 % change	2000	1990–2000 % change
World	40.0	23	29.1	183	8.8	226
Low income	41.3	55	4.8	60	1.6	220
Middle income	53.5	46	12.0	58	3.8	280
High income	37.1	16	33.6	205	10.1	237
East Asia & Pacific	65.6	34	13.3	151	3.9	160
Europe & Central Asia	65.6	129	13.6	n.a.	3.8	n.a.
Europe EMU	56.3	25	49.3	250	14.8	410
Latin America & Carib.	37.7	63	10.5	33	4.5	400
Middle East & N. Africa	51.6	14	7.5	-35	1.0	11
South Asia	24.3	47	3.1	121	0.6	500
Sub-Saharan Africa	56.8	38	11.0	116	1.8	80

Notes: a exports plus imports
    b sum of absolute values of inflows and outflows

Source: World Bank, *2002 World Development Indicators*

However, middle-income countries are the most 'open' in terms of international trade in goods. Among regions, openness increased the most during the 1990s in Europe and Central Asia (which includes the former Soviet countries), while there was relatively little change in trade openness in the Middle East and North Africa.

With respect to gross private capital flows, the high-income countries are responsible for most of these flows. In 2000, the ratio of gross private capital flows to GDP was 33.6 percent in the high-income countries, as compared with 12.0 percent and 4.8 percent in middle-income and low-income countries respectively. The relative growth in capital flows was also the fastest in the high-income countries.

Table 1.1 also shows that – as already pointed out by, for example, Lucas (1988) – most Foreign Direct Investment (FDI) flows between high-income countries. Gross FDI as a percentage of GDP was in 2000 only 1.6 percent in low-income countries, 3.8 percent in middle-income countries, but 10.1 percent in high-income countries. However, besides the Economic and Monetary Union (EMU) area of Europe, there was also rapid growth of FDI during the 1990s in South Asia and Latin America.

An interesting issue is the extent to which the growth in trade, financial and capital flows has been primarily *within* global regions rather than *between* such regions. Such issues are best addressed with gross flow data, such as a matrix of gross inter-country trade flows across the world.

Studying gross flow matrices is a popular research endeavour in regional science, where the gravity model that originated from physics is usually posited as a simple and robust mathematical model to describe the observed spatial patterns (e.g., Isard, 1999). There has been much criticism in economics of the gravity model, despite the popularity of empirical applications such as those with respect to trade – pioneered by Tinbergen (1962) and Pöyhönen (1963) – and to migration (see, e.g., the survey by Greenwood, 1975). The reason for the criticism was the assertion that the gravity equation cannot be derived from conventional micro foundations of producer and consumer behaviour. In recent years, however, the gravity model has witnessed a revival as an effective means to study the impact of economic and financial liberalisation on trade patterns. Christie Smith in Chapter 8 of this book and Tim Hazledine and Sara Lipanovic in Chapter 9 use gravity models for their empirical research. Better micro foundations have also been laid (see, e.g., Brown and Anderson, 2002).

An alternative way to study gross flows, and again popular in regional science circles, is the network perspective (e.g., Johansson and Westin, 1994). For most countries, most of the total volume of trade takes place with only a few major trading partners. In a mathematical sense, trade flows can be interpreted similarly to the now common 'hub and spoke' system of international air traffic. In 'hub and spoke' air travel, passengers travel between peripheries via 'feeder' spokes and a major hub at either end (resulting in what is referred to as 'three or more degrees of separation' between the peripheries). In the trade context, the connectivity between countries is particularly of interest when studying 'contagion' of economic shocks, such as those that occurred during the late 1990s Asian financial and economic crisis (e.g., Reynolds, 2001).

Spatial interaction and networks are the focus of Part B of this book. Laurie Schintler and Rajendra Kulkarni adopt a network perspective to study the global growth of exports in Chapter 4. Following Watts and Strogatz (1998), their key concept is that of 'small-world' connectivity. In a small-world network, much of the interaction is within 'cliques' while the cliques are connected through major hubs or nodes. In the trade context, regional free trade areas represent cliques and the largest trading nations act as hubs.

Are cliques becoming more important and has globalisation reduced the average degrees of separation between any two trading nations? Schintler and Kulkarni attempt to answer these questions by means of data on merchandise export growth in 77 nations for the periods 1985–1990, 1990–1995 and 1995–2000.

After defining measures of local and global connectivity, they find that more remote nations have strong local connectivity and weak global connectivity in each cross-section. Over time, however, global connectivity has increased for all countries. Local connectivity appears to have changed little over time except for the 'intermediate' group of countries that are neither remote nor share borders with many neighbours. Thus, while globalisation has indeed strengthened global and local connectivity in the world's network of merchandise trade, Schintler and Kulkarni's calculations provide no evidence that connectivity of remote countries has improved more than that of more centrally located countries.

Upali Wickramasinghe considers in Chapter 5 the impact of geography and connectivity on the spatial variation in income per capita. After assembling an international data set on 82 countries, Wickramasinghe estimates both conventional regression models of 1997 Gross National Product (GNP) per capita and models that take stochastic spatial spillover effects into account. The explanatory variables in the models include traditional ones resulting from neoclassical growth theory, such as the physical capital stock and education, plus indicators of institutions, policies, infrastructure and geographical features such as climate, access to the sea and distance from the equator.

Wickramasinghe explicitly accounts for spatial contiguity effects and distance between countries by means of spatial econometrics (see, e.g., Anselin, 1988). The possibility of spatial spillovers (modelled by spatial lags in dependent variables and spatial autocorrelation of residuals) seems very plausible, but is often ignored in the growth and development literature. The force that drives the spatial linkage in Schintler and Kulkarni's network analysis in Chapter 4 is export growth: growing exports in any given nation are leading to income gains that are, in turn, likely to lead to growing exports among the nation's trading partners, particularly those in close proximity. In contrast, Wickramasinghe emphasises spillovers related to income levels: these can include a common pool of resources such as technological know-how and regional infrastructure. Neighbours may also be attracted to each other due to common language, customs and institutions. Wickramasinghe finds that spatial proximity indeed matters: the autoregressive parameters are always significant.

An interesting finding is that contiguity (whether countries have common borders or not) matters more than distance between countries. Thus, countries that have few common borders may find this geographical feature to be to their disadvantage economically. On the other hand, access to the sea turns out to be a positive influence on income: land-locked countries have lower income, *ceteris paribus*. Overall, the spatial distribution of income is due to a mixture of factors that include geography, economic policies and institutions.

Island countries share, by definition, no common land borders with other countries at all. The importance of contiguity identified in Chapter 5 therefore suggests that 'being an island' may be an economic disadvantage (despite the positive effect of access to the sea). The economic disadvantage of being an island may be particularly pertinent in the Pacific Ocean, in which some of the most remote economies in the world can be found. In Chapter 6, Geoffrey Bertram and Özer Karagedikli focus on 22 Pacific island economies and investigate a form of spatial interdependence that is not based on distance but on the degree of political integration between an island economy and its former colonial ruler. This idea fits in well with the model of development of these Pacific islands proposed by Bertram and Watters (1985), who characterised the economies of the Pacific micro-states as driven by migration, remittances, aid and budget deficits. With these economic influences in mind, Bertram and Watters labelled the Pacific micro-states as Migration, Remittances, Aid and Bureaucracy (MIRAB) economies and the fact that this somewhat awkward acronym remains popular in the development literature testifies to the soundness of their theory. Interestingly, the form of spatial interaction that is observed here does not have the gravity property: islands that are relatively close may have development paths that are very different, depending on the strength and nature of the linkages with their 'metropolitan patron' economies.

Bertram and Karagedikli find by means of cross-section and panel data regression models that the per capita income of Pacific island economies can be explained by the income level of the relevant metropolitan patron, combined with the degree of political integration with that patron. Islands that are tightly linked to rich patrons have relatively high per capita income. Island nations with weak political linkages with the patron country, and islands with links to relatively poor patrons, have low per capita income. These results provide an explanation for the earlier finding by Cashin and Loayza (1995) that there is little evidence of income convergence among Pacific island economies.

One nation in the South Pacific is rather different from the other island nations in this part of the world. New Zealand is relatively large and affluent enough to be a 'metropolitan patron' in Bertram and Karagedikli's analysis of island–patron linkages. With a population of just over 4 million, the country is also beyond the size of the small states studied in Chapter 10 by Armstrong and Read, who adopt 3 million as a cut-off point. On the other hand, New Zealand's relative remoteness and relatively narrow export base, in which the processing of primary sector output and tourism are dominant, generate a vulnerability that is not unlike that of some of the small states and micro-states. In Chapter 7, Geoff Simmons investigates the impact of New Zealand's remoteness and small domestic market on the size distribution of firms and the relationship with firm performance.

The key hypothesis is that firm growth in New Zealand is constrained by the small size of the domestic market and by the difficulty, due to geographic isolation, of moving into exporting. While the hypothesis itself is straightforward, testing it turns out to be rather difficult. There is evidence that the proportion of small firms is unusually large in New Zealand. Almost all (close to 99 percent) of New Zealand firms have less than 50 employees and the distribution is increasingly skewed towards small firms. Simmons believes that New Zealand's dominance of small firms may have something to do with a relatively remote location and small scale. For example, Iceland and Atlantic Canada (an area of Canada including the provinces of New Brunswick, Nova Scotia, Newfoundland and Prince Edward Island) have a similar predominance of small firms. Cultural, institutional and compositional factors may surely matter too, but New Zealand's firm size distribution is quite different from, for example, that of its neighbour Australia.

Small firm size may in itself not be a barrier to successful exporting. For example, one large company, Fonterra, acts as the exporting arm of its many cooperative shareholder dairy farmers, who are not individually classified as exporters. Nonetheless, New Zealand firms in many industries may face difficulties in moving into export markets through an inability to obtain the necessary information on overseas markets, to adapt to local customs in those markets, to raise the necessary capital and to absorb a large variability in export orders. In addition, an increase in scale may exacerbate skill shortages (which tend to be common in small remote economies), push up wages and lower the return on assets.

Despite these difficulties, Simmons believes that the high rates of net growth of small firms in New Zealand – and the even higher rates of firm creation and destruction – generate a Schumpeterian process of creative destruction that eventually will lead to a larger proportion of firms with an export orientation (either directly or through linkages with producer boards and similar exporting agencies), and that barriers to exporting can be overcome.

Earlier in this chapter it was noted that the gravity model provides a useful framework to estimate the effect of distance on observed trade volumes. In this context, distance represents more than the cost of delivery of a good or service. Distance may also reflect the cost of face-to-face communication, co-ordination costs, and cultural and institutional differences. In addition, tariffs and other trade barriers may also be interpreted as increasing the effective distance between buyers in the importing nation and sellers in the exporting nation. Finally, the use of different currencies and regulation of financial flows also increase distance between trading partners. In this context, an interesting question is whether the adoption of a major currency would be a useful strategy for a peripheral nation to boost trade, and perhaps FDI as well.

Christie Smith investigates in Chapter 8 the impact of currency union on trade by re-analysis of a large data set of bilateral trade flows put together by Andrew Rose and collaborators (e.g., Rose and van Wincoop, 2001). The effect of currency union is estimated by a dummy variable that is set to one for any trade flows between nations that have the same currency and zero otherwise. In most of the specifications, the dummy variable is positive and significant, suggesting that currency union indeed enhances trade. There are some difficult econometric problems, however, in this type of regression analysis. Both income and the currency union dummy may be considered to be endogenous (i.e., affected by trade) and it is difficult to find exogenous instrumental variables that can act as substitutes. An alternative approach in which countries adopting currency union are compared with a 'control' group of structurally similar countries by means of a 'difference in differences' estimator is not straightforward either. Whenever the econometric problems are addressed in some way, the estimate of the effect of currency union is diminished.

In the end, Smith's gravity models suggest that any currency union benefit is dwarfed by the immutable effect of physical distance. Thus, while currency union may benefit a small open economy with several large neighbours close by, it does not appear to be an effective strategy for a more remote economy. It is interesting to compare the case of Ireland (where the adoption of the euro may be considered to have been advantageous – see Walsh's discussion in Chapter 13 of this book) with that of New Zealand, where it is not certain that the benefits of adopting the currency of Australia or the United States (both major trading partners) would outweigh the costs (see, e.g., Grimes and Holmes, 2000; Scrimgeour, 2002).

If countries differed only in the use of currency, then the effect of currency union could simply be gauged from estimating a gravity model on a trade flow matrix that includes both intra-national and international trade flows by a dummy variable set equal to one for the former type of flows. In empirical applications, which started with McCallum's (1995) study of Canada–US trade, such a dummy variable tends to be indeed highly significant. Nonetheless, the use of different currencies may only be a minor influence on this border effect: trade barriers, differences in the institutional environment, language and culture may play much bigger roles. This type of empirical research does nonetheless suggest a very simple method of assessing the impact of greater economic integration on trade: the 'border dummy' should become smaller.

Tim Hazledine and Sara Lipanovic focus on the border effect and address the general question of whether peripheral economies can benefit from closer integration with a larger neighbour (both in economic and in broader terms) by means of an Australia/New Zealand case study. They find a large border effect. However, this effect cannot be estimated very precisely and may be anywhere between six and 18 (so that, at least theoretically, trans-Tasman trade could increase six fold if the border effect could be fully removed). But, given the fact that Australia and New Zealand already have a free trade agreement, Hazledine and Lipanovic suggest that some 'home bias' may in fact be the outcome of efficient trading. In an imperfectly competitive environment, the equilibrium payoff from transactions that are between agents who share common values and institutions may be greater than those across international borders. Nonetheless, the consensus is that the closer economic integration of Australia and New Zealand has benefited the two countries (with benefits somewhat disproportionally to the latter, see, e.g.,

Lloyd, 1999), although the gravity model has – rather surprisingly – been unable to detect this in terms of the trade flows (Ratnayake and Townsend, 1999).

1.4 STRATEGIES

The analytical models that have been developed to describe the evolving configuration of economic activity, such as those discussed in Fujita and Thisse (2002), do not lend themselves easily to practical policy advice (see also Krugman, 1999). The main problem is that the outcomes of the 'new economic geography' models are often ambiguous, dependent on parameter values, and only tractable through computer simulation rather than analytically. In an important recent contribution, Baldwin et al. (2003) develop theoretical consequences of trade policy, tax policy and regional policy by means of a range of core–periphery and related models, but the conclusions are again rather sensitive to the exact specification of the models. Baldwin et al. do not provide any empirical evidence for their policy models and note that the empirical verification of the 'new economic geography' models is in any case as yet still in its infancy (p.4).

Given that it may be difficult to make simple theoretical predictions regarding the roles of geographical features such as location, size and density in the presence of global integration with declining transportation and communications costs, the authors of the chapters in Part C of the present book adopt purely empirical approaches to identify what matters in terms of economic outcomes and what role policy might play.

Harvey Armstrong and Robert Read have compiled data on 105 small states and island states around the world, with smallness being defined as a population of 3 million or less. In Chapter 10, Armstrong and Read assess whether smallness has been detrimental to economic performance in terms of real income per capita and economic growth.

A recurring theme throughout this book is that smallness can be detrimental due to the lack of economies of scope and scale, an absence of natural resources or too much reliance on a few abundant resources, a lack of skilled workers and Research and Development (R&D), vulnerability due to a narrow array of exports, and constraints on fiscal and monetary policy imposed by openness. Remote small states face of course the additional disadvantage of relatively higher transportation and communications costs. Yet rather surprisingly, Armstrong and Read find that the majority of small states exhibit a relatively strong performance in terms of economic growth and per capita income levels. Moreover, small states often perform better than their large neighbours. This rather optimistic conclusion cannot be taken lightly as the authors painstakingly carry out sensitivity analyses in terms of data sources, methodologies and model specifications. There is some evidence that islands perform worse than mainland states, but the effect is relatively small compared with other determinants of income.

Armstrong and Read find that the small size of the domestic market and relative labour scarcity can be constraints to development, suggesting that trade promotion that exploits niche markets (such as those derived from climate, natural resources and specialised know-how) will pay off. Consistent with the evidence of Bertram and Karagedikli in Chapter 6 on the Pacific micro-states, they also find that political sovereignty is inversely related to growth performance within a global data set, although this is not the case at the European level.

Within Europe, an interesting case is that of Finland. Nils Bjorksten and Laura Meriluoto point out in Chapter 11 that this country faces several geographical disadvantages: it has a small population, it is located on the periphery of Europe, separated from most of the continent by the Baltic Sea, has a cold climate and rather obscure language. Yet, except for a period of adjustment between 1990 and 1993, Finland has experienced a rate of growth that has been noticeably faster than the OECD average. Bjorksten and Meriluoto explain this outcome by means of a trade-driven development strategy combined with a social safety net that protected those workers who were negatively affected by the structural readjustment. The standard Heckscher–Ohlin model provides a simple explanation of Finland's relative specialisation in the exporting of ICT-related products, with the growth of telecommunications giant Nokia the often-cited success story. Relative to capital and unskilled labour, Finland had a relatively large endowment in skilled labour and technical know-how that gave it a comparative advantage in ICT-related products. This situation was fostered through education policies and active government involvement in R&D. Bjorksten and Meriluoto argue that the Finnish example can provide a blueprint for overcoming peripherality. Nonetheless, the large level of government intervention that was used to foster development and shield the labour market from growing unemployment of unskilled workers may generate long-term costs that may call into doubt the sustainability of the current growth path.

In a world of footloose firms and mobile workers, the balance of centripetal and centrifugal economic forces determines the distribution of activity. The positive externalities of agglomeration play an important role in the concentration of economic activity, but urban firms and residents may also experience negative externalities in the form of congestion, pollution and crime. In addition, the high density of economic activity pushes up land prices. Thus, quality of life provides another reason why geography may matter more rather than less in the New Economy and growth areas are emerging where amenities are good and land prices are, at least initially, low (e.g., Kotkin, 2000).

Lee Huskey investigates in Chapter 12 the potential tension between agglomeration advantages and quality of life in the location of high-tech employment. Estimating regression models of relative employment in high-tech manufacturing and services across US states, he finds that employment in both sectors is positively correlated with open spaces and quality of life scores. As expected, agglomeration matters too, although there is a difference between services and manufacturing in that accessibility to markets appears to matter only for the latter. High-tech services appear relatively concentrated in metropolitan-dominated states, while manufacturing tends to be located outside such states. Huskey suggests that marketing and exploiting local natural amenities can provide a useful development strategy for peripheral regions and countries. Naturally, there are limitations to this. For example, a pleasant climate is becoming increasingly attractive as incomes grow, since outdoor leisure activities are income elastic and populations are ageing. Yet not all peripheral areas are endowed with attractive climates.

Tax incentives provide of course another means of attracting investment, particularly when international trade is encouraged through giving exporting firms a more favourable treatment than firms supplying primarily to the domestic market. This is one of the development strategies adopted by Ireland, which is discussed in some detail by Brendan Walsh in Chapter 13.

It is no exaggeration to label Ireland as one of the most successful economies in the OECD during the 1990s, for example outperforming Finland in a macro sense, although Walsh notes that Irish firms have yet to develop a world-renowned brand name with the prominence of Finland's Nokia. Given its location between the USA and Europe, peripherality does not appear to have been a major obstacle to Irish growth, although it certainly entitled the country to EU subsidies.

Walsh attributes Irish growth to a convergence effect, favourable external developments (such as the ICT boom, the benefits from EU integration and declining costs of transportation and communications) and sound domestic policies (fiscal stabilisation, abundant and relatively cheap skilled labour, industrial policy and corporate tax policy). However, Walsh warns against the adoption of tax incentives as a non-cooperative development strategy. An unsustainable 'race to the bottom' in tax rates may result when countries compete for FDI. The high standard of living, relatively high inflation and the erosion of cost advantages may also call into doubt whether 1990s growth can be repeated.

In many cases, successful development in small open economies has built on ICT-related manufacturing and services. Can ICT developments promote higher growth and income in small peripheral economies through greater adoption of electronic commerce? Bronwyn Howell and Lisa Marriott have a first go at answering this question for the case of New Zealand in the final chapter of this book, Chapter 14.

They find that New Zealand is consistently among the top ten OECD countries in terms of indicators of e-commerce. Howell and Marriott develop an e-commerce measurement framework that distinguishes between connectivity, capability, uptake and performance. The fact that New Zealand does well in terms of connectivity, capability and uptake of e-commerce applications suggests that the predominantly small New Zealand firms (see also Chapter 7) have found this an effective strategy for strengthening their competitive position in the global economy. Howell and Marriott suggest that small remote economies must invest more in ICT than other countries in order to reap a sustainable advantage. However, while it is plausible that the rapid technology uptake in New Zealand during the 1990s contributed to its shift to a somewhat higher growth path, it is difficult – if not impossible – to carefully separate out this factor from the myriad of other influences on long-run growth. Recent studies, such as Pilat et al. (2002), suggest that the ICT manufacturing sector has experienced very high rates of productivity growth (spilling over to higher growth rates in countries such as Finland and Ireland) and certain ICT-using services have also benefited (e.g., in the USA and Australia). However, it remains fiendishly difficult to quantify the macro-level impact of the rapid adoption of e-commerce practices.

1.5 FINAL COMMENTS

Overall, the ICT and knowledge-driven economy of the 21st century provides both promise and challenge for small remote economies. While transportation, information transfer and communication costs have declined sharply, geography continues to matter – and perhaps even more so now than in the past. Information is ubiquitous and Internet cafes can be found in some of the most remote places in the world. Yet, face-to-face contact and a clustering of economic activity remain essential in the New Economy.

Some small and remote economies can benefit from the trend that footloose companies and workers are increasingly attracted to quality of life aspects of location. Negative externalities of large and dense urban conglomerations (e.g., congestion, pollution and crime) are a push factor in favour of small and island economies. A undulating landscape and sunny climate are attraction factors, and the often-found economic benefit of access to water may have less to do with transportation than with benefits to the residents along the shore.

The case studies in this book show that peripherality does not need to be a permanent disadvantage. Small remote countries can reach high growth paths and catch up or surpass leading economies. Nonetheless, small peripheral countries need greater government intervention and must devote more resources to overcoming their spatial disadvantage. There is no simple blueprint. They must try harder than the larger economies, for example in steering resources to education and R&D, finding the best niches to promote and perhaps investing more in ICT than larger competitors.

Small countries also suffer often from skill shortages and a brain drain. Given the mobility of professionals, there is no simple solution but to offer competitive wages in order to attract and retain the highly skilled. Nonetheless, some small distant economies may offer a high quality of life as a compensation for lower wages. In any case, small countries can make more effective use of their diaspora (Bergsten and Choi, 2003; Bedford, 2001).

It is also clear from the evidence presented in this book that peripheral countries and regions should not 'go it alone': they can benefit from integration with large neighbours or continue to exploit historical ties. Neighbourhoods do matter: small economies benefit from positive spillovers in rich global regions. International integration may include currency union, but this does not appear to be essential. However, many small remote economies remain vulnerable and will continue to depend on an international framework of international cooperation and assistance. Small remote economies may pay a premium to attract capital.

Theoretical developments in endogenous growth theory and economic geography suggest that a case can be made for a private–public partnership in developing a growth strategy. This is particularly the case where small firm sizes lower the opportunity to invest in private R&D and apprenticeships.

A major difficulty arises from reconciling such a pro-active and public expenditure-driven strategy with a desire to keep taxes low to minimise efficiency losses and attract FDI. Hence, governments need to tread carefully, as a strategy of 'picking winners' is all too easily likely to lead to rent-seeking behaviour. There is now ample evidence that infrastructure and education are most important (see, e.g., Nijkamp and Poot, 2004) but culture, institutions and social capital matter too. A critical success factor is the creation of the right incentives for growth (Easterly, 2001). Even then, some 'luck' in terms of favourable external developments helps too.

There is much scope for additional research in this area. For example, a better integration of analysis of domestic geography *vis-à-vis* international geography is desirable. Small city-like states such as Singapore are very different from small countries with similar population sizes but much lower density. Low density leads to higher production costs, thin markets and less competition. There is an important role for competition policy in such cases. Agglomeration forces that are encouraged by successful national strategies may increase the urban–rural divide within countries. A top-down driven decentralisation of firms and workers is less likely to be successful than decentralised 'bottom-up' regional development initiatives (e.g., Higano et al., 2002).

Finally, a rich family of models of economic geography has emerged in recent years. The assessment of the implications of these models for small remote economies and the explicit testing of these models have only just begun and are likely to be a fruitful avenue for further research.

NOTES

1. In terms of remoteness, Australia came a close second. The least remote economy was Japan, followed closely by Belgium, the United Kingdom and The Netherlands. The calculations by Evans and Hughes (2003, p.35) reinforce comments made by Hazledine and Lipanovic in Chapter 9 of this book (see Chapter 9, note 4).
2. In 1870, New Zealand had the fourth highest per capita income in the world and in 1950 the third highest (Maddison, 2001).
3. It is not implied here that New Zealand's physical geography does not possess economically attractive features. Mild temperatures and generous rainfall contribute to strong grass growth that, for example, provides the comparative advantage in pastoral agriculture, while the beauty of the mountainous regions, geothermal activity in some areas, etc. are major assets for the now highly important tourism industry.
4. Even in a peripheral region, population density may be relatively high in one or a few urban areas.
5. This figure has been kindly provided by the New Zealand Treasury.

REFERENCES

Acemoglu, D., Johnson, S. and J. Robinson (2001), 'The colonial origins of comparative development: an empirical investigation', *American Economic Review*, 91, 1369-1401.

Aghion, P. and P. Howitt (1998), *Endogenous Growth Theory*, Cambridge, MA: MIT Press.

Anselin, L. (1988), *Spatial Econometrics: Methods and Models*, Dordrecht: Kluwer Academic Publishers.

Baldwin, R., Forslid, R., Martin, P., Ottaviano, G. and F. Robert-Nicoud (2003), *Economic Geography and Public Policy*, Princeton: Princeton University Press.

Bedford, R. (2001), '2001: reflections on the spatial odysseys of New Zealanders', *New Zealand Geographer*, 57, 49-54.

Bergsten, C.F. and I. Choi (eds) (2003) *The Korean Diaspora in the World Economy*, Washington, DC: Institute for International Economics.

Bertram, G. and R.F. Watters (1985), 'The MIRAB economy in South Pacific microstates', *Pacific Viewpoint*, 26, 497-519.

Brown, W.M. and W.P. Anderson (2002), 'Spatial markets and the potential for economic integration between Canadian and U.S. Regions', *Papers in Regional Science*, 81, 99-120.

Bushnell, P. and W.K. Choy (2001), 'Go west, young man, go west?', Working Paper 01/7, Wellington: New Zealand Treasury.

Cairncross, F. (2001), *The Death of Distance*, Boston: Harvard Business School Press.

Cashin, P. and N. Loayza (1995), 'Paradise lost? Growth, convergence and migration in the South Pacific', *IMF Staff Papers*, 42, 608-641.

Easterly, W. (2001), *The Elusive Quest for Growth*, Cambridge, MA: MIT Press.

Ellison, G. and E.L. Glaeser (1999), 'The geographic concentration of industry: does natural advantage explain agglomeration?', *American Economic Review*, 89, 311-316.

Evans, L. and P. Hughes (2003), 'Competition policy in small distant open economies: some lessons from the economics literature', Working Paper 03/31, Wellington: New Zealand Treasury.

Evans, L., Grimes, A. and B. Wilkinson (1996), 'Economic reform in New Zealand 1984-1995: the pursuit of efficiency', *Journal of Economic Literature*, 33, 1856-1902.

Fujita, M., Krugman, P. and A.J. Venables (1999), *The Spatial Economy*, Cambridge, MA: MIT Press.

Fujita, M. and J.F. Thisse (2002), *Economics of Agglomeration*, Cambridge: Cambridge University Press.

Gallup, J.L., Sachs, J. and A. Mellinger (1999), 'Geography and economic development', *International Regional Science Review*, 22, 179-232.

Gould, J. (1982), *The Rake's Progress? The New Zealand Economy Since 1945*, Auckland: Hodder and Stoughton.

Greenwood, M. (1975), 'Research on internal migration in the United States: a survey', *Journal of Economic Literature*, 13, 397-433.

Grimes, A. and F. Holmes (2000), *An ANZAC Dollar? Currency Union and Business Development*, Wellington: Institute of Policy Studies, Victoria University of Wellington.

Higano, Y., Nijkamp, P., Poot, J. and J.J. van Wyk (2002), *The Region in the New Economy: An International Perspective on Regional Dynamics in the 21st Century*, Aldershot: Ashgate.

Isard, W. (1999), 'Regional science: parallels from physics and chemistry', *Papers in Regional Science*, 78, 5-20.

Johansson, B. and L. Westin (1994), 'Affinities and frictions of trade networks', *Annals of Regional Science*, 28, 243-261.

Kohno, H., Nijkamp, P. and J. Poot (2000), *Regional Cohesion and Competition in the Age of Globalization*, Cheltenham UK and Northampton, MA, USA: Edward Elgar.

Kotkin, J. (2000), *The New Geography*, New York: Random House.

Krugman, P. (1990), *Rethinking International Trade*, Cambridge, MA: MIT Press.
Krugman, P. (1991), "Increasing returns and economic geography', *Journal of Political Economy*, 99, 483-499.
Krugman, P. (1993), 'First nature, second nature, and metropolitan location', *Journal of Regional Science*, 33, 129-144.
Krugman, P. (1999), 'The role of geography in development', *International Regional Science Review*, 22, 142-161.
Landes, D. (1998), *The Wealth and Poverty of Nations: Why are Some so Rich and Some so Poor?*, New York: Norton.
Lloyd, P.J. (1999), 'The future of the CER agreement: a single market for Australia and New Zealand', in P.J. Lloyd (ed.) *International Trade Opening and the Formation of the Global Economy*, Cheltenham UK and Northampton MA, USA: Edward Elgar.
Lucas, R.E. (1988), 'On the mechanics of economic development', *Journal of Monetary Economics*, 22, 3-42.
Maddison, A. (2001), *The World Economy: A Millennial Perspective*, Paris: OECD.
McCallum, J. (1995), 'National borders matter: Canada–USA regional trade patterns', *American Economic Review*, 85, 615–623.
Neary, J.P. (2001), 'Of hype and hyperbolas: introducing the new economic geography', *Journal of Economic Literature*, 34, 536-561.
Nijkamp, P. and J. Poot (2004), 'Meta-analysis of the impact of fiscal policies on long-run growth', *European Journal of Political Economy*, 20, 91-124.
Nonaka, I. and H. Takeuchi (1995), *The Knowledge-Creating Company: How Japanese Companies Create the Dynamics of Innovation*, Oxford: Oxford University Press.
OECD (2003), *National Accounts of OECD Countries*, Paris: OECD.
Peretz, D. (2001), *Small States in the Global Economy*, London: Commonwealth Secretariat.
Pilat, D., Lee, F. and B. van Ark (2002), 'Production and use of ICT: a sectoral perspective on productivity growth in the OECD area', *OECD Economic Studies*, 0(35), 47-78.
Pöyhönen, P. (1963), 'A tentative model for the volume of trade between countries', *Weltwirtschaftliches Archiv*, 90, 93-99.
Ratnayake, R. and B. Townsend (1999), 'The geographical pattern of New Zealand's international trade: an application of the gravity model', *New Zealand Economic Papers*, 33, 27-38.
Reynolds, C. (2001), 'A conceptual model of global business growth in Southeast Asia', *Journal of the Asia Pacific Economy*, 6, 76-98.
Roos, M. (2002), 'How important is geography for agglomeration?', paper presented at the 42nd Congress of the European Regional Science Association, Dortmund, August 27–31.
Rose, A.K. and E. van Wincoop (2001), 'National money as a barrier to international trade: the real case for currency union', *American Economic Review*, 91, 386-390.
Scrimgeour, D. (2002), 'Exchange rate volatility and currency union; New Zealand evidence', *Journal of Policy Modeling*, 24, 739-749.
Storper, M. and A.J. Venables (2002), 'Buzz: the economic force of the city', paper presented at the DRUID Summer Conference on Industrial Dynamics of the New and Old Economy, Copenhagen/Elsinore, 6–8 June.

Streeten, P. (2001), *Globalisation: Threat or Opportunity?*, Copenhagen: Copenhagen Business School Press.

Tinbergen, J. (1962), *Shaping the World Economy*, New York: The Twentieth Century Fund.

Van Den Bulcke, D. and A. Verbeke, (2001), *Globalization and the Small Open Economy*, Cheltenham UK and Northampton, MA, USA: Edward Elgar.

van der Velde, M. and H. van Houtum (2000), *Borders, Regions and People*, London: Pion.

Watts, D.J. and S.H. Strogatz (1998), 'Collective dynamics of small-world networks', *Nature*, 393, 440-442.

2. Locality Matters: Myths and Facts on the New Economy

Gert-Jan M. Linders, Henri L.F. de Groot and Peter Nijkamp

2.1 A NEW SPATIAL-ECONOMIC LANDSCAPE

The currently popular perception of a 'death of distance' suggests that traditional location theory as formulated by Von Thünen and Weber has lost its validity and relevance in our era of virtual communication. In addition, the emergence of the global network society (Castells, 1996) suggests that location is not a stand-alone choice of a firm, but is embedded in world-wide market area connections, marketing channels, information technology regimes, transport systems and telecommunications infrastructure. It is also increasingly claimed that conventional international and interregional trade may now not only be determined by the comparative advantage based on factor inputs, but also by network access, knowledge infrastructure and product heterogeneity in the context of monopolistic competition (as advocated already in the path-breaking contribution of Dixit and Stiglitz, 1977). All such forces may have a dynamic, and less predictable, impact on location and allocation decisions of firms, including transport and trade flows. In more recent studies on economic development we have therefore also witnessed attempts to integrate trade and location issues (Fujita et al., 1999; Pohl, 2001). The advent of the ICT society has meant that information is a central element in the emerging geographic landscape of our world, not only for the transmission of data or the supply of non-material services, but also for an efficient logistic handling of material commodity flows (Gorter and Nijkamp, 2001).

In contrast to such global connectivity trends, we also witness a renewed interest in the locality. Local (or regional) networks of firms appear to become vital in exchanging tacit knowledge by means of face-to-face contacts, as can be observed for example in the so-called 'Third Italy'. Clearly, such network constellations may be incorporated in multi-layer higher-order networks. And consequently, the local–global divide is much more complicated than just a simple economic–geographic segmentation of our world. The cities or metropolitan areas play a particular role in our global network society. Although it is often argued that the 'death of distance' would make cities in the future almost redundant or would at least erode the traditional agglomeration advantages (scale, localisation and urbanisation economies), it is noteworthy that on a worldwide scale cities do not show any clear sign of decline. Cities are still the centre of economic activity and have managed to reinforce their position (see also Glaeser et al., 1992; Glaeser, 1998; and Rauch, 1993). Despite serious concerns about social costs such as congestion, crime and ethnic tensions, cities have demonstrated a remarkable ability and vitality to exploit economies of density, including those elements that belong to a virtual network society (such as an intense contact potential, a social protection network, a diversified highly skilled labour force and an international orientation). In other words, the city offers externalities of various kinds that are not significantly affected by the transition to a network society. On the contrary, cities tend to reinforce their position in the new economic–geographic landscape of our world and, consequently, one may wonder whether the future of our network society will be something other than a replication of the past. Despite rapid transformations in the area of ICT and in many other advanced technologies, the question arises whether the future of our world will be different from the current urbanisation pattern and whether new spatial–economic ramifications are likely to emerge (see also Leinbach and Brunn, 2001).

These questions are extremely relevant against the background of the current debate on the future viability of the so-called 'New Economy'. The transition from the material goods economy towards a service economy and next towards a virtual or electronic economy is often given this label. The New Economy concept, introduced for the first time in *Business Week* in 1995 by Chris Farrell, has prompted an avalanche of debates among economists in recent years. The New Economy is a network constellation in which the rapid use of ICT leads to increasing returns (see also Brynjolfsson and Hitt, 1995; Shapiro and Varian, 1999). In the meantime many economists have expressed some doubt as to whether the New Economy will be beneficial to all world citizens or whether it will just reinforce the existing geographic–economic powerblocs. Others are afraid that the New Economy will lead to a new divide among forerunners and backrunners in the global economy, so that a new spatial–economic fragmentation will emerge. This chapter addresses several of the above-mentioned issues from the viewpoint that 'locality matters'. After this introductory section, Section 2.2 will set the scene by investigating the relationship between ICT and information services, with production systems discussed in Section 2.3. Since global competition is central to the New Economy, Section 2.4 will focus on the relationship between ICT and international (or interregional) trade in information services, and the consequences for international (or spatial) patterns of specialisation and relative welfare. Section 2.5 then presents an analysis of the way in which these concepts may interrelate with growth and productivity. Empirical questions also receive some attention. The two final sections deal with the question of whether our findings have implications for the organisation of the new space-economy, and also make suggestions for future research.

2.2 THE INFORMATION AGE AS A NEW ECONOMY

The increased use of ICT has a pervasive impact on all economies. It not only leads to an efficiency increase in communication, but it also generates a drastic change in logistic value chains, labour relations, service provision, knowledge acquisition and management styles (Foray and Lundvall, 1996; Kohno et al., 2000; Lundvall, 1998). ICT is a network constellation and owes its economic importance to network externalities (Capello, 1994), which create increasing returns and a drastic decline in transaction costs (van Geenhuizen and Nijkamp, 2001; Westland and Clark, 1999).

The spatial–economic implications of ICT are still hard to foresee. The literature is rather ambiguous and comes up with different views of the future. On the one hand, there is the belief that ICT may overcome barriers of space and time, so that the space-economy becomes footloose with equal opportunities for all localities. This is supported by the 'death of distance' hypothesis and reflected in visions of 'electronic cottages' or the 'e-society' (see also Mitchell, 1995). But on the other hand, there are also scientists who argue that the economic and political power centres of our world will not vanish and that the concentration of knowledge will favour the continuation of cities (Gillespie and Williams, 1988; Graham, 1999). The reason is that ICT helps to execute remote control, to create a critical mass of knowledge infrastructure, to favour flexible specialisation and to exploit the socio-cultural and institutional basis of agglomerations. As a consequence, ICT is an efficiency-enhancing city-centric factor in the area of customer-driven production, client-oriented management, network and knowledge innovation, and work flexibility, through which it favours economies of density in urban areas. The blend of economies of scale and of scope in the ICT sector leads to a better compliance with idiosyncratic consumer demands, as modern ICT products tend to be customised and order based (Reich, 2001; Linders, 2001). The tendency to move from high volume to high value has been occurring since the 1970s, but accelerated in the early 1990s. The key behind these changes is the advent of information, communication and computer technologies.

Reich (2001) identifies three constraints to meeting individual consumer desires that become less significant, in large part as a result of ICT. First, the additional cost of producing highly customised products, as opposed to high volumes of identical products (mass production), has progressively disappeared in a growing proportion of industries. In fact, ICT allows easier fine tuning of machinery, which alleviates the inflexibility of equipment towards obtaining desired product characteristics. Second, the transport costs of information and goods have fallen rapidly. This enables consumers to get the best deals from almost anywhere and allows for worldwide competition in the provision of goods and services. Although the fall in the cost of physical transport is in large part directly due to progress in transportation technologies and equipment, ICT plays an important role here too. The use of computers and communication technologies has enabled a more efficient design of equipment and logistic processes, thus contributing indirectly as well as directly to falling transportation cost. Finally, the Internet combines information, telecommunication and computer technology in providing easy access to specific desired information from around the globe. This allows consumers to acquire comparative information from which they can select the best alternative. Hence, the Internet alleviates problems of incomplete and imperfect information and fosters effective global competition.

Clearly, information plays a crucial role in improving the customisation of products and the competitiveness of markets. Therefore, the New Economy has also become synonymous with the information age. But information has always been important. What's new now? In fact, the constraints that have been loosened by the rise of ICT all reflect a more or less prohibitive scarcity of information. Information was important in the past mainly because of its scarcity and/or the inability to incorporate it in production. Due to high search costs, information was expensive to acquire and provide. Production processes also lacked the flexibility to absorb real-time information on desired product specifications.

Nowadays, the cost of acquisition and provision of information has substantially decreased. Production processes and information systems have become increasingly linked together. This allows flexible and customized production. Thus, ICT has boosted the effectiveness of information and thereby the efficiency of market exchange. Because of the 'death of distance', inherent in the information age, market exchange has become truly global at the same time. The information age does not lead to customisation in all possible end-product sectors. The nature of a product and the position within the product life cycle are decisive. The emergence of global competition due to easy access to product information and falling costs of transportation and logistical planning holds nonetheless nearly everywhere. The information age causes a geographical extension of markets: previously separated markets have come to overlap.

The widening of markets has different consequences for the marketing of different kinds of products. Highly standardised products, such as books or petrol, have little need and/or ability to be customised. An extension of the market intensifies price competition in the entire commodity chain. Since the products are standardised, they can be marketed from anywhere in large quantities at low marginal costs now that information provision and access have become global and logistics are becoming ever cheaper. In the absence of trade barriers, regional price differences will be sharply reduced, especially for standard products.

Besides standardised mass products, we can distinguish two alternative kinds of products: special or exclusive products and flexible products. Special or exclusive products are available in limited supply and their market was already more extended – and less regionally differentiated – than for standardised products. People are willing to travel further to buy a hi-fi set by Bang & Olufsen than by Samsung. The information age does not yield comparable changes in marketing for these products. It will not intensify price competition with alternative products, since special products occupy a highly stable market niche, based on product status that results in low substitutability. Flexible products can be produced according to customer specifications. These products experience market widening in terms of both geography and variety (or scope). The information age causes customisation as well as price competition in these products (varying from cars, through apparel to retail services).

In summary, digital technologies enable consumers to choose the best possible deal from around the globe and producers to offer more customised products. Competition rises and shifts from costs to value, focusing on faster marketing, better matching and higher quality, as well as lower prices (especially in saturated markets). Product characteristics in many industries will satisfy customer desires better.

2.3 PRODUCTION SYSTEMS IN THE NEW ECONOMY

In light of the arguments given above we may conclude that the New Economy raises the 'information content' in the gross value of products and transactions (Reich, 2001). Information system applications are necessary to match and market customised products and to ensure precision quality. Moreover, global competition presses producers to optimise their supply chain, which is also made possible by easy access to information. This leads to international fragmentation of some parts of the supply chain while fostering regional agglomeration in others (Jones, 2000). In any case, co-ordination of logistics increases reliance on complex information systems. Developing and managing these information systems requires specialised, highly skilled labour and support services. Hence, information services are increasingly essential inputs, complementary to the production of customised end products. These information services can be provided more easily across large distances because of the developments in ICT. The importance of information services in particular in the economic system of the New Economy is crucial in our opinion.[1] They are both complementary to the customisation in consumer goods and services and the personification of the global information market place.

Fundamentally, the rise of the information age implies that cost structures change. The rising complexity of information system applications increases the necessary fixed ex-ante investments in human capital and the development of the applications. Information is costly to develop but becomes much cheaper to reproduce and provide (Shapiro and Varian, 1999). Therefore, economies of scale and imperfect competition are prominent features in the intermediate information service sector (Markusen, 1989).

Customisation of end products and vertical specialisation underlie the increasing demand for specialised intermediate information services. The complexity of information systems necessitates that producer services are highly flexible to the requirements of buyers. Therefore, information services will consist of different varieties that are close substitutes in demand as well as in production technology (Stibora and de Vaal, 1995). Thus economies of scope are also important in information services. Since services are by definition flexible and heterogeneous products, the difference in strategy between economies of scale and scope for the service provider is not as relevant, though. From the side of intermediate demand, returns to variety reflect the value placed on differentiated, customised services. For service providers, recouping the fixed investments in information development is central to their competitive strategy. In order to succeed in making such large investments, capital markets and educational institutions must support the human and financial capital requirements for information systems development. The availability of human capital, educational infrastructure and diversified financial markets are therefore essential to the absorption of ICT technologies and the lift-off of the New Economy.

In end-product sectors, the emerging information age results in a twofold development. On the one hand, advances in marketing due to the emergence of versatile and complex information systems have led to a widening of markets in standardised products. The geographical extension of these markets yields a rising importance of scale effects in competitive strategy. On the other hand, scale economies give way to economies of scope in many final products, in which information systems are increasingly crucial for co-ordination towards customised demand. Meeting varying needs becomes the key strategy there.

In the information age, markets become less predictable and the speed of adapting to changing conditions of demand becomes more important (i.e., markets and transactions become more complex). Therefore, vertical integration to stabilise the market is a less tempting option compared with outsourcing support services and other inputs in order to avoid demand uncertainty (de Groot, 2001). Moreover, since economies of scale related to complex skill requirements have gained importance in these support services, outsourcing is further advanced. However, such a change in the mode of organisation of production should also take into account the effects on the transaction costs of contract governance.

Summarising, several concepts that are central to an analysis of the New Economy have been identified: economies of scale, transport costs of information, returns to variety (economies of scope), outsourcing and transaction costs. The next section explores how these concepts interact and affect trade, specialisation and welfare.

2.4 TRADE IN SERVICES AND INTERNATIONAL SPECIALISATION

2.4.1 Returns to Scale and Variety, Transport Costs and Trade in Intermediates

The increasing importance of trade in intermediates and the reality of imperfect competition as a crucial factor for international economic relations have motivated the rise of a strand of literature grouped together as representing 'new trade theory'. A typical collection of contributions to new trade theory can be found in Krugman (1990). The inclusion of scale economies, both internal and external, allows the formal study of the emergence of regional concentration, retainable industries and trade conflicts. An important conclusion is that free trade does not necessarily benefit all nations. Nations can change their position in the international division of labour in favourable ways at the expense of other nations by subsidising industries towards export competitiveness (Gomory and Baumol, 2000).

For our purposes, the most interesting extension of new trade theory is the inclusion of transport costs in a setting of increasing returns to scale. A classic example is the article by Krugman and Venables (1995). They analyse the effect of globalisation (in our terminology, the rise of the New Economy) on specialisation patterns between countries. Globalisation is represented by a fall in the cost of transporting merchandise. The presence of external returns to scale, reflecting cost and demand linkages between sectors, stresses the central role played by trade in intermediates for the outcomes of specialisation patterns. Agglomeration effects are possible for intermediate levels of transport costs. This implies that globalisation does not necessarily raise real income and welfare in all regions.

This analysis, however, focuses on trade in merchandise and does not incorporate the most central aspect of the New Economy: the emergence of the information age. Consequently, the effects of trade in information services on the pattern of specialisation have not yet been analysed explicitly. Evidence on the rising importance of information services in intermediate demand and production supports the relevance of such analysis (see, for example, Francois and Reinert, 1995).

De Groot and Nordas (2001) provide a model to analyse the impact of the emerging information age on the international economy. Following contributions by Francois (1990) and Markusen (1989) to the literature on trade in intermediate services, De Groot and Nordas show that the possibility of trade in services can drastically affect specialisation patterns and welfare across countries. However, they add several features that enhance the coverage of the concepts that are at play in the rise of the information age.

Let's take a short look at one possible chain of effects of developments in ICT on specialisation patterns and welfare. First, the fall in trading costs (i.e., transport costs of information) enables more effective world-scale competition in the provision of information services. Production of these information services is subject to economies of scale. Since these services together enter as complementary inputs in the production of final products according to the principle of increasing returns to variety, changes in specialisation patterns may even result in a loss of welfare in countries that lack the human capital or information infrastructure needed.

2.4.2 Outsourcing and Transaction Costs

The rising demand for information services has been identified as one of the key changes in the New Economy. Together with the increased tradability of information services, rising demand implies a larger potential market. This is a further incentive for outsourcing of these services to specialised firms in the market. Economies of scale in the production of indirect inputs can be more fully exploited by specialisation in the market (de Groot, 2001).[2]

Whether intermediate services will remain to be provided in-house or will increasingly be provided by decentralised market exchange then depends on the change in transaction costs that ensues from such a shift in the mode of governance. Before contemplating the possible effects of ICT on the relative efficacy of market versus internal provision of information services, a short overview of the logic of transaction cost economics is presented.

Transaction cost economics appreciates the fact that transactions need to be aligned with varying governance structures (Williamson, 1998) in order to organise economic activity efficiently. The key insight behind this is that people have limited capabilities and lack perfect insight. Under these circumstances contractual partners tend to act opportunistically to some degree, depending on the balance of power in the transaction relation and the complexity (uncertainty) of events. For the respective partners, the extent of specificity of their assets related to the transaction determines the degree of bilateral dependencies between them. Potential conflict may thus arise surrounding an economic transaction. To prevent such conflict from undoing or upsetting opportunities to realise mutual gains, a governance structure has to be chosen that fits the characteristics of a given transaction. Not all transactions can be organised according to the governance of market exchange and still less can fully depend on the pure price mechanism of the invisible hand. Contracts are often necessary. This may even amount to the abandonment of market relations in favour of internalisation into hierarchical relations.

From this point of view, all costs that arise in relation to the chosen contractual arrangements for a transaction qualify as transaction costs. All of these costs are incurred in planning, adapting and monitoring task completion in its most general form on behalf of the transaction (de Groot, 2001). Think of costs of logistic management and organisation, search costs for contractual partners, costs of devising contractual safeguards, costs of bureaucratic distortions and consequential costs from the contractual hazards of task incompletion.

In general, market provision is associated with higher contractual hazards and higher costs of control, the more specific the assets are related to the transaction. Internalisation then becomes a relatively more beneficial option. Conversely, in a situation of low asset specificity the market becomes a relatively more efficient governance structure. Obviously, the opportunities for reaching economies of scale rise when assets are less specific. Market provision enlarges the scale of production relative to internal provision by pooling resources, thus realising the opportunities for economies of scale. Furthermore, the adaptability of the market to changing conditions of demand and supply is better in such a situation.

Transaction costs are generally related to the search for and acquisition and interpretation of information. How does ICT affect these costs? Access to information has become easier and the capacity to process information into knowledge has risen. This also implies that ICT has a significant administrative impact on the organisation of economic activity. What consequences does the change in organisational capacity have for the transaction costs of market and hierarchy?

First, ICT reduces the costs of logistic planning and organisation of transactions in both market and hierarchical contexts. Think, for example, of the costs related to stock management. This fall in transaction costs occurs across the board and reflects the productivity gains in the information infrastructure (more effective and productive information systems and networks). Second, faster and more comprehensive access to information and knowledge lowers the costs of search, control and, to a certain degree, the extent of asset specificity. The latter needs some further illustration.

A lack of information in a situation of bounded rationality caused part of the product differentiation in information services in the 'old' economy. Since the markets for information services were non-transparent and geographically constrained, each producer of end products entered into close relation with only a few intermediate service providers. In this way each intermediate producer faced firm-specific demand. Asset specificity thus generated an unfavourable balance of power for downstream producers. Often this would amount to the internalisation of these services within a vertically integrated hierarchy. The improvements in the conditions of information acquisition resulting from ICT lead to more transparent and geographically extended markets. Both customers and providers get easier access to larger markets. As a result, the extent of asset specificity falls and the degree of competition rises. Concluding the second category of effects, it can be said that the costs related to opportunism can be better contained because of the advent of the information age. Thus ICT reduces the consequential costs of market provision and therefore the need for devising detailed contracts of little adaptability.[3] As a consequence, the rationale of internal provision diminishes.

Combined with the arguments of increasing market unpredictability and scale effects that were discussed earlier, all of this suggests that ICT is an important driving force behind the increased tendency to outsource non-core activities. It tends to reduce transaction and transportation costs and thereby fosters the marked-mediated exchange of goods and services. The market has become more effective in providing high-powered incentives for transactions of diverse nature (de Groot, 2001). Outsourcing may complement the process of rising international trade and specialisation in information services. It allows further productivity gains in the presence of scale economies and returns to variety. Final good producers are enabled to focus on core activity, while information services become available and more easily substitutable on the market, at lower prices and larger variety.

Countries that most successfully install an effective and productive information infrastructure will succeed best in bringing transport and transaction costs down. As a result, outsourcing of intermediates and productivity gains in information services and end products will be highest there. These countries stand to gain most from the changes in costs, tradability of services and specialisation patterns that lie ahead in the emerging New Economy.

2.5 PRODUCTIVITY AND GROWTH IN THE INFORMATION AGE

In this section some of the most important findings so far are first recapitulated. Then the interpretation of transaction costs in relation to the nature of information services is sharpened. Subsequently, the analysis is extended by considering the dynamic implications of the New Economy.

2.5.1 Main Insights

It is argued in this chapter that the best way to understand the information age is to acknowledge that cost structures have changed drastically. ICT developments have lowered the costs of information acquisition, provision and processing. These changes result in falling variable costs of customisation, a geographical extension of markets and declining transaction costs. Consequently, the economic structure and the way of doing business are changing. Competition in the entire commodity chain becomes more global and transactions become more complex. Cost considerations increase the reliance on vertical specialisation (outsourcing of support services) and market incentives. Because of economies of scope in marketing, conglomeration becomes an alternative strategy to cope with increased market volatility (Reich, 2001). All of this has increased the dependence on complex information systems that exploit the advantages of the information age. The information systems themselves are costly to develop. Indeed, rising R&D intensity, a shift to fixed (sunk) costs and complementarity to human capital creation are important features of information services in the New Economy.

To appropriate the productivity benefits of the New Economy, the development of an effective information infrastructure is necessary. This requires the development of complicated information systems and the skills to apply these in production and marketing. Because of the complementarity to human capital building, learning effects and the need for efficient capital markets to finance the development cost, less developed countries are at risk.

2.5.2 Information Services and Transaction Costs

The analysis of the information age yields a paradox. The more efficient information infrastructure manifests itself through falling transaction costs. But the intensified competition that coincides with the New Economy also pushes the economy towards more complex transactions. What, then, is the total effect on transaction costs and how should we interpret the outcome?

A two-tier approach to transaction costs is adopted to solve the paradox. This interpretation further stresses the distinction between transaction costs and trading costs. Transaction costs arise because of the need to govern transactions that emerge as a result of specialisation of labour. Contracts have to be arranged between partners and information has to be collected to establish a division of tasks, execute them and control these activities (see Section 2.4). The collection and absorption of information are central to transaction costs.

Two layers of information activity can be identified. At the first layer, information services serve to collect and present information and knowledge to the contractual partners as input into their management process. These services can be identified formally as transaction costs and can be referred to as 'transaction cost-related support services'. Examples are computer services (software development and computer advice), data management services (such as inventory and order documentation, and accounting in general) and consultancy (marketing advice, management advice and accountancy). The (top and middle) management of the contractual relation can be found at the deeper, more fundamental, second layer of information activity. This layer supports the activities that absorb and process the information and knowledge provided by the first layer in order to plan, coordinate and control task completion in transactions (e.g., stock management, financial management and strategic planning). These activities are also transaction costs.[4] They are more fundamental transaction costs, because demand for first-layer intermediate services arises from the overhead service activity in this layer.

Transaction costs need to be distinguished from trading costs. Transaction costs are related to the coordination of interactions between contractual partners. Trading costs arise because of the physical exchanges that are part of transactions, such as the transport and storage of goods and people and the transmission of information. As such, transportation, storage, commerce and telecommunications are examples of services that qualify as trading costs.

The paradox referred to above arises because it may not be clear what role transaction costs and trading costs play in production. Economists interpret activities related to transactions as costs. This leads to the question of whether these activities are productive or a mere waste. All activities, from information services and transportation to commerce and management are productive, since they fulfil a need posed by economic scarcity of information, knowledge and physical movement.[5] The key to understanding the nature of these activities is to acknowledge their indirect (or derived) productivity as intermediates in the production of end products. In this indirect productivity lies the effect of ICT. As a result of ICT, both trading costs and some second-layer transaction costs have fallen. The need for middle management to coordinate task completion and control has diminished (de Groot, 2001). Top management can now focus more and more effectively on strategic planning, a type of transaction cost that yields the highest potential productivity gain for end production. Second, output scale and indirect productivity of information services (first-layer transaction costs) have risen. They have become cheaper and more effective in use. As a result, they have become more important as inputs in production. Evidence on the structure of production has indeed revealed growth of the importance of information-based services in production (Stibora and de Vaal, 1995; de Groot, 1998). Labour has substituted from end products to information services (Reich, 2001).

All in all, the information age allows a relocation of transaction costs to more productive ends by reducing scarcity of information as an input and improving the effectiveness of absorbing and processing this information. The implications of the information age for long-term economic growth can now be addressed. The strategy to be followed to find empirical corroboration or challenge of the theoretical expectations also warrants attention. The remainder of this section addresses these subjects briefly.

2.5.3 Dynamic Aspects of the New Economy

From the empirical literature on the dynamic consequences of the New Economy, a mixed picture arises. Accelerating productivity growth seems to concentrate in a small section of the economy, notably communication equipment, computer and related industries, and the rest of durable manufacturing (Gordon, 2000). Still, the effects of the New Economy may be delayed because of the required transformation of the economic structure for the absorption of ICT developments. Productivity growth could eventually accelerate if the New Economy proves to change the way business is done across the economy: doing different things differently. The information age and the emergent importance of complex information systems constitute a truly new economy. This argument conforms with the view of fundamental structural change, also called the 'general-purpose technology' view of ICT (Helpman, 1998). According to the view, at least for an extended period of time, the productivity growth trend would shift upwards. The information age of computer and Internet technology has a further potential benefit for long-term growth. Like the invention of script, the introduction of integrated computer, information and communication technologies may enhance research productivity on a permanent basis. The reason is that a new information technology is even more general than all previous general purpose technologies: it can be used in the production process of knowledge itself, besides its role as a source of inspiration for new developments in technology.[6]

Bartelsman and Hinloopen (2000) offered an analysis in line with this insight. They argue that the use of ICT products in knowledge production raises the rate of growth in knowledge at a constant level of R&D activity. They point out several motivations for their hypothesis. First, knowledge creation benefits considerably from more efficient communication and information processing. Information and communication technologies provide researchers with a vast increase in available data. Computer technologies enable them to process and analyse data in a much more versatile and efficient fashion. Second, ICT products may contribute to wider diffusion and easier absorption of newly developed knowledge by fostering the digital codification of knowledge. Finally, the information age may facilitate matching between demand for knowledge and supply of innovations. Faster and more comprehensive access to information and knowledge lowers the transaction costs of search and monitoring. Thus, ICT leads to more effective communication and better assessment of success during R&D. The productivity of R&D activity rises because efficient matching and interaction help ensure the effectiveness of R&D efforts. The higher productivity of knowledge creation will permanently raise overall technological development and growth in productivity.

Although these arguments seem plausible, some interesting opposition has emerged. First, Gordon (2000) has suggested that the advantages of ever-rising computing power are bound to meet natural limits. Society is moving downward along the demand curve for computing power, in the direction of progressively lower marginal utility of new computing advances. Although interesting, the criticism of Gordon (2000) is rather deterministic. He might have failed to appreciate sufficiently a fundamental feature of general-purpose technologies: they change the way of doing business across the economy and thus shift the demand curve for (additional complementary) innovations outward. Certainly, the information age coincides with rising complexity, which will endogenously call for more R&D. A rising R&D and human capital intensity ensues and may do so without raising productivity growth. But, for now, this seems to be a derived, second-order effect. Human capacity is redirected and complex computer outputs constitute an improvement on previous knowledge, despite the time that needs to be invested in interpreting such outputs.

Second, several theorists have challenged the argument of increased diffusion and absorption of knowledge in the information age.[7] The critique centres around the discussion of the complementarity between tacit and codified knowledge. It is generally accepted that ICT improves the diffusion and absorption of codified knowledge. Analysts disagree, however, on the possibility that a higher percentage of knowledge can become codifiable and whether actors in R&D will even wish to increase codification. Probably tacit knowledge remains important to be able to absorb codified knowledge and generate new knowledge. The increased efficiency in codifying parts of knowledge serves as a stimulus for investments in tacit knowledge too. After all, tacit knowledge allows the producers and/or users of new knowledge to appropriate the economic benefits of this knowledge better. Overall investments in, and output of, knowledge creation may still increase as a result of ICT. Yet, an improvement of productivity in terms of codified knowledge may just as well lead to less overall investment in knowledge creation and lower technological progress, since tacit knowledge becomes relatively expensive and free riding on knowledge created by others increases.

2.5.4 Empirical Issues

In order to assess the changes in the services trade and specialisation patterns that occur in the information age, empirical research is very important. Unfortunately, empirical research on trade in services is relatively rare because of the lack of detailed international trade statistics on services. Still, sectoral studies may allow a comparison of trade in information services for a selected group of countries. Several empirical questions emerge to test the theoretical expectations regarding trade patterns.

First, the importance of trade in services must be assessed. The question arises as to whether services trade has kept up with or even surpassed the fast pace of growth in merchandise trade in recent decades. As shown in Linders (2001), it turns out that trade in services accounts for about 20 percent of world trade. Since 1980, the share of services has risen slightly from 17 percent. Interestingly, the evidence shows that the share of information-based business services has grown steadily. While the position of services has matured within the composition of global trade, some countries clearly specialise relative to others in exporting services. The second question, therefore, is to determine patterns of relative export specialisation in services across countries. The special emphasis on information services may, however, limit the range of countries for which detailed trade patterns can be acquired. More sensible and detailed research may be possible on the next empirical question: 'what are the determinants of specialisation patterns in services trade flows?' Given the heterogeneous nature of information services and the presence of economies of scale, intra-industry trade and trade under imperfect competition are expected to be relevant. Also, as noted earlier, the New Economy is characterised by increased complexity and interdependence of industries. Therefore, external economies of scale within the information infrastructure – due to learning and complementarity to human capital – can be expected to be relevant too. The challenge will be to capture these economies in empirical indicators. A crucial part of the effort will focus on the measurement of differences in transaction costs between countries, as resulting from differences in the productivity of the information infrastructure.

2.6 ICT, KNOWLEDGE AND LOCALITY

Knowledge is a particular good in an information economy. Although in an ICT world knowledge might in principle be accessible everywhere, both knowledge-rich and knowledge-poor areas are observed in reality, depending on the investment efforts in knowledge creation, diffusion and use. In particular, the creation of new knowledge is a phenomenon that is fraught with lack of insight. Indeed, knowledge incubation is a rarely studied phenomenon, in contrast to firm incubation. Not only the presence of a knowledge infrastructure (e.g., universities, laboratories, research institutes) but also the local attitude (sense of intellectuality, open mind, interest in knowledge transfer) play a critical role. From a regional–urban perspective, the openness of the locality is also an important factor. Knowledge acquisition most likely follows the Schumpeterian view on the production of new insights in a competitive environment (Acs and Varga, 2001).

It should be added that the local knowledge base is also of utmost importance for local economic development. In a knowledge society, many firms are critically dependent on the access to new knowledge. And therefore, knowledge is also a major characteristic of a locality (van Geenhuizen and Nijkamp, 2001). When attracting new activities and investments, regions can follow two basic strategies, viz. competing with low costs or competing with high value-added. The latter strategy encapsulates many policy challenges. Competing with high value-added means competing with creativity, the best and latest information, the highest standards of production, and an easy access to resources and companies around the world (Andersson, 1991; Kanter, 1995; Mayinger, 2001). Thus, this strategy is based upon the production and use of knowledge as an essential economic resource. Therefore, the first reason for focusing on knowledge as the outcome of learning processes is likely to be the better performance of knowledge-based economic growth. A second reason is the expected structural change of the economic base of many city regions in advanced economies, reflected in a transformation of this economic base from commodity-based activities in the production sector to knowledge-based activities in the broader service sector. In addition, there tends to be a move from mass production to more flexible modes of production, the latter requiring greater variation in knowledge and knowledge application (Acs, 2002). Another important reason for addressing knowledge is its potential contribution to sustainable development, in terms of application of new technology and new organisational formats. A fourth and final reason for paying attention to knowledge is the nature of policy making itself. There is an increasing uncertainty in regional policy making, caused by factors such as conflicting outcomes in related policy fields, varying support of the stakeholders involved and macroeconomic developments. Policy making becomes a learning activity in itself by including methods of policy design that take uncertainty into account (e.g., Friend and Hickling, 1997). Regional and urban policy makers, therefore, may treat knowledge and the underlying learning processes as essential sources of economic power, competitiveness and sustainable development.

Knowledge is part of our modern ICT society. It is a *sine qua non* for its emergence and survival. It is also a tradable good, but usually only in the form of codified knowledge. Creative knowledge or tacit knowledge is normally not for sale. It has to be generated and facilitated at favourable locations.

An important lesson is that the much-praised concept of the 'death of distance' suggests that free market access is abundantly available all over the world and that space is a free good. This is a mistake, as space remains scarce and its relative scarcity leads to significant price differences in land use. In addition, greater logistic efforts are needed to ensure an efficient delivery of an ever-growing variety of physical goods. Despite ICT, material consumption will rise ('kilobytes cannot be eaten'). A second reason why the tyranny of space will still prevail in the future is that there is no free access to ICT. To reap the fruits of ICT in a competitive international environment requires much investment in hardware, software and intellectware. In this context, endogenous growth theory offers an important lesson: there is 'no ICT manna from heaven'. Thus, the question arises under which conditions specific regions are able to attract more ICT activities than others. This will be decisive for the distribution of welfare and hence for global equity (Lall and Yilmaz, 2001). The answer to the above question cannot be given by simple comparative cost arguments nor by neoclassical trade theory. It requires an evolutionary perspective with a blend of endogenous growth theory, innovation and incubation theory, and new economic geography, complemented by sustainability theory.

2.7 POSSIBLE FUTURE RESEARCH DIRECTIONS

Many interesting questions concerning the impact of ICT on the international economy remain. This final section briefly sketches the directions for future research on this subject. Given the importance of the information infrastructure for reaping the potential benefits of the information age, future research should focus on the links between ICT, transaction costs and the productivity of the information infrastructure.

Information systems, physical and intangible networks, and human capital that together form the information infrastructure can potentially revolutionalise the organisation of economic activity by reducing trading and transaction costs. The productivity of the information infrastructure, however, may crucially depend on the intangible, informal network of trust and convention between economic agents. In the end, trust is the key determinant behind transaction costs (Fukuyama, 1995) and hence for realising the full potential of ICT to lower these costs. This aspect strengthens the case for the thesis that ICT is enforcing agglomeration trends and reinforcing cities. The 'comparative advantage' of cities in generating the network externalities associated with ICT has already been mentioned. Issues surrounding trust may help explain the geographical dimension of the ICT revolution. Indeed, then, the local–global divide in the information age is much more complicated than the visions of 'electronic cottages' or the 'e-society' suggest. High-value production, especially of information services, is likely to be localised in areas with dense networks of trust and human capital. In these regions, the full potential of the information age can be reached. An efficiently operating information infrastructure yields a superior productivity of information services and human capital as inputs into the production of end products.

The question then remains whether ICT will lower trading and especially transaction costs of information services sufficiently for lagging regions to benefit from increased tradability without falling further behind in the technological capability to attract new industries. Here, the question is also whether ICT will largely substitute electronic networking for intensive person-to-person interaction in the provision of key information services, or will rather complement these 'handshake' institutions in localised agglomerations of high-tech activity. Sales of end products, however, are likely to be global, as the costs of transport and information transmission have plunged.

The importance of the locality of the information revolution puts forward the need for comparative data on the issues identified above. The construction of a database in which ICT and institutional factors, such as trust, play a prominent part in a geographical context will be of central importance for further study of the development of relative welfare in the New Economy.

NOTES

1. For convenience, intangibles will be equated to services throughout the chapter. In this way, information systems and the provision of information are both among information services. See, for example, Hirsch (1989), Stibora and de Vaal (1995) and Linders (2001) for specific discussion of the nature and characteristics of services and information. Hill (1977) has provided the most widely accepted academic definition of services.

2. The interdependence between rising demand and outsourcing also indicates that we should not attribute the entire rise in the share of intermediate services in output to rising demand. Part of it reflects outsourcing of already existent activity and represents organisational rather than structural changes. Still, much of this organisational change in turn reflects structural changes in cost and demand parameters (Postner, 1990).
3. Alternatively some argue that information systems can be deliberately used to create bureaucratic distortions and serve conflicting interests and opportunistic behaviour. Competitive pressure can either induce individual agents' learning efforts in order to become more competitive, or to hamper and obstruct knowledge creation more effectively. Ultimately, the outcome depends on the nature of informational asymmetries and the capability of information systems to alleviate or strengthen these asymmetries. Asset specificity is a crucial variable for the ability to appropriate quasi-rents by opportunistic acts. If anything, ICT seems to reduce such specificities somewhat. Therefore, the ultimate total effect of ICT on transaction costs tends to be beneficial.
4. The consequential costs of task incompletion are also transaction costs and part of this second management layer.
5. It will be clear that consequential costs, as part of transaction costs, are pure waste. These costs are clearly different from other transaction costs, since they are not produced but result as a by-product of some failure.
6. One can argue that the same holds for electricity or the wheel. With electricity, light, motion and even measurement came to be applied in much more sophisticated ways than before. Of course, all of these phenomena are ingredients in the research process. Still, information is even more crucial for and akin to knowledge creation. It is the basic source of all knowledge.
7. The challenge arose at a workshop on ICT, organised by the Netherlands Bureau for Economic Policy Research (CPB) and the Dutch Ministry of Economic Affairs, The Hague, in spring 2000.

REFERENCES

Acs, Z. (2002), *Innovation and the Growth of Cities*, Cheltenham, UK and Northampton, MA, USA: Edward Elgar.

Acs, Z. and A. Varga (2001), 'Geography, endogenous growth and innovation', *International Regional Science Review*, 25, 132-148.

Andersson, A.E. (1991), 'Creation, innovation and diffusion of knowledge - general and specific economic impacts', *Sistemi Urbani*, 3, 5-28.

Bartelsman, E. and J. Hinloopen (2000), 'De verzilvering van een groeibelofte', in L. Soete (ed.), *ICT en de Nieuwe Economie*, Utrecht: Lemma, pp. 61-81.

Brynjolfsson, E. and L. Hitt (1995), 'Information technology as a factor of production', *Economics of Information and New Technology*, 3, 183-199.

Capello, R. (1994), *Spatial Economic Analysis of Telecommunications Network Externalities*, Aldershot: Avebury.

Castells, M. (1996), *The Rise of the Network Society*, Malden: Basil Blackwell.

de Groot, H.L.F. (1998), *Economic Growth, Sectoral Structure and Unemployment*, PhD Thesis, Tilburg: Tilburg University.

de Groot, H.L.F. (2001), 'Macroeconomic consequences of outsourcing: an analysis of growth, welfare and product variety', *De Economist* 149, 53-79.

de Groot, H.L.F. and H.K. Nordas (2001), 'Trade in information services and economic development: on the implications of ICT for less developed countries', SNF Working Paper, no. 32/01, Bergen.

Dixit, A.K. and J.E. Stiglitz (1977), 'Monopolistic competition and optimum product diversity', *American Economic Review*, 67, 297-308.

Foray, D. and B.-A. Lundvall (1996), 'The knowledge based economy', in OECD (ed.), *Employment and Growth in the Knowledge Based Economy*, Paris: OECD, pp. 11-32.

Francois, J. (1990), 'Trade in producer services and returns due to specialization under monopolistic competition', *Canadian Journal of Economics*, 23, 109-124.

Francois, J. and K. Reinert (1995), 'The role of services in the structure of production and trade: stylized facts from a cross-country analysis', CEPR Discussion Paper, no. 1228, London: Centre for Economic Policy Research.

Friend, J. and A. Hickling (1997), *Planning Under Pressure. The Strategic Choice Approach*, Oxford: Butterworth-Heinemann.

Fujita, M., Krugman, P. and A.J. Venables (1999), *The Spatial Economy: Cities, Regions and International Trade*, Cambridge, MA: MIT Press.

Fukuyama, F. (1995), *Trust: The Social Virtues and the Creation of Prosperity*, New York: The Free Press.

Gillespie, A. and H. Williams (1988), 'Telecommunications and the reconstruction of regional comparative advantage', *Environment and Planning*, 20, 1311-1321.

Glaeser, E. (1998), 'Are cities dying?', *Journal of Economic Perspectives*, 12, 139-160.

Glaeser, E., Kallal, H., Scheinkman, J. and A. Shleifer (1992), 'Growth in cities', *Journal of Political Economy*, 100, 1126-1152.

Gomory, R.E. and W.J. Baumol (2000), *Global Trade and Conflicting National Interests*, Cambridge, MA, MIT Press.

Gordon, R.J. (2000), "Does the 'New Economy' measure up to the great inventions of the past?", *Journal of Economic Perspectives*, 14, 49-74.

Gorter, C. and P. Nijkamp (2001), 'Location theory', in S. Hanson (ed.), *Encyclopedia of the Social Sciences*, Amsterdam: Elsevier.

Graham, S. (1999), 'Global grids of glass: on global cities, telecommunications and planetary urban networks', *Urban Studies*, 36, 929-949.

Helpman, E. (1998) (ed.), *General Purpose Technologies and Economic Growth*, Cambridge, MA: MIT Press.

Hill, T.P. (1977), 'On goods and services', *Review of Income and Wealth*, 23, 315-338.

Hirsch, S. (1989), 'Services and service intensity in international trade', *Weltwirtschaftliches Archiv*, 19, 45-59.

Jones, R.W. (2000), *Globalization and the Theory of Input Trade*, Cambridge, MA: MIT Press.

Kanter, R.M. (1995), *Thriving Locally in the Global Economy*, New York: Simon & Schuster.

Kohno, H., Nijkamp, P. and J. Poot (2000), *Regional Cohesion and Competition in the Age of Globalisation*, Cheltenham, UK and Northampton, MA, USA: Edward Elgar.

Krugman, P. (1990), *Rethinking International Trade*, Cambridge, MA: MIT Press.

Krugman, P. and A.J. Venables (1995), 'Globalization and the inequality of nations', *Quarterly Journal of Economics*, 110, 857-880.

Lall, S. and S. Yilmaz (2001), 'Regional economic convergence: do policy instruments make a difference?', *Annals of Regional Science*, 35, 153-166.

Leinbach, T.R. and S.D. Brunn (2001), *The Wired Worlds of Electronic Commerce*, London: John Wiley.

Linders, G. (2001), 'Theory, methodology and descriptive statistics on services and services trade', CPB Memorandum 10, The Hague: CPB Netherlands Bureau for Economic Policy Analysis.

Lundvall, B.-A. (1998), 'The learning economy', in B. Johnson and K. Nielsen (eds), *Institutions and Economic Change*, Cheltenham, UK and Northampton, MA, USA: Edward Elgar, pp. 33-54.

Markusen, J. (1989), 'Trade in producer services and in other specialized intermediate inputs', *American Economic Review*, 79, 85-95.

Mayinger, F. (2001), *Mobility and Traffic in the 21st Century*, Berlin: Springer Verlag.

Mitchell, W.J. (1995), *City of Bits, Space, Place, and the Infobahn*, Cambridge, MA: MIT Press.

Pohl, N. (2001), *Mobility in Space and Time*, Heidelberg: Physika-Verlag.

Postner, H.H. (1990), 'The contracting-out problem in service sector analysis: choice of statistical unit', *Review of Income and Wealth*, 36, 177-186.

Rauch, J. (1993), 'Productivity gains from geographic concentration of human capital: evidence from the cities', *Journal of Urban Economics*, 34, 380-400.

Reich, R.B. (2001), *The Future of Success*, New York: Alfred A. Knopf.

Shapiro, C. and H.R. Varian (1999), *Information Rules*, Cambridge, MA: Harvard University Press.

Stibora, J. and A. de Vaal (1995), *Services and Services Trade: A Theoretical Inquiry*, Amsterdam: Thesis Publishers.

van Geenhuizen, M. and P. Nijkamp (2001), 'Knowledge as a crucial resource in policy making for mainport Rotterdam', in M. van Geenhuizen and R. Ratti (eds), *Gaining Advantage from Open Borders*, Aldershot: Ashgate, pp. 285-304.

Westland, J.Ch. and T.H.K. Clark (1999), *Global Electronic Commerce: Theory and Case Studies*, Cambridge, MA: MIT Press.

Williamson, O.E. (1998), 'Transaction cost economics: how it works, where it is headed', *De Economist*, 146, 23-58.

3. Geography, Transactions Costs and Economic Performance

Philip McCann

3.1. INTRODUCTION

During the last decade, there has been a renewed growth of interest in the role which geography plays in determining economic performance. The recent interest in the economics of geography has arisen due to three major and concurrent influences: technological, institutional and analytical.

The principal technological influences that have contributed to the recent growth of interest in the economic impacts of geography are the technological developments that have significantly reduced the transactions costs associated with distance. The rapid growth and improvements in information, communication and transportation technologies have improved the ability of decision makers to coordinate market and organisational activities across larger spatial areas. These new technologies permit better planning and control of productive activities across multiple locations, resulting in an improved ability to exploit intra-marginal differences in international and interregional rates of return. As such, a cursory analysis would suggest that the economic importance of geographical location, and in particular the adverse consequences of geographic peripherality, may appear to become rather less important than they might previously have been.

The institutional influences, which have recently encouraged more discussion about the economic consequences of geography, are the movements towards free trade and integrated market areas such as the EU, NAFTA, ASEAN and MERCOSUR. While the underlying logic behind the creation of these zones is the assumption of overall mutual welfare gains, the exact geographical distribution of these gains is an important question for policy makers (Yeung et al., 1999; Clement et al., 1999). Within these integrated market areas, the falling importance of national borders as arbiters of economic performance raises issues such as possible spatial differences in the types and quality of investment both within and between countries, and also possible differential growth impacts between central and peripheral locations (Krugman and Venables, 1990). In these discussions, the question of whether or not there are any adverse consequences associated with geographical peripherality depends primarily on whether or not economic integration is seen as a universal equilibrating growth mechanism (Barro and Sala-i-Martin, 1992).

The final influence behind the recent increase in interest in the economics of geography comes from analytical developments. In particular the work of two key commentators, Paul Krugman (1991) and Michael Porter (1990), has opened up discussions of the role which geography plays in economics and business to a much wider academic and policy-making audience than was previously the case. Their work has spawned two huge literatures. The work of Krugman (1991) has led to the development of the so-called 'new economic geography' literature, which argues that the uneven distribution of industrial activities across space is a natural result of market processes. Meanwhile the work of Porter (1990) has fostered the literature promoting the importance of industrial 'clusters'. Both of these literatures have also pervaded the popular press as well as national and international policy-making circles. As such, the influence of these arguments concerning the economic aspects of geography now goes well beyond the domain of academic research environments and extends widely into public policy spheres. The primary lessons from these two literatures are that geography really does matter in determining economic performance and geographic peripherality can have adverse consequences.

The three principal influences behind the recent growth of interest in the economics of geography each appear, at least at face value, to somewhat contradict each other in terms of the potential adverse impacts of geographical peripherality. The technological influence appears to argue for a reduced importance of differential location, and the institutional influence appears to suggest that the importance of differential location depends on returns to scale, while the current academic influence appears to suggest that location has significant consequences. How can we reconcile these different influences?

The aim of this chapter is to consider these issues from the perspective of the transactions costs involved in the overcoming of space. By examining the nature, extent and role of spatial transactions costs we can begin to identify the conditions under which location does or does not play a significant economic role. The chapter is organised as follows. In Section 3.2 we review the various arguments that suggest that spatial transactions costs have fallen over time, and we then compare these with the arguments that suggest not only that they may not have fallen over time, but that in some cases they may have risen over time. In order to do this, we focus in each case initially on information transactions costs, and then subsequently on goods-shipments costs. In Section 3.3 we review the analytical models that argue for proximity as an essential economic advantage under certain conditions. On the basis of these arguments we then adopt a transactions costs approach to present various stylised sets of relationships between the nature of transactions costs, firm behaviour and industry location, which exist in conditions where geographical proximity is deemed to be advantageous. Section 3.4 briefly reviews some of the evidence identifying the spatial extent over which proximity is perceived to be advantageous. Section 3.5 provides some broad conclusions.

3.2   SPATIAL COMMUNICATION AND TRANSPORTATION COSTS

In this section we review the evidence and arguments that suggest that spatial transactions costs have fallen or risen over time. To do this we initially review the arguments that imply that spatial transactions costs have fallen. We then compare these with the counter arguments implying that in some cases spatial transactions costs have risen over time. In each case, we initially review the issues surrounding information transactions and then consider the issues surrounding goods-shipments costs. We also consider here the reasons why the role played by distance-transport costs have often been overlooked by analysts, and provide evidence arguing for a more careful consideration of these issues.

3.2.1 Geography is Becoming Less Important

There are many arguments and much evidence to suggest that spatial transactions costs are falling over time, such that the importance of geographical location becomes progressively less over time. In order to consider these perspectives, we can split the arguments into those that relate to the transactions of information across space and those that relate to the transactions of goods across space.

Falling information transmission costs
The last two decades have seen dramatic improvements in the ability of decision makers and planners to coordinate activities across space. The

primary reason for this is that new developments in information technology mean that complex operations can now be managed both more efficiently and more effectively than was previously possible. There are two aspects to this.

First, the new information technologies have reduced the real cost of communicating across space, in order to more efficiently control existing spatial arrangements of activities (*The Economist*, 1999a). This is a common observation in activities where physical goods are being moved across space, such as in the management of international supply chains (*Financial Times*, 1999) or the coordination of multinational manufacturing sites (*The Economist*, 1999b). Similarly, where information is moved across space, information technologies also allow for more efficient control mechanisms. This is evident in, for example, international accounting, where New York banks transfer their bookkeeping requirements overnight to firms in Dublin, in order to have them updated in time for the opening of the money markets the next day.

Second, the existence of these new information technologies also allows decision makers to undertake the coordination of spatial arrangements of activities that were previously not possible. An example in the case of activities where physical goods are being moved across space is the ability to control just-in-time (JIT) production and supply systems across space. In JIT production and distribution arrangements (Nishiguchi, 1994; Schonberger, 1996), it is necessary to control the flows of goods between firms to a very high degree, in order to ensure the timeliness of deliveries. The ability to track and monitor the speed of movements of goods therefore becomes essential, particularly if the goods are being shipped over significant distances. Similar arguments also hold for the case of customised high-speed mail services. Meanwhile, in the case of service industries such as finance and marketing, the new possibilities provided by information technologies for the supply of information-based services across space appear almost unlimited, at least at first glance (*The Economist*, 1999b).

Each of these arguments suggests that new information technology systematically improves our ability to coordinate activities across space, such that the supply of existing activities will become cheaper due to better management, and also the range of activities supplied across all spatial areas will increase. As such, the advent of these new communication technologies suggests that differences in location would appear to become successively less important over time in determining the range of products and activities available at any location. Some authors have even assumed that eventually this would lead to the death of cities, or even the death of geography as an issue in its own right (Toffler, 1980; Naisbitt, 1995).

The apparent unimportance of transport costs

Many economists have often regarded the role played by transport costs, in determining economic performance or affecting allocative efficiency, as a relatively minor issue. There are three reasons for this. The first reason is that in aggregate production statistics, apart from the case of extraction industries in which transport costs are often of the order of 15 percent, transport costs are empirically found to be rarely above 2–3 percent for most industries, and even less in many modern industries, whereas labour costs will typically be at least of the order of 40–50 percent of total costs (Tyler and Kitson, 1987). Therefore, industrial economists have often argued that marginal changes in local labour prices have a relatively much greater impact on economic behaviour of most industries than do equivalent changes in transport costs. Consequently, discussions have tended to focus on the role played by factor price changes, largely ignoring the role played by transport costs.

The second reason for the disregard of transport costs is that trade economists have often assumed that the effects of these costs can be analysed more or less in the same manner as trade barriers, and that the impacts of high transport costs are primarily to limit trade over large distances only to high value–weight ratio products.

The third reason is that both of the above arguments as to why transport costs should only be of minor importance, also fitted neatly into the prevailing pedagogical framework. Post-war Ricardian trade models based on assumptions of fixed national factor endowments appeared, at least on the surface, to be reasonable in a world of largely closed economies and restricted currency flows (Casson and McCann, 1999).

All three of these arguments can be challenged directly with evidence showing that transport are a much more significant economic issue. The first argument against the prevailing view is that aggregate statistics on transport costs actually tell us very little about the importance of distance costs. The reason for this is that the true costs involved in the overcoming of distance are the total *logistics costs* involved in the shipping, holding and handling of flows of inventories of goods across space, and these are much greater than simply transport costs (McCann, 1993, 1998). These logistics costs comprise the transport costs, the (opportunity) capital costs tied up in inventories, plus the space and labour costs involved in the storage and handling of inventories. Since all of these costs are interrelated, conclusions based on observations of transport costs can be very misleading. For example, in an industry shipping low value–weight ratio goods such as coal, the transport costs involved in moving the coal will be a high proportion of total costs. On the other hand, for firms shipping very high value–weight ratio goods such as electronics components, transport costs will account for a very low share of the total cost. However, this is not to say that distance costs are unimportant, because in this case the majority of the distance costs will be hidden in the very high capital costs tied up with inventory holding and shipping. The total logistics costs arising from shipping goods are always very significant (McCann, 1998; Johnson and Kaplan, 1987).

The second argument against the unimportance of distance transport costs is that real-world observations provide us with many counter examples. Simple rules of thumb suggesting that distance and transport costs mitigate the delivery of low value–weight ratio goods are useless in many cases. New Zealand is a case in point. Many of New Zealand's global exports are agricultural products with very low value–weight ratios. The relationship between distance, spatial patterns of production and the nature of traded goods is thus clearly far from obvious.

The third argument against the conventional wisdom is that the institutional framework of modern international markets is completely different from that which gave respectability to Ricardian trade models. Production factors are now highly mobile. Capital, in particular, is globally mobile, and processes of economic integration are progressively increasing the mobility of labour across both regions and nations. Therefore, production and trade models based on assumptions of fixed factor endowments become increasingly unrepresentative of the types of structural changes being faced by developed modern integrating economies. In these cases, the location of factors, activities and the resulting patterns of interregional and international trade can no longer be assumed as being exogenous for the majority of sectors.

While these arguments suggest that distance costs are actually more significant than many previous analytical approaches imply, that is not to say that in reality they are much more significant than they were previously. Most observers would suggest that distance-transport costs have fallen dramatically in real terms over recent years due to the advent of new technologies such as roll-on roll-off vehicles, containerisation, more fuel-efficient aircraft and ships with lower port-handling costs. The evidence suggests that the aggregate share of total output accounted for by transportation costs has fallen markedly over time (Glaeser, 1998). Therefore, even though we should take transport costs into consideration in a more explicit manner in our models than was previously the case, many observers still assume that the effect of these costs will be relatively marginal.

3.2.2 Geography is Becoming More Important

The arguments outlined above which suggest that information transmission costs have fallen, and consequently geography has become much less critical, must be treated with a certain amount of caution. This is because the validity of these arguments depends implicitly on two assumptions: the transactions costs of moving goods and people across space have fallen; and the changes in transport behaviour should not have led to an increase in transportation costs. In contrast, there are other arguments that suggest that the spatial transactions costs involved in transmitting information may actually be increasing over time. If any of these counter arguments can be substantiated, it would imply that geographical location is becoming an even more important economic consideration nowadays than was previously the case, even after allowing for the information technology developments described above. Once again, we can consider these issues by splitting the arguments into those that relate to the transactions of information across space and those that relate to the transactions of goods across space.

Increasing information transmission costs

In Section 3.2.1 it was explained why most people assume that the increasing development and usage of information technologies will progressively reduce spatial transactions costs, thereby reducing the importance of geography over time. However, there are some other arguments which suggest that the development of these information technologies is actually leading to increases in the costs of transmitting information across space, thereby increasing the importance of geography over time. At issue here is the question of how we define costs. Information technology obviously reduces the costs associated with transmitting particular quantities and types of information across space, but an additional aspect of these technologies is that they also lead to an increase in the quantity, variety and complexity of the information being produced. What are the costs involved in transmitting this additional information across space?

The argument here is that an increase in the quantity, variety and complexity of information produced itself increases the costs associated with transmitting this information across space. This is because much of the information will be of a non-standardised tacit nature, and the transmission of this type of information essentially requires face-to-face contact. The opportunity costs involved in not having face-to-face contact will consequently increase with the quantity, variety and complexity of such information. The greater is the quantity, variety and complexity of the information produced, the more frequent will be the requirement for face-to-face contact. Therefore, in order to consider the information transmission costs between any two agents separated by a given geographical distance, it is necessary to calculate their total transport commuting costs plus the opportunity costs they incur during periods when they are not in face-to-face contact, *at the optimised commuting frequency*. Both of these costs can be shown to be a function of the frequency of their interaction, with the transport-commuting costs being directly related to the commuting frequency and the opportunity costs inversely related to the commuting frequency (McCann, 1995). This itself leads to a frequency optimisation problem, of which the (envelope) result turns out to be a non-linear square root function of each of the spatial and non-spatial cost variables (for details, see the Appendix). Therefore, for any given geographical distance between agents, the general result is that the spatial transactions costs of distance increase as the opportunity costs associated with not having continuous face-to-face contact increase (McCann, 1995). The spatial outcome of this argument is that, *ceteris paribus*, agents will move closer to each other as the variety and complexity of information increases in order to reduce the resulting opportunity costs of distance.

There are two sources of evidence that support this argument that spatial information transactions costs have increased over recent decades as the level of information technology usage increases. The first source of evidence comes from observations on the rate of global urbanisation. Over the last three decades, the proportion of people living in urban areas has increased in all parts of both the developed and developing world (United Nations, 1997). While the reasons for this are complex, particularly in relation to the out-migration of labour from rural areas in developing economies, the ubiquitous urbanisation phenomenon in the developed parts of the world where information technologies are mostly applied suggests that the geographical proximity of firms and people is becoming relatively more advantageous over time.

This observation can also be bolstered by evidence from interpersonal interactions in these economies. The second source of evidence suggesting that information transactions costs have increased over time has been provided by Gaspar and Glaeser (1998) and involves an assessment of telephone usage patterns. Using data from Japan and the USA Gaspar and Glaeser observe that there is a relationship between the density and frequency of telephone usage and the location of the users. First, they find that users who are geographically closer together, and for whom greater face-to-face contact is therefore easier, spend more time talking to each other on the telephone than do users who are at greater distances from each other. Second, the same result also holds for urban size, in that users in larger urban areas talk to each other relatively more frequently than users in smaller urban centres. Third, the frequency of airline business travel has increased more or less in line with the growth in telecommunications usage.

The implication of these observations is that information and communication technologies and face-to-face contact are not substitutes for each other, but complements. In other words, an increased usage of information and communication technologies leads to an increase in the quantity, variety and complexity of information produced, which itself leads to an increase in spatial information transactions costs, and an associated increased need for spatial proximity to facilitate face-to-face contact. At the same time, an increase in the levels of spatial proximity encourages a greater usage of information and communication technologies, and the production of more varied and complex information.

Increasing transportation costs
In Section 3.2.1 it was argued that the distance costs associated with shipping goods are actually much greater in reality than many previous analytical commentators have assumed. However, irrespective of these pedagogical or paradigmatic changes, exactly how this argument relates to the question of whether geography is really becoming more or less important as an economic issue depends on whether such distance transactions costs themselves have become more or less significant over recent years. The evidence on this point is along similar lines to that presented above for the case of information transactions.

Moreover, transportation technologies have improved dramatically over recent years with the growth in roll-on roll-off trucking, containerisation, rapid-turnaround shipping, and the increased efficiency and frequency of airline services. The reduced real costs of transporting goods and people would suggest that geography is becoming less important as these new technologies appear. However, as we have noted above, the quantity, variety and complexity of market information generated in the modern economy are increasing. Therefore, this also implies that in many industries, which involve the production or shipping of goods across space, the variety and complexity of the logistics operations being undertaken will also increase. The reason for this is that as modern consumer demand is becoming more sophisticated, there is an increasing preference for goods shipments characterised by speed, reliability and timeliness. In other words, the consumer's opportunity costs of time have also increased for goods shipments. As such, there is a direct parallel with the argument regarding information costs. However, the opportunity (time) costs of goods shipments are in this case tied up in the levels of inventory being held, rather than the opportunity (time) costs of not having face-to-face contact. Modern household and industrial consumers now require a level of service customisation and delivery speed which previously were not considered as important or even possible. As the demand for delivery speed increases, the associated opportunity costs of lead-times also increase. The effects of this on distance costs can be explained by adopting a similar argument to that employed in the case of information transmission costs. For any two agents at a given distance apart, the optimised delivery frequency increases as the opportunity costs of time increase. As with the case above, the (envelope) result turns out to be a non-linear square root function of all cost variables (McCann, 1993, 1998, 2001b). Once again, analytically, the effect of this is to increase the transactions costs associated with shipping goods over any given distance.

There is a range of empirical evidence which suggests that the spatial transactions costs involved in the shipping of goods has actually increased over the last two decades because of the demand for more frequent deliveries. First, the average inventory levels for almost all manufacturing and distribution sectors in the developed world have fallen dramatically since the 1980s, relative to the value of output (Schonberger, 1996; *Financial Times'* 1998). This implies that the average lead-times of goods shipments have fallen over recent years, with a concomitant increase in goods-shipment frequencies. Second, by carefully disentangling the various components of transport costs it becomes clear that the proportion of global output which is accounted for by logistics and transportation activities in the economy has not fallen over recent decades (Hummels, 1999; *Financial Times*, 1997). Third, while the transportation cost component of bulk materials has generally fallen, there is evidence that this proportion has actually increased over recent decades, in spite of the improvement in transportation and logistics technologies (Hummels, 1999).

The most extreme example of this trend towards more frequent shipments is the application of JIT manufacturing and distribution techniques, the influence of which has pervaded all areas of modern production, distribution and retailing. In this case, the inventory levels are minimised and the frequency of shipments is maximised. From the above commuting-frequency arguments, the goods-shipments transportation costs between two agents located at any given distance will be maximised by the adoption of a JIT logistics arrangement. As such, geographical distance will become more significant as a cost issue. Therefore, this will provide the firm with the incentive to offset the cost increases associated with the adoption of a JIT logistics strategy, particularly by reducing the average distance between itself and its suppliers or customers. Observations of local expenditure patterns confirm that this type of location-substitution behaviour has taken place in a range of industries in response to the adoption of JIT techniques (Reid, 1995; McCann, 1998). Moreover, this behaviour is even evident in industries in which the product value–weight ratios are extremely high (McCann and Fingleton, 1996). In other words, this localisation behaviour is present in the very industries that traditional Ricardian trade theories would have ruled out.

3.3 WHICH SECTOR OR WHICH GEOGRAPHY IS IMPORTANT? THE ANALYTICAL ARGUMENTS

Sections 3.2.1 and 3.2.2 provide a range of arguments and evidence that suggest that the real costs involved in transacting information and goods across space have both decreased and increased over recent decades. These apparently conflicting conclusions can be reconciled in that the different types of changes in transactions costs described above have tended to take place in different types of sectors and activities. The sectors in which spatial transactions costs have indeed fallen significantly over recent decades are generally those sectors in which the nature of the spatial transactions undertaken have not changed fundamentally over time, in terms of the required frequency of interaction. This is typically the case in many raw material or extraction industries, and in industries producing manufactured products at a mature stage within their product cycles (Vernon, 1966). This is also the case in service sector industries in which the nature of the information being transacted is rather standardised, such as retail banking. In these cases, geographical peripherality would appear to be less of a disadvantage. On the other hand, in production sectors in which the demand lead-times have fallen dramatically, or in industries in which the variety and complexity of information generated have increased significantly, spatial transactions costs would appear not to have fallen over recent decades, while in some cases they have actually increased. In these cases, the requirement for geographic proximity as well as the potential disadvantages of peripherality would appear to have increased.

So far, we have been able to identify the ways in which the different types of spatial transactions costs involved in different industries may have changed over time. However, what we have not yet been able to do is to indicate the extent to which geographic proximity is economically advantageous or, conversely, the extent to which geographical peripherality is disadvantageous. In order to do this, we have to identify the spatial extent over which differences in the levels of such transactions costs become crucial.

As discussed earlier, the increased generation of complex and variable information encourages spatial proximity, to avoid the opportunity costs of distance. This kind of logic underlies one of Alfred Marshall's (1920) externality explanations for the existence of industrial agglomeration. Marshall's first observation concerned the existence of 'informal' information spillovers, where 'informal' refers to the fact that they are non-traded information spillovers between agents, primarily of a tacit nature. Such informal and tacit information spillovers can take place between geographically proximate agents or units of labour. Marshall's assumption is that information spillovers operate specifically at the level of the *individual urban area*, and it is over this spatial extent that transactions costs are assumed to become critical. In other words, from the point of view of information transactions, it is the geographical scale of the individual urban area which is critical in terms of determining economic performance. This is also the particular spatial logic that has been adopted by the 'new economic geography' models of Krugman (1991) and Fujita et al. (1999).

There are, however, other models of industrial location that are rather more circumspect in terms of their perception of the critical spatial extent of information transactions. While the 'new economic geography' models are based on the assumption that the individual urban area is the critical spatial extent which defines geographic advantage or disadvantage, the clustering model of Porter (1990, 1998) and the 'new industrial spaces' model of Scott (1988) are much less specific about the particular spatial dimension which is critical in terms of information transactions costs. The clustering model of Porter allows for information flows between firms and individuals within the same urban area, the primary effect of which is to stimulate local competition by increasing the transparency associated with competitive improvements. In other words, the beneficial competitive effects of technological gains are assumed to be most easily manifested within individual urban environments, and this transparency itself acts as a spur to further local competition. However, both the Porter and Scott models also allow for the fact that such information effects may be spread over much larger regional areas than individual cities, particularly where 'trust' relations (Granovetter, 1973) exist between firms. Trust relations between key decision makers in different firms are assumed to reduce inter-firm transactions costs, because firms do not face the problems of opportunism. As such, these trust relations circumvent many of the information issues raised by the markets and hierarchies dichotomy (Williamson, 1975). Where such relations exist, the predictability associated with mutual non-opportunistic trust relations can partially substitute for the disadvantages associated with geographic peripherality. In cases where there are small-firm industrial structures, the spatial extent over which such trust relations operate will tend to be a small sub-national regional scale (Scott, 1988; Porter, 1990). On the other hand, in industrial structures characterised by large vertically integrated firms, such trust relations may operate over much larger regional spatial scales; and in the case of contiguous small-area nations, these regional scales may extend beyond the individual country boundaries (Casson and McCann, 1999).

Notwithstanding the fact that the precise spatial extent over which transactions costs become critical is not always clear, it also varies according to the sector and location in question. In conditions where the quantity, variety and complexity of information produced are great, or the desired frequency of goods shipments is high, the argument still holds that geographical proximity is required to reduce the transactions costs associated with distance. In these cases where geographical proximity is evidently perceived to be advantageous from the variety of analytical and empirical evidence currently available, we can adopt a transactions costs approach to present three stylised sets of geography–firm–industry organisational relationships (Gordon and McCann, 2000; McCann, 2001a; Simmie and Sennet, 1999). The three stylised characterisations of industrial clusters are distinguished in terms of the nature of firms in the clusters, the nature of their relations and the transactions undertaken within the clusters. These three distinct types of industrial clusters can be termed the *pure agglomeration*, the *industrial complex* and the *social network*. In reality, all spatial clusters or industrial concentrations will contain characteristics of one or more of these ideal types, although one type will tend to be dominant in each cluster. The characteristics of each of the cluster types are listed in Table 3.1 and, as we shall see, the three ideal types of clusters are all quite different.

First, in the model of pure agglomeration, inter-firm relations are inherently transient. Firms are essentially atomistic, in the sense of having no market power, and they will continuously change their relations with other firms and customers in response to market arbitrage opportunities, thereby leading to intense local competition. As such, there is neither loyalty between firms nor any particular long-term relationship. The cost of membership of this cluster is simply the local real estate market rent. There are no free riders; access to the cluster is open, and consequently it is the growth in the local real estate rents that is the indicator of the cluster's performance. This idealised type is best represented by Marshall's (1920) model of agglomeration, as adopted by the new economic geography models (Krugman, 1991; Fujita et al., 1999). The notion of space in these models is essentially urban space, in that this type of clustering only exists within individual cities.

Table 3.1 Industrial clusters

Characteristics	Pure agglomeration	Industrial complex	Social network
Firm size	atomistic	some firms are large	variable
Characteristics of relations	non-identifiable unstable and frequent trading fragmented	identifiable stable and frequent trading	trust loyalty joint lobbying joint ventures non-opportunistic
Membership	open	closed	partially open
Access to cluster	rental payments location necessary	internal investment location necessary	history experience location necessary but not sufficient
Space outcomes	rent appreciation	no effect on rents	partial rental capitalisation
Example of cluster	competitive urban economy	steel or chemicals production complex	new industrial areas
Analytical approaches	models of pure agglomeration	location-production theory; input–output analysis	social network model (Granovetter)
Notion of space	urban	local or regional but not urban	local or regional but not urban

Second, the industrial complex is characterised primarily by long-term stable and predictable relations between the firms in the cluster, involving frequent transactions. This type of cluster is most commonly observed in industries such as steel and chemicals. Analytically, this type of spatial cluster is the type typically discussed by classical (Weber, [1909] 1929) and neoclassical (Moses, 1958) location-production models, which represent a fusion of locational analysis with input–output analysis (Isard and Kuenne, 1953). Component firms within each spatial grouping undertake significant long-term investments, particularly in terms of physical capital and local real estate, in order to become part of the grouping. Access to the group is therefore severely restricted both by high entry and exit costs, and the rationale for spatial clustering in these types of industries is that proximity is required primarily in order to minimise inter-firm transport costs. Rental appreciation is not a feature of the cluster because the land, which has already been purchased by the firms, is not for sale. The notion of space in the industrial complex is local, but not necessarily urban, and may extend across a sub-national regional level. In other words, these types of complexes can exist either within or far beyond the boundaries of an individual city, and depend crucially on transportation costs.

The third type of spatial industrial cluster is the social network model. This is associated primarily with the work of Granovetter (1973) and is a response to the hierarchies model of Williamson (1975). The social network model argues that mutual trust relations between key decision-making agents in different organisations may be at least as important as decision-making hierarchies within individual organisations. These trust relations will be manifested by a variety of features, such as joint lobbying, joint ventures, informal alliances and reciprocal arrangements regarding trading relationships. However, the key feature of such trust relations is an absence of opportunism, in that individual firms will not fear reprisals after any reorganisation of inter-firm relations. Inter-firm cooperative relations may therefore differ significantly from the organisational boundaries associated with individual firms, and these relations may be continually reconstituted. All of these behavioural features rely on a common culture of mutual trust, the development of which depends largely on a shared history and experience of the decision-making agents.

This social network model is essentially aspatial, but from the point of view of geography it can be argued that spatial proximity will tend to foster such trust relations over a long time period, thereby leading to a local business environment of confidence, risk taking and cooperation. Spatial proximity is thus necessary, but not sufficient, to acquire access to the network. As such, membership of the network is only partially open, in that local rental payments will not guarantee access, although they will improve the chances of access. The geographical manifestation of the social network is the so-called 'new industrial spaces' model (Scott, 1988), which has been used to describe the characteristics and performance of areas such as the Emilia-Romagna region of Italy (Piore and Sabel, 1984; Scott, 1988). In this model space is once again local, but not necessarily urban, and usually extends over a sub-national regional level. In this case, both information transactions costs and transportation costs may play a role in determining the importance of geographical peripherality.

In each of the three stylised models of industrial clustering, geographic proximity is required in situations where the quantity, variety and complexity of information produced are great, or the desired frequency of inter-firm transactions is high. In each case, the exact level of spatial concentration required in order to offset the associated spatial transactions costs is either at an urban or at a regional scale, but generally much less than at a national scale, unless the country areas are very small. The obvious implication here is that the types of traditional trade models alluded to in Section 3.2.1, which assumed factor allocations to be exogenous and ignored the role of geography, are largely inappropriate for analysing economic behaviour in any of these types of industry-organisational environments.

3.4 WHICH SECTOR OR WHICH GEOGRAPHY IS IMPORTANT? THE EVIDENCE

Glaeser (1998) argues that if we consider goods transportation costs alone, then the rationale for modern cities disappears. On the other hand, he argues that the transportation costs involved in ensuring that people have regular face-to-face contact are the crucial driving force behind the generation of modern cities. In other words, the overcoming of increased modern information transactions costs is the primary rationale underlying the existence of modern cities. Yet, although in principle we can accept various arguments suggesting that geographical proximity is highly advantageous in many cases where information is varied and complex, empirically identifying the critical spatial extent which defines whether a location is advantageous or not is very difficult (Glaeser et al., 1992; Henderson et al., 1995). Indirect methods have to be employed, such as observing the spatial patterns of patent citations (Jaffe et al., 1993) or observing the capitalisation effects on local real estate prices (Gordon and McCann, 2000; McCann, 2001a). These techniques tend to confirm that information spillovers are constrained primarily within the individual urban area, thereby implying that the urban area is the critical geographical range of advantage. On the other hand, other empirical techniques such as observing the formal inter-firm outcomes of informal information exchanges (Arita and McCann, 2000; Audretsch and Feldman, 1996; Suarez-Villa and Walrod, 1997) or the spatial patterns of joint-lobbying activities (Bennett, 1998) suggest that the spatial extent of such information spillovers may be much greater than that of a single city, and may extend across whole sub-national regional areas. In the case of multinational manufacturing firms, Cantwell and Iammarino (2000) argue that the critical spatial areas which define geographic advantage or disadvantage for information spillovers may be far larger than any of the Marshall, Glaeser, Krugman, Porter or Scott arguments imply.

3.5 CONCLUSIONS

While communication and transportation technology has evolved over time, the transactions costs associated with overcoming geographical distance have not necessarily fallen for all industries and all locations. In many cases, these transactions costs continue to encourage economic agents to seek geographical proximity, resulting in the growth of cities or regional industrial systems. While the empirical evidence here suggests that the existence of modern urban concentrations is primarily related to information transactions costs, the assumption that urban concentrations are driven solely by localised information transactions may be somewhat overstated. As such, transportation costs will still play a role in urban development, as suggested by the arguments outlined in Section 3.2.2. Meanwhile, at the larger regional, interregional or international scales, transport cost and information transactions costs are clearly significant in determining the spatial patterns of trade, industry location and product consumption. This assumption is explicit both in traditional regional economics approaches and also in the 'new economic geography' models of spatial competition and trade. The result of all these analytical, empirical and institutional developments is that it is generally now acknowledged that spatial transactions costs are important in determining economic behaviour and performance. In other words, geography confers advantages and disadvantages both below and beyond national boundaries, the outcomes of which depend on the location and sector in question.

APPENDIX

A Simple Model of the Relationship between Transactions Frequency, Location and Total Distance-Transactions Costs

It is quite easy to demonstrate how both aggregate distance costs and transport costs are related to the frequency of interaction between economic agents. Following McCann (1995), we can set up a trip or transactions frequency optimisation problem, in which a firm faces the following cost minimisation problem:

$$C = \phi d^{\rho} f^{n} + \theta f^{-m} + rS \tag{A.1}$$

where d is the distance to the city centre or market point, f is the frequency of the trip or transaction, r is the rent per unit area,[1] S is the land area, C is the total cost per time period, and m, n, ϕ and ρ are positive constants, such that ϕd^{ρ} is the total distance costs per journey. Finally, θ is the opportunity cost of less than continuous face-to-face contact (i.e., f is less than infinite) or goods shipments that are less than pure JIT.

The first term in equation (A.1) reflects the fact that total transport costs per time period are a function of the trip or transactions frequency, while the second term indicates that the opportunity cost of the lost market revenues of a firm may be negatively related to the trip or transactions frequency. In other words, as the trip or transactions frequency increases the firm will increase its market share up to a maximum when continuous face-to-face contact or immediate JIT deliveries are maintained.

In a situation such as this, the firm must determine its optimum trip or transactions frequency. In order to calculate this, we differentiate with respect to f and set the derivative equal to zero:

$$\frac{\partial C}{\partial f} = n\phi d^{\rho} f^{n-1} - m\theta f^{-m-1} = 0 \tag{A.2}$$

The second-order condition can be shown to be positive so that this is the expression for minimum costs (McCann, 1995). Rearranging (A.2) gives:

$$f^{n+m} = \frac{m\theta}{n\phi d^{\rho}} \tag{A.3}$$

Therefore, the optimum trip or transactions frequency per time period F can be written as:

$$F = \left(\frac{m\theta}{n\phi d^{\rho}}\right)^{\frac{1}{n+m}} \tag{A.4}$$

Consequently, what we see is that the optimum number of trips or transactions per time period is inversely related to the distance of the firm from the city centre or market point. In order to calculate the rent payable at each location, assuming that all trips or transactions are undertaken at the optimum frequency $f = F$, for each particular location, we can apply the envelope theorem (Takayama, 1985) to (A.1) and obtain:

$$\frac{\partial C}{\partial d} = \rho \phi d^{\rho-1} F^n + \frac{\partial r}{\partial d} S = 0 \qquad \text{(A.5)}$$

Hence

$$\frac{\partial r}{\partial d} = \frac{-\rho \phi d^{\rho-1} F^n}{S} \qquad \text{(A.6)}$$

Therefore (A.6) can be rewritten as

$$\frac{\partial r}{\partial d} = -d^{\left(\frac{m\rho}{n+m}-1\right)} \left[\frac{\rho\phi}{S} \left(\frac{m\theta}{n\phi} \right)^{\frac{n}{n+m}} \right] \qquad \text{(A.7)}$$

This is always convex in d as long as ρ is less than or equal to one. In other words, as long as total transport costs are concave; that is, they are linear or less than with distance, even where the land area of the firm or household is fixed, the rent gradient will still be convex with distance. Equation (A.7) provides the analytical conditions under which the rent gradient is convex with distance. However, for illustrative purposes we can impute various parameter values which most commonly pertain in reality, namely that $n = m = \rho = 1$. This is the case where transport costs of commuting are linear with distance, and where there are costs directly and inversely related to the commuting frequency. Under these circumstances equation (A.7) becomes:

$$\frac{\partial r}{\partial d} = -\frac{(\phi\theta)^{\frac{1}{2}}}{S} d^{-\frac{1}{2}} \qquad \text{(A.8)}$$

In other words, the standard bid-rent result is therefore achieved here even without substitution between land and non-land inputs. The point is that where trip frequency is itself a decision variable, as in the case of all transport, distribution, retail and consumer shopping activities, plus all activities where the level of face-to-face contact or immediacy of delivery affects the market share, substitution takes place in terms of the frequency of transactions. The rent-gradient convexity is determined by this optimised trip frequency.

Now, in order to investigate how the total distance costs are related to the transport costs plus the opportunity costs of less than continuous face-to-face contact, we can define the total optimised transport costs per time period as:

$$F\phi d^{\rho} = \left(\frac{m\theta}{n\phi d^{\rho}}\right)^{\frac{1}{n+m}} \phi d^{\rho} \qquad\qquad (A.9)$$

Assuming once again for simplicity that $n = m = \rho = 1$, which is the usual case, we have:

$$Fd = \left(\frac{\theta}{\phi}\right)^{\frac{1}{2}} \sqrt{d} \qquad\qquad (A.10)$$

In other words, total transport costs rise in proportion to the square root of the haulage distance, *ceteris paribus* (McCann, 2001b). Moreover, we see that the total transport costs also rise in proportion to the square root of the opportunity costs θ of having less than face-to-face contact or less than immediate JIT deliveries of goods shipments.

Finally, an expression for the optimised total distance costs, which comprise both the transport costs and the opportunity costs of less than continuous face-to-face contact or JIT deliveries, can be given by inserting (A.10) into (A.1) as follows:

$$C = 2d^{\frac{1}{2}}(\phi\theta)^{\frac{1}{2}} + rS \qquad\qquad (A.11)$$

In words, total distance costs are a concave function of distance, as well as transport costs. This explains why the rental gradients (A.7) and (A.8) are convex functions of distance.

NOTE

1. We can assume for simplicity that local nominal wages will vary according to the nominal land price, in order to maintain real wages in spatial equilibrium, and that the production coefficients between local land and labour inputs are fixed. In other words, we can assume here that the parameter r represents the price of all location-specific factor inputs, and the parameter S represents the total stock of all location-specific inputs employed.

REFERENCES

Arita, T. and P. McCann (2000), 'Industrial alliances and firm location behaviour: some evidence from the US semiconductor industry', *Applied Economics*, 32, 1391-1403.

Audretsch, D. and M.P. Feldman (1996), 'R&D spillovers and the geography of innovation and production', *American Economic Review*, 86, 630-640.

Barro, R. and X. Sala-i-Martin (1992), 'Convergence', *Journal of Political Economy*, 100, 223-251.

Bennett, R.J. (1998), 'Business associations and their potential to contribute to economic development: re-exploring an interface between the state and the market', *Environment and Planning A*, 30, 1367-1387.

Cantwell, J.A. and S. Iammarino (2000), 'Multinational corporations and the location of technological innovation in the UK regions', *Regional Studies*, 34, 317-332.

Casson, M. and P. McCann (1999), 'Globalisation, competition and the corporation: the UK experience', in M. Whitman (ed.), *The Evolving Corporation: Global Imperatives and National Responses*, New York: Group of Thirty.

Clement, N.C., del Castillo Vera, G., Gerder, J., Kerr, W.A., MacFadyen, A.J., Shedd, S., Zepeda, E. and D. Alercon (1999), *North American Economic Integration: Theory and Practice*, Cheltenham: Edward Elgar.

Dluhosch, B. (2000), *Industrial Location and Economic Integration: Centrifugal and Centripetal Forces in the New Europe*, Cheltenham: Edward Elgar.

Financial Times, (1997), 'Survey: logistics', 7 October.

Financial Times, (1998), 'Survey: supply chain logistics', 1 December.

Financial Times, (1999), 'Survey: supply chain logistics', 17 June.

Fujita, M., Krugman, P. and A.J. Venables (1999), *The Spatial Economy: Cities, Regions and International Trade*, Cambridge, MA: MIT Press.

Gaspar, J. and E.L. Glaeser (1998), 'Information technology and the future of cities', *Journal of Urban Economics*, 43, 136-156.

Glaeser, E.L. (1998), 'Are cities dying?', *Journal of Economic Perspectives*, 12, 139-160.

Glaeser, E., Kallal, H.D., Scheinkman, J.A. and A. Shleifer (1992), 'Growth in cities', *Journal of Political Economy*, 100, 1126-1152.

Gordon, I.R. and P. McCann (2000), 'Industrial clusters, complexes, agglomeration and/or social networks?', *Urban Studies*, 37, 513-532.

Granovetter, M. (1973), 'The strength of weak ties', *American Journal of Sociology* 78, 1360-1389.

Henderson, J.V., Kuncoro, A. and M. Turner (1995), 'Industrial development in cities', *Journal of Political Economy*, 103, 1067-1085.

Hummels, D. (1999), 'Have international transportation costs declined?', Department of Economics Working Paper, Purdue University.

Isard, W. (1999), 'Further thoughts on future directions for regional science: a response to Fujita's remarks on the general theory of location and space-economy', *Annals of Regional Science*, 33, 383-388.

Isard, W. and R.E. Kuenne (1953), 'The impact of steel upon the greater New York–Philadelphia industrial region', *Review of Economics and Statistics*, 35, 289-301.

Jaffe, A., Trajtenberg, M. and R. Henderson (1993), 'Geographic localization of knowledge spillovers as evidenced by patent citations', *Quarterly Journal of Economics*, 108, 577-598.

Johnson, H.T. and R.S. Kaplan (1987), *Relevance Lost: The Rise and Fall of Management Accounting*, Cambridge, MA: Harvard University Press.

Krugman, P. (1991), *Geography and Trade*, Cambridge, MA: MIT Press.

Krugman, P. and A.J. Venables (1990), 'Integration and the competitiveness of peripheral industry', in C. Bliss and J.B. de Macedo (eds), *Unity with Diversity in the European Economy*, Cambridge: Cambridge University Press.

Marshall, A. (1920), *Principles of Economics*, (8th edition), London: Macmillan.

McCann, P. (1993), 'The logistics-costs location-production problem', *Journal of Regional Science*, 33, 503-516.

McCann, P. (1995), 'Rethinking the economics of location and agglomeration', *Urban Studies*, 32, 563-577.

McCann, P. (1998), *The Economics of Industrial Location: A Logistics-Costs Approach*, Heidelberg: Springer.

McCann, P. (2001a), *Urban and Regional Economics*, Oxford: Oxford University Press.

McCann, P. (2001b), 'A proof of the relationship between optimal vehicle size, haulage length and the structure of distance–transport costs', *Transportation Research A*, 35, 671-693.

McCann, P. and B. Fingleton (1996), 'The regional agglomeration impacts of just-in-time input linkages: evidence from the Scottish electronics industry', *Scottish Journal of Political Economy*, 43, 493-518.

Moses, L. (1958), 'Location and the theory of production', *Quarterly Journal of Economics*, 78, 259-272.

Mundell, R.A. (1957), 'The geometry of transport costs in international trade theory', *Canadian Journal of Economics and Political Science*, 23, 331-348.

Naisbitt, R. (1995), *The Global Paradox*, New York: Avon Books.

Neary, J.P. (2001), 'Of hype and hyperbolas: Introducing the New Economic Geography', *Journal of Economic Literature*, 39, 536-561.

Nishiguchi, T. (1994), *Strategic Industrial Sourcing: The Japanese Advantage*, Oxford: Oxford University Press.

Piore, M.J. and C.F. Sabel (1984), *The Second Industrial Divide: Possibilities for Prosperity*, New York: Basic Books.

Porter, M. (1990), *The Competitive Advantage of Nations*, New York: Free Press.

Porter, M. (1998), 'Clusters and the new economics of competition', *Harvard Business Review*, November–December.

Reid, N. (1995), 'Just-in-time inventory control and the economic integration of Japanese-owned manufacturing plants with the county, state and national economies of the United States', *Regional Studies*, 29, 345-355.

Samuelson, P.A. (1952), 'The transfer problem and transport costs: the terms of trade

when impediments are absent', *Economic Journal*, 62, 278-304.
Schonberger, R.J. (1996), *World Class Manufacturing: The Next Decade*, New York: Free Press.
Scott, A.J. (1988), *New Industrial Spaces*, London: Pion.
Simmie, J. and J. Sennett (1999), 'Innovative clusters: global or local linkages?, *National Institute Economic Review*, 170, October, 87-98.
Suarez-Villa, L. and W. Walrod (1997), 'Operational strategy, R&D and intrametropolitan clustering in a polycentric structure: the advanced electronics industries of the Los Angeles basin', *Urban Studies*, 34, 1343-1380.
Takayama, A. (1985), *Mathematical Economics* (2nd edn), Cambridge: Cambridge University Press.
The Economist (1999a), 'The world in your pocket: a survey of telecommunications', 9 October.
The Economist (1999b), 'The net imperative: a survey of business and the Internet', 26 June.
Toffler, A. (1980), *The Third Wave*, New York: Bantam Books.
Tyler, P. and M. Kitson (1987), 'Geographical variations in transport costs of manufacturing firms in Great Britain', *Urban Studies*, 24, 67-73.
United Nations Centre for Human Settlements (1997), *Human Settlements Basic Statistics*, Nairobi, ISBN: 92-1-0031003-9.
Vernon, R. (1966), 'International investment and international trade in the product cycle', *Quarterly Journal of Economics*, 80, 190-207.
Weber, A. (1909), *Uber den Standort der Industrien*, translated by C.J. Friedrich, (1929), *Alfred Weber's Theory of the Location of Industries*, Chicago: University of Chicago Press.
Williamson, O.E. (1975), *Markets and Hierarchies*, New York: Free Press.
Yeung, M.T., Perdikis, N. and W.A. Kerr (1999), *Regional Trading Blocs in the Global Economy: The EU and ASEAN*, Cheltenham: Edward Elgar.

PART B

Connectivity and Spatial Interaction

4. Physically Isolated Nations, Trade and 'Small-World' Network Connectivity

Laurie Schintler and Rajendra Kulkarni

4.1 INTRODUCTION

Advancements in information technology along with the application of new technologies to transportation are easing the movement of goods, information and people between nations of the world and in this sense bringing the world closer together. There is a question, however, as to whether or not certain countries – particularly those that are located in physically remote areas surrounded by topographical or other natural boundaries, or situated at the periphery of a continent – remain less connected economically, socially or otherwise despite improvements in communication and transportation technologies. One hypothesis advanced in this chapter is that through participation in regional or global trading agreements or pacts, physically isolated countries can benefit economically by being associated in some manner with nations that are major players in the global marketplace or that are closely tied to countries of this type. For example, Canada, which is located just to the north of the United States but physically separated from much of the rest of the world, may have an indirect but strong link to the rest of the world through its participation in the North American Free Trade Agreement (NAFTA).

During the last few decades there has been a proliferation of regional and global trading blocs and agreements, many of which involve nations that are relatively remote from the rest of the world in a geographical sense. The trend towards regionalism seems to suggest that a 'small-world' network is evolving in international trading relations. A 'small-world' network has a high degree of local clustering and a short average minimum path through the network facilitated by a few highly connected nodes in each regional cluster. Such a 'small-world' network turns out to be highly efficient in terms of moving information, goods, people or anything else through the network. Within this context, the benefits to a physically remote nation of participating in regional and global trading agreements should be much greater than they would be in the absence of a 'small-world' network topology.

This chapter addresses a range of questions with regard to this issue. First, is there a 'small-world' network evolving in international trade? And, if so, how does location in the network affect a nation? More specifically, are geographically remote nations more likely to be less regionally connected and therefore more likely to deviate from their neighbours in terms of trading activity or the rate of growth or decline in exports? At the same time, are these nations less likely to be linked to the global market or, more precisely, less likely to converge to the average rate of growth in international trade? Furthermore, does the regional and global connectivity of a nation influence the degree to which its exports grow or decline, and does geography play a role in affecting this relationship?

The chapter contains four sections in addition to this introduction. Section 4.2 describes how a 'small world' is evolving in international trade based on the emergence and strengthening of local, regional and global trade agreements. Local and global connectivity are defined in Section 4.3 by means of a set of indices. Here we focus on actual trading activity rather than the mechanisms put in place to facilitate interaction and economic cooperation. One index, a measure of local connectivity, captures how similar a nation is to its neighbours in terms of export growth. The other index, a measure of global connectivity, quantifies how similar a nation and the region in which it is located are to the rest of the world in terms of changes in trading activity, also measured by means of the growth in the volume of exports. The indices are subsequently applied in Section 4.4 to merchandise trade data for 77 nations in the world over three distinct time periods: 1985–1990, 1990–1995 and 1995–2000. Lastly, Section 4.5 offers some conclusions and directions for future research.

4.2   'SMALL-WORLD' NETWORK CONNECTIVITY AND TRADE NETWORKS

4.2.1   'Small-World' Network Connectivity

'Small-world' network connectivity is a new concept that has been receiving a lot of attention. Introduced by Watts and Strogatz (1998), a 'small-world' network is based on 'six degrees of separation', or the notion that everyone in the world is related to everyone else by at most six acquaintances. 'Six degrees of separation' is a phenomenon that stems from the formation of cliques and the existence of a few popular individuals that provide connections between cliques.

'Small-world' networks are similar in that they have a high degree of local clustering or cliquishness, like a regular lattice, and a relatively short average minimum path, like a completely random network. Watts and Strogatz (1998) assert that this phenomenon is probably universal and applies to many natural and manmade networks. They cite the United States power grid, the neural network of a particular type of worm and the network of actors and actresses as diverse examples of 'small-world' networks.

'Small-world' networks are characterised by their average path length $L(p)$ and the degree to which there is local connectivity in the network, measured by a clustering coefficient $C(p)$. The variable $L(p)$ measures the average minimum path in the network and $C(p)$ the connectivity of an average neighbourhood in the network. More specifically, $L(p)$ is the smallest number of links it takes to connect one node to another, averaged over the entire network, and clustering is the fraction of adjacent nodes connected to one another. One may view $L(p)$ as a global property of the network and $C(p)$ a local property.

Watts and Strogatz (1998) show that a 'small-world' network lies somewhere in between a regular lattice and a random network. To demonstrate this, they begin with a regular lattice with n vertices and k edges, and rewire it in such a way that it approaches a random network. Specifically, beginning with a vertex, the edge connected to its nearest neighbour is reconnected with probability p to another vertex chosen randomly from the rest of the lattice. No rewiring occurs if a connection to that vertex already exists. This process continues by moving clockwise around the lattice and randomly rewiring each edge with probability p until the lap is completed. Next, the same process is repeated for vertices and their second nearest neighbours. Because they consider a network with only first-order and second-order connections in each direction of the vertex, the rewiring process terminates after two laps.

In general, for a network with k nearest neighbours, rewiring will stop after $k/2$ laps. As the network is rewired, shortcuts through the network are created, resulting in an immediate drop in $L(p)$. Local clustering, or $C(p)$, remains relatively high up to a point, after which it begins to drop rapidly. The results of this process suggest that the global connectivity of a regular network can significantly improve with the addition of just a few shortcuts.

In essence, a 'small-world' network is one with a high degree of local clustering and a short average minimum path.

The huge interest in 'small-world' networks is due to the impact they can have on dynamical systems. According to Watts and Strogatz (1998), for example, 'models of dynamical systems with small-world coupling display enhanced signal propagation speed, computational power, and synchronizability'. Furthermore, contagious diseases tend to spread more freely in 'small-world' networks. These findings have profound implications for many manmade and natural systems. In a telecommunications network, for example, 'small-world' network connectivity may improve the ease with which information diffuses through the system.

4.2.2   Trade Agreements and 'Small-World' Network Topology

Over the last decade, the number of regional trading alliances and pacts has grown tremendously, implying that $C(p)$, that is, the level of cliquishness associated with each nation in terms of its policies and actions to cooperate with neighbouring nations, has strengthened. Over the same time period, the number of multilateral and bilateral agreements between nations of different regions has also proliferated, in essence creating 'short-cuts' or connections between cliques that contribute to greater global connectivity or, in 'small-world' network terminology, a lower $L(p)$.

The trend towards greater regionalism and globalism began a few decades ago although it became most apparent during the 1990s. Currently, there are over a hundred regional trading agreements.[1] The Association of Southwest Asian Nations (ASEAN), for example, was founded in 1967 by the nations of Indonesia, Malaysia, the Philippines, Singapore and Thailand. Brunei Darussalam later joined in 1984, Vietnam in 1995 and Burma and Laos in 1997. The original purpose of the organisation was to enhance regional cohesion through cooperative arrangements. The ASEAN Declaration states that the aims of the organisation are to '(1) accelerate the economic growth, social progress and cultural development in the region through joint endeavours in the spirit of equality and partnership in order to strengthen the foundation for a prosperous and peaceful community of Southwest Asian nations, and to (2) promote regional peace and stability through abiding respect for justice and the rule of law in the relationship among countries in the region and adherence to the principles of the United Nations Charter' (http://www.asean.or.id).

During the late 1980s and the 1990s, some of the regional trading alliances that had formed previously strengthened. In addition, a number of new alliances were formed. For example, the Andean Group was re-energised in 1991 with the ratification of the Act of Barahona. This agreement was designed to promote the development of a free trade zone and the establishment of a common tariff with four levels (ranging from 5 percent to 20 percent). Columbia, Ecuador and Venezuela have since formed a free trade zone and have implemented a common external tariff (CET) along with Bolivia. Peru also increased its participation in the group, but only on a transitional and modest basis.

ASEAN also recruited new members during this time period. As noted above, Vietnam joined in 1995 and agreed to reduce its tariffs by up to 5 percent by 2006. Furthermore, the Philippines agreed to make a concerted effort to liberalise its trade with other ASEAN nations. Member nations agreed in 1992 to nearly eliminate intra-ASEAN trade tariffs on most goods by 2007, thereby establishing an ASEAN free trade area.

In 1989, the United States and Canada entered into a free trade agreement, which called for the elimination of bilateral tariffs on trade by 1998. NAFTA, ratified in 1993, extended this agreement to Mexico and expanded the scope of the earlier free trade agreement.

Australia and New Zealand adopted a free trade agreement, the so-called 'Australia–New Zealand Closer Economic Relations Trade Agreement' (ANCERTA, or CER for short) in 1983. The original CER provided the schedule for the achievement of free trade by 1995, but a 1988 review led to a speeding up of the implementation and by 1990 virtually free trade in goods between the two countries had been achieved.

During the 1990s a number of other bilateral and multilateral agreements were initiated between nations of different regions, providing connections between cliques. In 1991, for example, the Andean Trade Preference Act came into force. This agreement reduced the cost of trading between South American countries and the United States by eliminating duties on certain exports going to the United States. In 1997, Canada and Chile entered into a free trade agreement. Some of the provisions of the arrangement include duty-free access for a large share of Canadian exports and the elimination of Chile's import duty on a range of goods. Negotiations to include Chile in NAFTA began in 1995.

The Asia-Pacific Economic Cooperation (APEC) organisation, formed in 1989, includes the countries of Japan, China, Australia, New Zealand, Russia, Chile, Peru, Brunei Darussalam, Canada, Indonesia, Republic of Korea, Malaysia, the Philippines, Singapore, Thailand and the United States. While not viewed as a trading bloc per se, it does promote policies that reduce trade barriers between participating nations. The nations of APEC include in fact some of the fastest growing economies in the world.

In 1994, Mexico signed a free trade agreement with Columbia and Venezuela. This was one of the most liberal trade agreements in Latin America, offering price advantages over US goods and services for member nations. Mexico and Chile also signed an agreement during the 1990s. In 1994, Chile entered into a free trade agreement with Ecuador. By 1995, tariffs on most merchandise trade between Chile and Ecuador had been eliminated. Over the last decade, Ecuador has made an effort to abandon the protectionist trade policy it had in the 1980s by means of a more liberal trading regime. Chile also formed a free trade agreement with Columbia in 1994 with the intent of reducing import duties over a five-year period.

While a 'small-world' topology of the network of trading nations of the world is plausible, the question is whether this topology has had any impact on the actual regional and global connectivity of a nation in terms of trading activity. If a 'small-world' network exists, then one would expect to see nations within regions being affected by each others' trading and at the same time they would be connected to the global market through dominant players within their region. For example, a regional agreement such as NAFTA would in a 'small-world' network not only enhance economic interaction between the United States, Mexico and Canada, but it would assist the latter two nations in becoming more connected to the rest of the world *vis-à-vis* the United States.

In the section that follows, two indices are developed that allow examination of 'small-world' network connectivity in terms of trading activity. The indices are unique to the literature on 'small-world' networks in that they are based on weighted links and nodes. Most of the research that has been done on 'small-world' networks to date focuses on graphs and networks with unweighted nodes and links. While there have been a few attempts to move beyond such networks, the results of these studies are still quite preliminary (Yook et. al., 2001).

4.3 MEASURING 'SMALL-WORLD' CONNECTIVITY

The first index, $LOCAL_i$, is a measure of $C(p)$ for nation i. Specifically, it captures the degree to which changes in a nation's trading activity (measured here by merchandise exports) are influenced by what is occurring in neighbouring countries in terms of exports. The measure is defined mathematically as follows:

$$LOCAL_i = \frac{1}{n}\sum_j m_{ij}\left(g_i^w - g_j^w\right)^2 \tag{4.1}$$

where n is the number of nations as defined by the symmetric n by n matrix **M** with elements m_{ij}, which is a contiguity matrix. In this matrix, $m_{ij} = 1$ if nations i and j are contiguous, otherwise $m_{ij} = 0$. The variable g_j^w is the weighted rate of change in exports of nation j. The weight is given by the total volume of exports of that country during the base year, divided by the total global volume of exports. The closer the value of $LOCAL_i$ is to zero, the more similar nation i is to its neighbours in terms of changes in trading activity. This is interpreted as a greater degree of regional connectivity in terms of merchandise trade.

The global connectivity of a nation i, equivalent to L(p) in 'small-world' network terminology, is defined by a modified auto-covariance equation as follows:

$$GLOBAL_i = \frac{1}{n}\sum_j m_{ij}\left|g_i^w - \bar{g}_D^w\right|\left|g_j^w - \bar{g}_D^w\right| \tag{4.2}$$

where $\bar{g}_D^w$ is the median or mean change in exports in the world. This equation deviates from that conventionally used to calculate the covariance between two variables in a few respects. First, it incorporates the impact of geography through the contiguity matrix **M**. Second, it uses the absolute values of the deviations rather than actual differences between each variable and the respective mean or median value associated with the global level. The rationale for doing this is that it is desirable to create an ordinally scaled index, which ranges in value depending on how connected a nation and the region in which it is located are to what is occurring at the global level. Traditional auto covariance is not ordinally scaled. It produces negative values when there is negative association between the two variables of interest, positive values when there is positive association and a zero for no dependence. The index $GLOBAL_i$ can only be non-negative, with a value closer to zero for any given nation i implying that changes in its exports, as well as the exports of the surrounding countries, closely resemble changes occurring at the global level. In other words, nation i has a high degree of global connectivity in this context.

One can assess whether or not a 'small-world' network has been evolving in international trade by tracking the values of the $LOCAL_i$ and $GLOBAL_i$ measures over time, and examining whether or not they are moving towards zero, which would imply that this is the case.

4.4   AN EMPIRICAL APPLICATION

In this section we apply the indices presented in the previous section to
merchandise exports (valued in millions of US dollars) for three distinct time
periods: 1985–1990, 1990–1995 and 1995–2000. The data were collected
from the World Bank website (www.worldbank.org). Figure 4.1 shows all 77
nations selected for the analysis, and the spatial relationships between these
countries in terms of contiguity. A line between two nations indicates that
they are neighbours.[2]

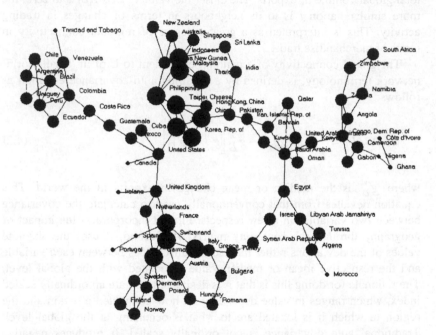

Figure 4.1   Grouping of nations in terms of degree of physical isolation

K-core analysis was used to partition the nations into three categories
based on their degree of physical isolation. Category one, indicated by the
smallest dots in Figure 4.1, represents countries that are adjacent to only one
other nation or that in graph-theoretic terms have a relatively low degree of
connectivity and few higher-order neighbours.[3] For example, Portugal and
Spain fall into this category, as they are located at the periphery of the
European continent. The second category, designated by the medium-sized
dots, includes moderately isolated nations or those that generally have only a

few adjacent countries. Category three, which is represented by the large dots, includes countries that have several immediate neighbours.

For most of the nations included in the analysis, the measures of local and global connectivity ($LOCAL_i$ and $GLOBAL_i$ respectively) have declined over time, implying that a 'small-world' network is evolving in international trade when one considers actual trading activity. This is true even for nations that share only a single border or that are islands located in remote areas of the world, such as New Zealand. Hence this finding is consistent with the broad globalisation trend driven by advancements in information, communication and transportation technologies. In addition, it suggests that the bilateral and multilateral trade agreements between different nations since 1985 are indeed contributing to greater trade between them.

Some groupings have become more connected regionally. The regional grouping of the United States, Mexico and Canada constitutes one example. Hence the measures provide evidence of the strengthening of the economic relationship between the three participating countries by means of the NAFTA agreement. The politically relatively isolated nations of Libya, Pakistan and Syria, on the other hand, show increasing values of $LOCAL_i$ and $GLOBAL_i$ over time, implying that they appear to have distanced themselves from the rest of the world in terms of economic association (as measured by merchandise trade).

While regional and global connectivity have generally increased for nations located in remote areas, Figure 4.2a shows that these nations are still on average less tied to the global economy than other countries, at least in terms of merchandise exports. At the same time though, they remain more locally connected, as illustrated in Figure 4.2b. In fact, local connectivity does not necessarily imply global connectivity. $GLOBAL_i$ and $LOCAL_i$ have relatively low positive correlation coefficients for each time period (see Table 4.1). Over time, however, the association between these two factors has strengthened somewhat. This suggests that the effect of regionalism on a nation's ability to become more globally connected has increased, perhaps through linkages with other nations within their own region that are dominant players in international trade. The latter are in 'small-world' network terminology the countries that provide linkages between regions, or cliques, creating short-cuts through the network and enhancing overall global connectivity.

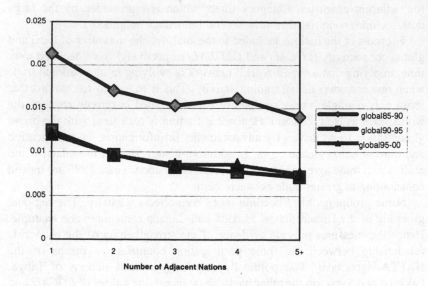

Figure 4.2a   Location and change in global connectivity

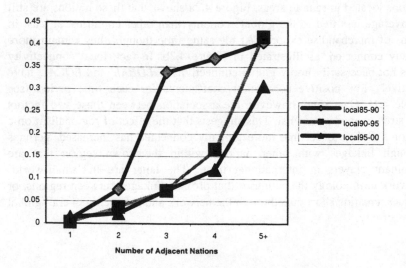

Figure 4.2b   Location and change in local connectivity

Table 4.1   Correlation coefficients between global and local effects

Period	1985–1990	1990–1995	1995–2000
Correlation coefficient	0.13	0.16	0.19

4.5 CONCLUSIONS

This chapter has introduced the concept of 'small-world' connectivity in a network with weighted nodes and links. It should be noted that much research carried out on 'small-world' networks to date has focused exclusively on the case of non-weighted nodes and links. Here, 'small-world' connectivity was examined by comparing the growth in merchandise exports across nations. Special attention was paid to the role of remote nations in the global network.

It was found that both local and global connectivity have generally been increasing since 1985. Moreover, although local and global connectivity are only weakly correlated, the correlation has been increasing over time. Finally, physically isolated nations are becoming more regionally and globally connected in terms of trade. However, the effectiveness of regional trade arrangements *vis-à-vis* global trade arrangements remains a key issue that should be further explored both in terms of the network analysis and other methodologies.

NOTES

1. See www.worldbank.org for more information on these and other free trade agreements.
2. In most cases, contiguity between two nations was defined as whether or not they share a common border. However, distance was used to indicate adjacency in the case of islands or non-landlocked countries.
3. Some discretion was used here given that the data set contained only a subset of the world's nations.

REFERENCES

Watts, D.J. and S.H. Strogatz (1998), 'Collective dynamics of "small-world" networks', *Nature*, 393, 440-442.
Yook, S.H., Jeong, H., Barabasi, A.L. and Y. Tu (2001), 'Weighted evolving networks', *Physical Review Letters*, 86, 5835-5838.

5. Geographical Proximity and Economic Performance of Nations

Upali Wickramasinghe

5.1 INTRODUCTION

Any inquisitive person glancing at a world map showing the distribution of per capita GNP would notice that the world is fragmented neatly into rich and poor regions. The poor are mostly concentrated in the tropics (between the latitudes of 23.45 degrees North and South) and the rich mostly in the temperate zones of the Northern and Southern hemispheres, with a few exceptions. It seems as if countries at differing levels of economic progress have clustered together by some force (Table 5.1).

This observation has led to the belief that geographical proximity plays an important role in the process of economic development. Gamini Corea, a former Secretary General of UNCTAD, asked: '...why economists have been somewhat remiss in not analysing the effects of proximity and contiguity on economic and development experiences' (Corea, 1998, p.6). Kamal Dervis, Vice President Middle East and North Africa Region of the World Bank, noted in 1997 that countries of a particular region seem to experience something of a commonality of growth outcomes that cannot be fully explained simply by individual countries' domestic policies. Mellinger et al. (2000) show sharp differences in per capita income according to eco-zones. These observations, as Clark et al. (2000) put it, challenge us to document and explain the spatial scale and global allocation of economic activity. This clustering behaviour can have great implications for the growth prospects of countries on the edge of the world, particularly if geography has such a strong influence on economic performance. In this light, the role of economic policies *vis-à-vis* geographical determinism needs to be carefully examined.

While there have been several attempts to quantify spillovers of growth across countries,[1] relatively few attempts have been made to document and analyse the impact of proximity on spatial distribution of global economic activity.

Table 5.1   Distribution of per capita income

Regions	Per capita GNP (1998)	
	Mean	Std. Dev.
North America	25,204	3,675
Europe & Central Asia		
European Union	21,695	5,181
Economies in transition	7,265	3,791
Russian Federation		
and Central Asia	4,091	3,664
East Asia & the Pacific		
Australia & New Zealand	19,014	3,299
East Asia	10,361	10,216
East Asia 1	19,759	7,176
East Asia 2	13,784	10,642
East Asia 3	1,811	646
Pacific islands	3,377	939
Latin America & the Caribbean	5,603	2,946
Middle East & North Africa	8,242	7,354
South Asia	1,999	830
Africa	1,880	1,997
Southern Africa	5,348	2,203
Sub-Saharan Africa	1,049	436
Others	4,010	3,740

Note:
Country classifications are as follows: *East Asia 1*: Japan and South Korea; *East Asia 2*: Singapore, Brunei, Hong Kong, Malaysia, Thailand, Philippines and Indonesia; *East Asia 3*: China, Lao PDR, Vietnam, Mongolia and Cambodia; *Southern Africa*: South Africa, Botswana, Namibia, Swaziland and Zimbabwe; *Africa Others*: Mauritius, Madagascar and Cape Verde; *Economies in transition*: Albania, Belarus, Bulgaria, Croatia, Czech Republic, Cyprus, Estonia, Hungary, Latvia, Lithuania, Poland, Romania, Macedonia FYR, Slovak Republic, Ukraine; *Central Asia*: Armenia, Azerbaijan, Georgia, Kazakhstan, Kyrgyz Republic, Moldova, Slovenia, Tajikistan, Turkmenistan and Uzbekistan

Source: Author's calculations based on World Bank (2000)

Since GDP is the common measure of national economic activity, per capita income is one of the most reliable and readily available measures of the stage of development and the extent of global income inequality. As Sen (2001) pointed out that the primary concern is the level of inequality, not its marginal change. This chapter uses per capita income in a cross-section of countries to analyse the spatial distribution of economic activity in the world, and is organised as follows. The next section reviews the literature to identify factors that might explain why proximity matters in the economic performance of regions and nations. Section 5.3 develops the analytical framework. Section 5.4 describes the selection of explanatory variables and data. Section 5.5 discusses empirical results and Section 5.6 concludes the chapter.

5.2   RECONSIDERING PROXIMITY

The influence of neighbours on economic performance has been a source of debate among economists and geographers for a long time. Both groups sought explanations for such an influence within the confinement of their disciplinary boundaries. However, a cross-disciplinary convergence of ideas and methods has emerged during the last decade or so.

There is a wider acceptance now that physical geography plays a major role in shaping the structure of global development. Physical geography affects the patterns of agriculture, the process of innovation, productivity of labour and a host of other socio-economic processes. In this sense, the evolution of global civilisations has much to do with physical geography. Mellinger et al. (2000) show that climate, coastal access and soil quality can explain a major proportion of the global differences of economic performance. Their study confirms sharp differences in per capita income according to eco-zones. According to their estimates, tropical regions are nearly uniformly poor while temperate regions have a wide income range, with only 7 percent of the temperate-zone populations at income levels below $2,000, compared with 42 percent of the tropical zone population.

The acceptance of geographical factors as determinants of economic performance should not be conceived as accepting the notion of 'geographical determinism'. Instead, it only recognises that geography plays a role in economic development through its impact on labour productivity, the process of generating knowledge and disease prevalence.

The impact of economic policies can be transmitted across national boundaries, particularly to neighbours, through several channels. Ever since

Marshall wrote about the emergence of Manchester's cotton mills in the 19th century (Marshall, 1932), economists have been discussing the formation of industrial clusters and the influence of 'pioneering' firms on others. This idea can be applied to the case of the nation state with a few exceptions. For one, location is a choice variable for industries while it is fixed in space as far as countries are concerned. For another, the connectivity among nation states, or even within regions, depends on the extent of 'openness', and regional and international borders seem to dampen the externalities (e.g., Jaffe et al., 1993; Eaton and Kortum, 1996; Cabellero and Jaffe, 1993). Keeping these caveats in mind, the theory of industrial cluster formation can be extended to nation states.

In the case of a nation state, positive spillovers may emerge when one or more countries in its region achieve high rates of growth. A growing economy can create several positive externalities on its neighbours (and some negative ones, such as pollution, also). Among the positive externalities are better employment opportunities, the potential for higher intra-regional trade among neighbours and technology transfers across borders. Moreover, an advanced economy is more likely to offer its neighbours better transportation networks, including shipping liners, supply chains, marketing channels and a larger market. One major reason for the emergence of such externalities is the existence of a 'common pool of resources'. Chua (1993; as cited in Moreno and Trehan, 1997) postulates the existence of regional production functions, almost along the same line of argument as in the case of industrial agglomeration suggested by Marshall and others. Output of a country may not only depend on its own inputs but also on inputs of contiguous countries. This is relevant for many manufacturing and services industries. For example, tourism in a small country may depend on the attractiveness of the region as a whole, since visitors attempt to maximise benefits of a long journey by combining visits to many destinations. However, this does not negate the ability of a particular country to work as a gravitational force in attracting tourists into a region. Dynamic externalities, which are derived from technological advances, increased specialisation and division of labour that accompanies and/or drives growth and development (Young, 1928), can also play critical roles in the process of economic growth. The diffusion of knowledge and the enhanced flow of information are two more benefits that accrue to countries located close to a growing economy.

International trade is a vehicle that transmits positive and negative 'shocks' across borders. Since there is evidence that distance and the volume of trade are inversely related, it is conceivable that transmission of economic shocks is also higher among neighbours. Such transmission across borders tends to increase with the dismantling of trade barriers, the development of transportation infrastructure and communication networks, the simplification of customs procedures and several other policy interventions, and invigorates economic dynamism within a whole region, sometimes even when individual countries may not be enthusiastic about free trade. Low intra-regional trade may perpetuate poverty as it limits the potential for greater division of labour within a region and the extent of the market, further magnifying the global income inequality. This may seem to be happening in the cases of Sub-Saharan Africa and South Asia, two regions where intra-regional trade is almost insignificant compared with developed regions such as the European Union, North America and East Asia.

'Neighbourhoods' are thought to be important in attracting foreign investment into a region. According to this view, investors generally have a certain perception of a region which determines their investment decisions. The experience gained by investing in a country determines further expansion within the region. In the case of an outflow of capital, investors seem to exit from a whole region within a short period of time even if the problem is restricted to one country. Both entry and exit of capital show that investors rely on the average conditions in 'regions' as against individual countries. Two recent examples are the financial crises in East Asia in 1997 and Latin America in 1995, precipitated in Thailand and Mexico respectively. In addition, there is evidence to believe that investors choose a neighbour rather than a distant country for investment, particularly when resources and experience are limited. A neighbour can be attractive due to a combination of factors such as the availability of better information, the knowledge of local institutions, customs and languages, and cultural affinity. Eaton and Tamura (1994) find that distance and foreign direct investment are negatively correlated. Similarly, Shatz and Venables (2000) observe that adjusting for market size, a large share of investment stays close to home. The relocation of industries from Hong Kong to Mainland China, from Singapore to nearby countries and from Japan to East Asia could be viewed as examples. These investment flows are often associated with the transfer of advanced technology to neighbours, spurring growth momentums in capital-importing countries.

The emergence of a country within a region as a 'growth centre' seems to be an accident in many cases and such accidents have far-reaching implications for the economic performance of a whole region. Growth episodes generally reverberate through neighbours and create ripple effects, mostly through investment and trade, particularly when the growing nation develops capacity constraints, forcing industries to relocate elsewhere. Economic growth can also lead to currency appreciation, rendering domestic production less profitable. As Dervis (1997) argues, Germany's *Wirtschaftswunder* was arguably the initial driving force behind Europe's good performance in the 1950s and 1960s while Japan seems to have provided the initial impetus for East Asian dynamism. The appreciation of the Japanese yen is considered to be responsible for the shifting of industries to East Asia in the 1980s and 1990s.

The 'flying geese' hypothesis of Akamatsu (1961) provides a structured view of this transformation. According to this view, industries within a country and groups of countries 'catch up' with more advanced countries through production and international trade. The industrialisation experience of Japan and the Newly Industrialised Countries neatly fits into this description. Japan followed at its initial stage of development the example of the then five advanced countries, viz. the United Kingdom, United States, France, Germany and Russia. The maturity of industrialisation in Japan forced Japan to relocate industries and gave rise to the emergence of other East Asian countries as centres of production. Kojima (1973, 1978) recognises that firms move abroad when a firm in a comparatively disadvantaged industry can make a higher rate of profit abroad than from an alternative investment project at home. The dynamic version of this theory (Lee, 1990, p.61) suggests that 'capital outflows facilitate structural adjustment in the investing country by transferring abroad the industries in which the country is losing its comparative advantage'. In all these episodes, sustained growth at home for an extended period of time has been observed, triggering an outward flow of investment and technology.

The role of multinational corporations (MNCs) has been emphasised as a factor that led regions to emerge as growth centres. MNCs contribute to economic development 'as conduits for the flow of knowledge between countries' (Almeida and Grant, 1998, p.1). The superiority of MNCs in diffusing knowledge is the result of their flexibility in utilising a wide range of knowledge transfer mechanisms and the result of embedding the transfer mechanisms within a social context that enhances their effectiveness. Several mechanisms of knowledge spillover have been identified, which include the transfer of personnel, the availability of expatriate experts and internal consultants, on the job training in other countries, short visits and electronic data exchange (e.g., electronic mail, groupware, video conferencing, telephone and fax messages, and seminars). The transfer of knowledge among neighbours can be much more intense than among distant countries due to closer interactions, lower travelling and communication costs, easy communication, similarity of languages and cultural backgrounds, and regional cooperation arrangements.

These theories show that a multitude of factors are responsible for economic growth and performance of countries, ranging from geography to institutions and policy. While geography does play a role in the economic growth of nations, economic policy and institutions play an even bigger role through their influence on the nature of spillovers and externalities of growth outcomes, as well as contagion effects across national boundaries. The casual observation that there is spatial dependence in economic performance and that 'neighbourhoods' matter needs to be scrutinised in a model that combines geography, institutions and policy. Neoclassical growth theory provides a framework where these factors can be juxtaposed and compared.

5.3   ANALYTICAL FRAMEWORK

The standard neoclassical growth model provides a useful starting point for investigating the global distribution of economic activity. Let Y denote the total output and N the quantity of labour input. Following Durlauf and Quah (1999), assume that the stock of human capital H is embodied in the labour force. The effective labour input is then defined as $L = NH$. The different kinds of physical capital K_1, K_2, ..., are assumed to be aggregated in a measure of the capital stock K. The state of technology in the economy is denoted by A. The output of such an economy is given by $Y = F(K, L, A)$. It is convenient to focus on income per head $y = Y / N$, effective income per head $\tilde{y} = Y / NHA$ and effective capital per head $\tilde{k} = K / NHA$. Finally, assuming constant returns to scale and a Cobb–Douglas production technology, effective income per head is related to effective capital per head according to

$$\tilde{y} = \left(\tilde{k}\right)^{\alpha} \tag{5.1}$$

Because the focus of this chapter is on contemporaneous spatial spillovers rather than endogenous growth over time, we will assume that only physical capital is accumulated (i.e., $H = 1$), while population and the state of technology grow at the exogenous rates v and ξ respectively.[2] Given all the assumptions above, physical capital accumulation is given by the following equation:

$$\dot{\tilde{k}} / \tilde{k} = \sigma f(\tilde{k}) / \tilde{k} - (\delta + v + \xi) \tag{5.2}$$

where δ and σ are, respectively, the rate of depreciation of the capital stock and the fraction of savings out of income. The dot above a variable indicates the rate of change over time. Using (5.1) and (5.2), the steady-state effective level of income is:

$$\tilde{y}^* = \left(\tilde{k}^*\right)^\alpha = \left[\left(\delta + v + \xi\right)^{-1}\sigma\right]^{\alpha/(1-\alpha)}$$

(5.3)

With technical change assumed to be exogenous, the time path of technology can be described by

$$A(t) = A(0)e^{\xi t}$$

(5.4)

Noting that the observed per capita income $y = Y/N = \tilde{y}HA = \tilde{y}A$ when $H = 1$, Durlauf and Quah (1999) derive:

$$\log y(t) = \log \tilde{y}^* + \left[\log \tilde{y}(0) - \log \tilde{y}^*\right]e^{-\lambda t} + \log A(0) + \xi t$$

(5.5)

This equation has two components: a level component and a convergence component. The evolution of income per head is fully described by equation (5.5), initial values of effective income and technology, and the steady-state level of effective income given by equation (5.3).

   Anselin (1988) provides an econometric framework that can be readily utilised for empirically testing equation (5.5) in a way that also takes proximity into account. The general specification is

$$y = \rho W_1 y + X\beta + u$$
$$u = \lambda W_2 u + \varepsilon$$

(5.6)

$$\varepsilon \sim N(0, \sigma^2 I_n)$$

where y is a $n \times 1$ spatial cross section of observations on a dependent variable, X is a $n \times k$ matrix of explanatory variables and W_i ($i = 1,2$) are weight matrices of size $n \times n$ in which the elements reflect some measure of distance between the cross-sectional units, with weights varying inversely with distance.

   Estimation of the full model (5.6) can be quite cumbersome and requires the use of maximum likelihood techniques. For example, LeSage (2000) suggests a grid search in which ρ is constrained to be between the inverses of the minimum and maximum eigenvalues of the standardised spatial weight matrix. Standardisation of the matrix **W** is achieved by dividing the values in each row by the row total. A major drawback of the method, as Manski (1993) notes, is the statistical problem arising from the adjustments needed to calculate the spatial correlation and the identification of spillovers. Some argue that spillovers may simply reflect the influence of omitted variables (Temple, 1999).

5.4 SELECTION OF EXPLANATORY VARIABLES AND THE DATA

A data set for a cross section of 82 countries was assembled for carrying out the empirical analysis.[3] Data availability dictated the selection of countries. Unless otherwise indicated the data are from the *World Development Indicators* 2000 CD ROM   (World Bank, 2000). The variables and their empirical proxies are discussed below. The dependent variable is per capita GNP in 1997.

The two most fundamental variables contained in the neoclassical production function are the physical capital stock (K) and the stock of human capital (H). The capital stock available from Nehru and Dhareshwar (1993) was updated using standard procedures.[4] Human capital is approximated by the average number of years of schooling of the population between the years 25 and 64. Krueger (1968) found that education explains a substantial proportion of per capita income variation across countries. Mankiw et al. (1992) also show that education is an important factor behind cross-country income variation. Sala-i-Martin (1997) included lagged primary-school enrolment and lagged life expectancy as fixed variables, which were assumed to be robust determinants of human capital. While Sala-i-Martin considered the growth of output, the logic applies even more to the level of per capita income. For several countries, the data pertaining to the average number of years of schooling are not available. In those instances, the values were approximated using the Education Attainment Index (EAI) (UNDP, 2000), which is found to be a good predictor of the average years of schooling of adults wherever data are not available.[5]

The geographical variables used in similar studies include: the climatic zone, 'tropicality', access to the sea, distance from the coast, distance from the equator, disease prevalence (e.g., malaria) and regional dummies. With respect to the climatic zone, previous studies have used several approximations. A common one is the proportion of a country's land area within a particular climatic zone based on a global ecological classification scheme (Gallup et al., 1998; Mellinger et al., 2000). Similarly, distance from the equator is a popular measure of tropicality.

The variables used in this study are proximity measured by contiguity or distance (which determine the spatial weight matrix **W**), the climatic zone (*CLIM*), access to the sea (*ACCESS*) and 'tropicality' (*TROP*). The variable *CLIM* is approximated by a dummy variable defined according to the Koppen–Geiger climate zones, as given by the global map in Mellinger et al. (2000, p.175).[6] The distance of a country from the equator was treated as an indicator of tropicality (*TROP*), and the distances were estimated using the Microsoft Encarta Interactive World Atlas (2000). *ACCESS* is approximated by a dummy variable assigning one to those countries with access to the sea and zero for others. A regional dummy (*REGD*) is calculated by assigning numerical values for regions.[7]

The importance of institutions and policies for economic performance is well known. Hall and Jones (1999) and Bassanini et al. (2001) attribute a large part of cross-country variation in income to 'institutions' and 'policies' in OECD countries. Several institutions that seem relevant in explaining the observed variation of per capita income across countries are considered in the present study. These include political instability (*POL*), rule of law (*ROL*), extent of corruption (*CORR*), general price level, the extent of government involvement in the economy, the extent of financial development and exposure to foreign trade. The data on *POL*, *ROL* and *CORR* were taken from the World Bank data set on governance (World Bank, 2001).[8] The general price level is approximated by the GDP deflator (*GDPD*), while government revenue (*GREV*) and government consumption (*GCON*) are measured as percentages of GDP. Since government revenue and consumption fluctuate over the business cycle, a ten-year average of both variables was calculated over the period 1987–1997.[9] The influence of financial development was captured by two variables: credit provided to the private sector (*CREDIT*) and liquid liabilities of the financial system (*LIQ*), both as percentages of GDP. To capture the impact of income inequality on economic performance, the Gini coefficients (*GINI*) were used, and the data on this are from the Deininger and Squire (1996) data set.[10] Trade openness is approximated by the percentage share of the sum of imports and exports to GDP (*TRADE*).

In order to capture the impact of infrastructure on economic performance, two key variables were considered: the availability of roads (*ROADS*) and electricity production per capita (*ELEC*). The extent of roads was measured by the percentage of paved roads. Data deficiencies in this area abound even for larger countries such as China. In many of these instances, the average values pertaining to the region, for example East Asia, were used. The data on *ELEC* were obtained from the World Resources Institute (1999).[11]

Proximity, one of the most critical elements of this study, was measured by the contiguity structure, or by distances between countries. The contiguity structure provides one of the simplest methods of quantifying proximity. As LeSage (2000) points out,

> contiguity, reflecting the relative position in space of one regional unit of observation to other such units. Measures of contiguity rely on the knowledge of the size and shape of the observational units depicted on a map. From this, we can determine which units are neighbours (have borders that touch) or represent observational units in reasonable proximity to each other. Regarding spatial dependence, neighbouring units should exhibit a higher degree of spatial dependence than units located far apart. For spatial heterogeneity, relationships may be similar for neighbouring units. (p.10)

A contiguity weight matrix was constructed using the so-called 'rook contiguity' by defining $w_{ij} = 1$ for countries i and j that share a common border, and $w_{ij} = 0$ otherwise. As noted above, the elements of **W** are normalised to have sums that add to unity. In the case of distance weights, these are defined as

$$w_{ij} = \frac{1/d_{ij}}{\sum_{j} 1/d_{ij}} \qquad (i \neq j); \qquad w_{ii} = 0 \qquad (5.7)$$

where d_{ij} is the distance between the capitals of the countries in the sample. This weighting matrix links all the countries in the sample to each other, and the relative importance of each country in a particular neighbourhood varies inversely with its distance from the country. For measuring the distance, 'the great circle distance' is employed.

5.5　EMPIRICAL RESULTS

First, consider the 'gross spatial dependence' of income per capita, defined as the extent of variation that can be explained solely by the spatially weighted dependent variable. This model assumes that nothing other than spatial dependence matters in explaining the distribution of per capita income across countries. The model can be derived from equation (5.6) by assuming $\mathbf{X} = \mathbf{i}$ (a vector of ones), $\mathbf{W_2} = \mathbf{0}$ and $\mathbf{y}$ is a vector containing the logarithm of per capita GNP. The matrix **W** is the weighting matrix described previously. Hence

$$y = b + \rho\mathbf{W}_1y + \varepsilon \tag{5.8}$$

The empirical analyses were carried out using the Spatial Econometrics Toolbox developed by LeSage (2000), available on the Internet at http://www.econ.utoledo.edu.

The results are reported in Table 5.2, which suggests that spatial dependence measured by contiguity or distance weights can respectively explain 51 and 40 percent of the variation in per capita income across countries. Both the contiguity weight and distance weight estimates of ρ are highly significant. Based on these estimates, one may be tempted to conclude that proximity is a highly significant variable in explaining economic performance of nations. As will be argued later, specification errors and data deficiencies must be carefully evaluated before arriving at such a definitive conclusion.

Table 5.2   Estimates of the first-order spatial autoregression model of 1997 per capita GNP

Variables	Contiguity weight		Distance weight	
Constant term	3.7667	(7.0866)	0.3516	(1.2333)
Proximity ρ	0.5327	(8.1211)	0.9481	(26.44)
$\bar{R}^2$	0.5119		0.4023	
Log-likelihood	-249.53		-255.52	

Note: Asymptotic t statistics are given in parentheses

Next we consider an ordinary least squares model of the distribution of per capita income across countries that includes all the variables discussed above but disregards spatial dependence. This provides a useful benchmark for comparing results of models that include spatial dependence. The substitution of $\mathbf{W}_1 = \mathbf{W}_2 = 0$ into equation (5.6) yields the standard regression model

$$y = \mathbf{X}\boldsymbol{\beta} + \mathbf{u} \tag{5.9}$$

The results of estimation of equation (5.9) are reported in Table 5.3. Variables introduced in the previous section that contributed little to the regression model have been excluded. The model explains 92 percent of the variation of per capita income across countries, and all the variables are of the expected sign. Of the variables used in the model, *H*, *CLIM*, *ELEC* and *TRADE* are significant at the 10 percent level or better; *K*, *ACCESS* and *ROL* are significant at the 20 percent level and the remaining variables, namely *TROP*, *REGD*, *ROADS* and *CREDIT*, are significant only at low probability levels.

Although the estimates of equation (5.8) (Table 5.2) suggest that the simple spatial effect alone can explain 51 percent of the variation of per capita GNP across countries, the estimates of equation (5.9) (Table 5.3) show that much of this variation can also be attributed to standard variables. As such, spatial effect can explain only a small portion of the total extent of variation of per capita GNP across countries. Models that claim to explain a substantial proportion of economic activity across countries by a single variable such as 'tropicality' need careful scrutiny, as they are likely to have overlooked many relevant factors.

Table 5.3 Ordinary least squares estimates of the regression model of 1997 per capita GNP

Variable	Coefficient	
Constant term	0.8845	(3.8592)
Physical capital stock per capita (*K*)	0.0385	(1.3039)
Human capital stock (*H*)	0.3619	(1.7597)
Climate dummy (*CLIM*)	0.1226	(2.5075)
Index of tropicality (*TROP*)	-0.0344	(-0.5603)
Access to the sea (*ACCESS*)	0.1053	(1.3055)
Regional dummy (*REGD*)	-0.0108	(-0.6152)
Percentage of paved roads (*ROADS*)	0.0890	(0.8904)
Electricity production per capita (*ELEC*)	0.5943	(6.4306)
Rule of law (*ROL*)	0.0684	(1.2918)
Government consumption as a % of GDP (*GCON*)	-0.0050	(-1.1511)
Domestic credit as a % of GDP (*CREDIT*)	0.0006	(0.8006)
Trade openness (*TRADE*)	0.0015	(1.9013)
R^2	0.9247	
$\bar{R}^2$	0.9116	

Note: *t* statistics are given in parentheses

To further investigate the impact of proximity on the distribution of economic activity, a more general model was estimated that assumes a non-zero weight matrix **W**. This yields the so-called 'spatial autoregression' model:

$$y = \rho W_1 y + X\beta + \varepsilon \tag{5.10}$$

where the exogenous explanatory variables are again given by the matrix **X**. Table 5.4 provides the estimates of this model.

Table 5.4   Estimates of the spatial autoregression model of 1997 per capita GNP

Variable	Contiguity weight		Distance weight	
Constant	0.6595	(3.3142)	-0.1326	(-0.3379)
K	0.0250	(1.0150)	0.0304	(1.1837)
H	0.2695	(1.5689)	0.3324	(1.8630)
CLIM	0.0482	(1.1189	0.0701	(1.5541)
TROP	-0.0357	(-0.6996)	-0.0698	(-1.2822)
ACCESS	0.1255	(1.8744)	0.0784	(1.1132)
REGD	-0.0263	(-1.7183)	-0.0144	(-0.9364)
ROADS	0.0989	(1.1919)	0.0439	(0.4979)
ELEC	0.5901	(7.6889)	0.5914	(7.3752)
ROL	0.0824	(1.8738)	0.0720	(1.5659)
GCON	-0.0049	(-1.3554)	-0.0047	(-1.2321)
CREDIT	0.0008	(1.2205)	0.0007	(0.9969)
TRADE	0.0011	(1.6241)	0.0011	(1.4932)
Proximity ρ	0.1524	(4.0913)	0.4101	(3.0758)
R^2	0.9384		0.9327	
Log-likelihood	-91.3840		-94.8200	

Notes:
1. Definitions of variables are as in Table 5.3
2. Asymptotic *t* statistics are given in parentheses

First, note that the inclusion of spatial dependence has increased the explanatory power only marginally. Second, only 5 out of the 13 variables included (namely *ACCESS, REGD, ELEC, ROL* and ρ) are significant at the

90 percent probability level in the model with contiguity weights. In the model with distance weights, only *H, ELEC* and ρ are significant. Two variables (*ACCESS* and *REGD*) have become less significant. The R^2 and the log-likelihood of both the models are almost the same.

The correlation between proximity and the geographic variables, namely *CLIM, TROP* and *ACCESS*, was tested using Pearson correlation coefficients. It was found that the variables *CLIM* and *TROP* are correlated with proximity. To avoid possible misspecification errors, *CLIM* and *TROP* were therefore dropped from the model. As the previous estimates show, proximity adds only marginally to the explanatory power of the regressions. However, R^2 is not a reliable guide for assessing the importance of the proximity effect. Several direct test statistics, namely Moran's *I*, the likelihood ratio, the Wald ratio and the Lagrange Multiplier, were computed to ascertain the existence of spatial dependence.[12] The marginal probabilities pertaining to the least-squares residuals were found to be small, which confirms the existence of spatial correlation in the residuals. Moran's *I* statistic also suggested spatial correlation. Comparing contiguity and distance weights, contiguity weights capture spatial dependence better than the distance weights. This finding suggests that neighbourhoods matter more than distances.

So far we have only considered first-order dependence, determined by the matrix $\mathbf{W}_1$, while $\mathbf{W}_2 = 0$. However, it is plausible that a whole cluster of nations within a supranational region may affect a country's economic performance, because the immediate neighbours share borders with the second set of neighbours, and so on. This idea can be captured by the full model (5.6) above, in which $\mathbf{W}_1$ and $\mathbf{W}_2$ measure first-order and second-order dependence respectively. The influences of either tier can be associated with the dependent variable or the residuals. The precise form of this relationship is not known and a formal method for identifying the true structure does not exist, which necessitates the use of trial and error methods. Several tests were carried out and the best results are reported in Table 5.5. As can be seen, a model that takes the second-tier neighbours into account performs better, having R^2 of about 95 percent, and both the first-order and second-order spatial relationships are highly significant. This confirms the existence of neighbourhood clusters.

Table 5.5   *Estimates of the general spatial autoregression model of 1997 per capita GNP*

Variables	Contiguity weights $W_1 = W_C$ $W_2 = W_C W_C$		Interaction with distance weights $W_1 = W_C$ $W_2 = W_C W_D$	
Constant	0.8375	(5.1338)	0.8456	(4.9919)
K	0.0324	(1.3229)	0.0312	(1.2905)
H	0.1827	(1.0709)	0.1771	(1.0621)
$ACCESS$	0.1209	(1.9852)	0.1293	(2.0810)
$ELEC$	0.5714	(7.8152)	0.5604	(7.6868)
ROL	0.1289	(3.2915)	0.1213	(3.0215)
$GCON$	-0.0041	(-1.2786)	-0.0043	(-1.2295)
$CREDIT$	0.0009	(1.4416)	0.0010	(1.5723)
$TRADE$	0.0011	(2.0509)	0.0012	(2.0247)
Proximity:				
First order	0.1303	(4.5664)	0.1341	(4.0827)
Second order	0.3527	(7.2745)	0.8856	(2.0526)
R^2	0.9579		0.9475	
Log-likelihood	99.6937		93.7040	

Notes:
1. W_C contains contiguity weights and W_D contains distance weights
2. Asymptotic t statistics are given in parentheses

5.6   CONCLUSIONS

Casual observation of the distribution of per capita income across countries suggests that there is a strong spatial dependence of poverty and affluence. This observation has given rise to a belief that 'economic neighbourhoods' do indeed exist and that geography plays a role in economic growth. The location of a country seems to affect its 'success' or 'failure' at the levels of households, industries and nation states. There are several channels that seem to transmit growth as well as poverty across national boundaries. Of these, externalities and spillovers appear to be the two most important. Although several studies have evaluated growth spillovers across countries, the spatial distribution of economic activity in the world has received little attention.

This chapter looked at how and to what extent proximity might matter in explaining economic performance in a cross section of countries. An econometric model based on the standard neoclassical growth model was developed for evaluating the hypothesis that proximity affects economic performance of countries. A weight matrix based on rook contiguity was constructed to capture proximity, while another weight matrix was constructed based on the distance between capital cities of countries in the sample.

The econometric modelling reinforces the casual observation that there is spatial dependence in the distribution of per capita income in a cross section of countries. The study attributes the global distribution of economic performance to a combination of factors, including geography, economic policies and institutions. In addition, the study found that proximity is more relevant and significant in explaining spatial distribution than distance, which suggests that neighbourhoods matter more than distance in determining economic performance of a country. The existence of better-performing neighbours has created a positive impact on neighbours' economic performance, depending on the extent of integration. In addition to proximity and a few select geographical variables such as access to coastal areas, a large part of the variation of per capita income across countries can be attributed to standard economic variables such as human capital accumulation, the availability of basic infrastructure, the rule of law and better governance. Prudent economic policies seem to be capable of circumventing the negative implications solely arising from the factors related to location, even when a country is located on the edge of the world.

NOTES

1.   See, for example, Temple (1999), Ades and Chua (1997), Easterly and Levine (1997), and Moreno and Trehan (1997).
2.   The simple theoretical model described here does not consider explicitly the accumulation of human capital, although the level of human capital is proxied by education outcomes. Moreover, many of the benefits that flow from human capital accumulation, such as improved health, better governance, the establishment of rule of law and R&D intensity, that feed back into economic growth have been taken into consideration in the empirical analyses.
3.   The list of countries in the sample: Algeria, Angola, Argentina, Australia, Austria, Bangladesh, Belgium, Bolivia, Brazil, Cameroon, Canada, Chile, China, Colombia, Costa Rica, Cote d'Ivoire, Denmark, Dominican Republic, Ecuador, Egypt, El Salvador, Ethiopia, Finland, France, Germany, Ghana, Greece, Guatemala, Haiti, Honduras, India, Indonesia, Iran, Ireland, Israel, Italy, Jamaica, Japan, Jordan, Kenya, Korea Rep.,

Madagascar, Malawi, Malaysia, Mali, Mauritius, Mexico, Morocco, Mozambique, Netherlands, New Zealand, Nicaragua, Nigeria, Norway, Pakistan, Panama, Paraguay, Peru, Philippines, Portugal, Rwanda, Senegal, Sierra Leone, Singapore, South Africa, Spain, Sri Lanka, Sudan, Sweden, Switzerland, Tanzania, Thailand, Trinidad and Tobago, Tunisia, Turkey, Uganda, United Kingdom, United States, Uruguay, Venezuela, Zambia, Zimbabwe.

4. The capital stock was updated by $K(t+1) = K(t) + I(t) - \delta K(t)$. Fixed gross capital formation in constant prices was estimated by dividing the local currency values by the GDP deflator. The depreciation rate, δ, was assumed to be 5 percent. Special cases: the capital stocks of Bolivia, El Salvador, Malaysia, Israel and Uruguay were updated using the fixed investment levels given in the World Bank (2000) CD ROM. Data for Argentina, Morocco and Sudan are from 1990; the capital stock for Thailand is from 1996.

5. The regression of schooling on EAI yielded $y = 0.532 \exp(2.923x)$, $R^2 = 0.8868$. This was used in estimating the average years of schooling wherever data were not available.

6. The numerical values assigned for Koppen–Guiger climate zones are: tropical A and sub-tropical Cw climates = 1; steppe and desert B climates = 2; temperate Cf, Cs, DW and Df climates = 3; highland H climate = 4; and polar E climate = 5.

7. The values assigned are as follows: Sub-Saharan Africa = 1, South Asia = 2, South Asia = 3, Central Asia = 4, East Asia and the Pacific = 5, South and Central America = 5, Europe = 6 and North America = 7.

8. For Rwanda, in the case of political instability and corruption, the average value for Sub-Saharan Africa is used.

9. For El Salvador, the value is for 1971; for Mozambique and Tanzania, the average for Sub-Saharan Africa in 1992; for Rwanda the four-year average 1989–1992; and for Sudan, the 1972–1982 average.

10. For Angola, Mozambique and Haiti, the average of African countries was used.

11. For those African countries where data are not available, electricity production is generally insignificant.

12. The results were not included in the chapter due to space limitations.

REFERENCES

Ades, A. and H.B. Chua (1997), 'Thy neighbour's curse: regional instability and economic activity', *Journal of Economic Growth*, 2, 297-304.

Akamatsu, K. (1961), 'A theory of unbalanced growth in the world economy', *Weltwirtschaftliches Archiv*, 86, 196-217.

Almeida, P. and R.M. Grant (1998), *International Corporations and Cross-Border Knowledge Transfer in the Semiconductor Industry*, Pittsburgh: The Carnegie-Bosch Institute.

Anselin, L. (1988), *Spatial Econometrics: Methods and Models*, Dordrecht: Kluwer Academic Publishers.

Bassanini, A., Scarpetta S. and P. Hemmings (2001), *Economic Growth: The Role of Policies and Institutions*, *Panel Data Evidence from OECD Countries*, Paris: OECD.

Cabellero, R.J. and A.B. Jaffe (1993), 'How high are the Giants' shoulders?' in, *NBER Macroeconomics Annual*, Blanchard, O.J. and S. Fisher (eds), London and Cambridge: MIT Press, pp. 15-74.

Chua, H.B. (1993), 'Regional spillovers and economic growth', Centre Discussion Paper No. 700, Economic Growth Centre, Yale University.

Clark, G.L., Feldman, M.P. and M.S. Gertler (2000), 'Economic geography: transition and growth', in Gorden, L.C., Marymann P. F. and M.S. Gertler (eds), *The Oxford Handbook of Economic Geography*, Oxford: Oxford University Press.

Corea, G. (1998), '50 years economic development in Sri Lanka', Independence Commemoration Lecture, Central Bank of Sri Lanka Colombo.

Deininger, K. and L. Squire (1996), 'A new data set measuring income inequality', *World Bank Economic Review*, 10, 565-591.

Durlauf, S.N. and D.T. Quah (1999), 'The new empirics of economic growth', *Handbook of Macroeconomics Volume 1A*, Amsterdam, New York and Oxford: Elsevier Science, North-Holland, pp. 235-308.

Dervis, K. (1997), 'Growing together: why the regional neighbourhood matters for the Middle East and North Africa', paper presented at the Middle East/North Africa Economic Conference, 16-18 November.

Easterly, W. and R. Levine (1997), 'Africa's growth tragedy: policies and ethnic division', *Quarterly Journal of Economics*, 112, 1203-1250.

Eaton, J. and S. Kortum (1996), 'International patenting and technology diffusion', NBER Working Paper, No. 4931, National Bureau of Economic Research.

Eaton, J. and A. Tamura (1994), 'Bilateralism and regionalism in Japanese and U.S. trade and foreign direct investment patterns', *Journal of the Japanese and International Economies*, 8, 478-510.

Encarta Interactive World Atlas (2000), Microsoft Corporation.

Gallup, J.L., Sachs, J.F. and A.D. Mellinger (1998), 'Geography and economic growth', *International Regional Science Review*, 22, 179-232.

Hall, R.E. and C.I. Jones (1999), 'Why do some countries produce so much more output per worker than others?', *Quarterly Journal of Economics*, 114, 83-116.

Jaffe, A., Trajtenberg, M. and R. Henderson (1993), 'Geographical localization of knowledge spillovers as evidenced by patent citations', *Quarterly Journal of Economics*, 108, 577-598.

Kojima, K. (1973), 'A macroeconomic approach to foreign direct investment', *Hitotsubashi Journal of Economics*, 14, 1-21.

Kojima, K. (1978), *Direct Foreign Investment: A Japanese Model of Multinational Business Operations*, New York: Praeger Publishers.

Krueger, A. (1968), 'Factor endowments and per capita income differences', *Economic Journal*, 78, 641-659.

Lee, C.H. (1990), 'Direct foreign investment, structural adjustment, and international division of labour: a dynamic macroeconomic theory of direct foreign investment', *Hitotsubashi Journal of Economics*, 31, 61-72.

LeSage, J.P. (2000), *Spatial Econometrics*, http://www.wvu.edu/WebBook.

Manski, C.F. (1993), 'Identification of endogenous social effects: the reflection problem', *Review of Economic Studies*, 60, 531-542.

Marshall, A. (1932), *Industry and Trade*, London: Macmillan.

Mankiw, N.G., Romer, D. and D.N. Weil (1992), 'A contribution to the empirics of economic growth', *Quarterly Journal of Economic Growth*, 107, 407-432.

Mellinger, A.D., Sachs, J.D. and J.L. Gallup (2000), 'Climate, coastal proximity, and development', in Gorden, L.C., Marymann P.F. and M.S. Gertler (eds), *The Oxford Handbook of Economic Geography*, Oxford: Oxford University Press.

Moreno, R. and B. Trehan (1997), 'Location and the growth of nations', *Journal of Economic Growth*, 2, 399-418.

Nehru, V. and A. Dhareshwar (1993), 'A new database on physical capital stock: sources, methodology and results', *Rivista de Analisis Economico*, 8, 37-59.

Pace, R.K. and R. Barry (1998), 'Simulating mixed regressive autoregressive estimators', *Computational Statistics*, 13, 397-418.

Sala-i-Martin, X. (1997), 'I just ran two million regressions', *American Economic Review*, 87, 178-183.

Shatz, H.J. and A.J. Venables (2000), 'The geography of international investment', in Gorden, L.C., Marymann P. F. and M.S. Gertler (eds), *The Oxford Handbook of Economic Geography*, Oxford: Oxford University Press.

Sen, A. (2001), 'A world of extremes: ten theses on globalization', *The Times of India*, 16 July.

Temple, J. (1999), 'The new growth evidence', *Journal of Economic Literature*, 37, 112-156.

UNDP (2000), *Human Development Report 2000*, New York: United Nations.

Young, A. (1928), 'Increasing returns and economic progress', *Economic Journal*, 38, 527-542.

World Bank (2000), *World Development Indicators 2000*, CD ROM.

World Bank (2001), www.worldbank.org/governance.

World Resources Institute (1999), *World Resources 1998-99*, Washington, DC: World Resources Institute.

6.   Core–Periphery Linkages and Income in Small Pacific Island Economies

Geoffrey Bertram and Özer Karagedikli

6.1 INTRODUCTION

The persistence of wide disparities in productivity and per capita incomes across the world economy is a long-standing puzzle for neoclassically minded economists. The intuition derived from the Solow–Swan growth model is that in a world where technology is a public good shared by all, each individual country's process of capital accumulation should eventually bring it to the same level of per capita income as other countries except insofar as national savings rates differ.[1] This result ought to emerge even in the absence of trade, labour migration and capital flows among countries, provided that technology (knowledge) is an international public good and that the rate of labour force growth is identical across countries.

The convergence intuition is not exclusive to neoclassical economists. The expectation that the capitalist industrial revolution in Western Europe would eventually transform the entire world order in its own image came as naturally to Marx ([1848] 1973, pp.71-72) as it did to Rostow (1960).

Once consistent cross-country time-series data became available in the 1980s, with the publication of the Penn World Tables (e.g., Summers and Heston, 1991), statistical investigations focused on the evidence for long-run global absolute convergence among national economies.[2]

The data for the past couple of centuries have turned out to be discouraging for the neoclassical hypothesis of a global trend towards equality (Barro, 1991; Maddison, 1994, 2001; Pritchett, 1996; Romer, 1994). Some economies have indeed converged into clusters ('convergence clubs') somewhat akin to galaxies in space. The high-income economies of the OECD, for example, seem to have converged over the past fifty years (Dowrick and Nguyen, 1989; Brander, 1992).

Countries within the OECD, the states of the USA, prefectures of Japan and the regions of Western Europe have converged towards their respective mean per capita income levels (Barro and Sala-i-Martin, 1991, 1992; Barro and Grilli, 1994, Chapter 14). The seven separate colonies of Australia and New Zealand similarly converged from 1861–1901 and stayed in step thereafter until 1991 (Cashin, 1995) although this cluster may have begun to disperse in the past two decades (Cashin, 1998).

The existence of these clusters of mutually convergent economies, however, has not implied global convergence. On the contrary, the global gap between rich and poor countries has widened over the past century. As Maddison (2001, p.48) comments, 'the major problem in growth analysis is to explain why such a large divergence developed between the advanced capitalist group and the rest of the world'.

Convergence or divergence is, in short, a live topic, and the search for convergence clusters has extended to the Pacific islands as to most other geographically defined regions.

6.2 THE CONCEPT OF REGIONAL CONVERGENCE

Western Europe, North America and Australasia are examples of geographically contiguous regions which sometimes exhibit converging tendencies in their economic as well as cultural and political dimensions. These regions also (not coincidentally) exhibit strong within-region trade and migration flows, relative to flows to and from other regions. Not all geographical regions, however, exhibit such intra-regional convergence of per capita income.

Latin America, Africa, the Caribbean, the Pacific and South–Southeast Asia exhibit far less intra-regional economic integration, and have had correspondingly greater difficulty than the OECD core countries in creating and maintaining regional economic blocs. The trade, migration and capital flows of the individual economies in many of these regions are dominated by bilateral external links to counter parties outside the region. Such dominance of extra-regional over intra-regional economic linkages leads to an unfavourable environment both for policy initiatives such as common currency areas and free trade areas, and for the market-driven process of economic convergence towards a regional average level of real income.

The fact that the OECD 'convergence club' is geographically dispersed shows the importance of elements other than geographical location in driving a convergence process. Although scattered around the world, the OECD economies share sufficient common economic linkages to be drawn together in terms of their per capita GDP and participation in what is sometimes described as the 'core' of the global economy.

When looking for convergence outside the OECD, then, one should bear in mind that geographical proximity is probably not the basic determinant of convergence or non-convergence. Maddison's (1994) continent-by-continent classification of relative growth performance over two centuries, and Cashin and Loayza's (1995) testing of the hypothesis of convergence in the Pacific islands region, throw up the same essentially negative result: economies located within geographically defined regions on the global periphery have tended not to exhibit regional absolute income convergence, in contrast to regions within the global core which have converged (Western Europe, North America, Australasia at least in some historical periods).

While peripheral economies do not seem to converge with each other, convergence forces could be at work along the 'spokes' linking former colonial powers in the world economic hub to former colonies on the periphery. Convergence might operate more strongly along the global spokes than around the rim (for a model along these lines, see Sunkel, 1973).

There continue, for example, to be strong links between Pacific island territories and the larger metropolitan states, which, over the past 150 years, have jockeyed for geopolitical position in the Pacific Ocean. Most of the metropolitan powers have retained aid, trade and labour market links with former or actual colonies, dependencies and overseas territories. These linkages provide the dominant external conditioning factors for each island economy's internal economic performance.

Figure 6.1 presents a simple schematic model of such a global system. The core comprises four countries, A, B, C and D. Each of these has trade, aid, migration and investment linkages with a particular segment of the global periphery or peripheries. In the diagram, imagine the entire core–periphery system as a 'solar system' with peripheral economies orbiting the core in three belts, like asteroids. The inner belt is populated by territories that are closely integrated politically as well as economically with patron states in the core. The next belt out is populated by periphery states with looser political/economic linkages ('self-governing in free association' is the code for this status in the Pacific). The outer belt contains sovereign independent states. Strong economic linkages, represented by heavy spokes, run to the closely integrated satellites. The weakest links (thinnest spokes) run to the outer belt of independent states. The gravitational attraction between income levels in core and periphery is strongest for closely linked states and weakest for independent (weakly linked) states. The spokes are the transmission belts for a wide variety of processes, which tend to bind islands to their patrons.

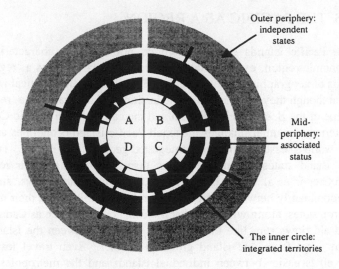

Outer periphery: independent states

Mid-periphery: associated status

A B
D C

The inner circle: integrated territories

Figure 6.1 A schematic core–periphery global system

Besides trade flows (especially the sourcing of consumption-goods imports, since islands tend to acquire and maintain the tastes of their metropolitan patron economies and societies), the spokes correspond to flows of aid and budgetary support; military treaties or arrangements; modes of incorporation in the patrons' political culture and international groupings such as the Commonwealth and the French Overseas Territories; migration paths for workers in search of jobs and opportunities in the global core; conduits for technology transfer; and educational ladders for ambitious islanders.

There is no relationship between the length of spokes in the diagram and the geographical distance of territories from their patron states. France's island territories in the Pacific are integral parts of metropolitan France despite being on the other side of the globe. But Papua New Guinea is independent of Australia and separated from it by a widening political and economic gulf, despite the two countries being geographic neighbours.

In addition, the hub and spoke model operates in the Pacific Ocean in spatial terms in a sense 'inside-out': the Pacific Rim is the core/hub, while the sea of islands is the region's economic periphery.

6.3 THE PACIFIC AS A REGION

The Pacific islands on their own do not have the characteristics of an economic region, even though they are often classified as a 'region' on the basis of geographical location, cultural similarities and political rhetoric; and even though they have acquired the institutional apparatus of a 'region' in the shape of the South Pacific Forum and the earlier South Pacific Commission. In terms of mutual linkages the small Pacific island economies are probably the world's least economically integrated geographical region. Trade among the island states accounts for less than 2 percent of their total exports (McGregor et al., 1992, pp.20-21). Labour migration flows, similarly, are predominantly between individual island communities and their metropolitan patron states, along with other Pacific Rim countries such as Canada. Capital and aid flows run, like the spokes of a wheel, between the islands and the Rim – not from one island group to another.[3] Even travel (especially air travel) is easier between individual islands and the metropoles than from island group to island group.

The characterisation of Pacific island communities as national economic units is also problematic. This is reflected in the nature of the economic data that are available as well as in the political status of the islands and the general tone of outside commentary on economic development prospects in the region.

Of the 22 entities covered by this study only nine (Papua New Guinea, Western Samoa, Fiji, Kiribati, Solomon Islands, Tonga Vanuatu, Nauru and Tuvalu) are sovereign independent nation states. Only six (Papua New Guinea, Western Samoa, Fiji, Solomon Islands, Tonga, and Vanuatu) have their own currencies. Only nine (Papua New Guinea, Western Samoa, Fiji, Solomon Islands, Tonga, Vanuatu, Marshall Islands, Federated States of Micronesia and Kiribati) are members of the World Bank, Asian Development Bank and/or IMF. Major parts of the regional economy such as Hawaii, New Caledonia and French Polynesia, as well as the smallest units (Tokelau, Niue, Easter Island, Norfolk Island, Galapagos Islands) are politically integrated parts of larger countries whose metropolitan economies are located around the Pacific Rim or in Europe. Several other island states are constitutionally 'self-governing in free association' with larger countries to whose currency areas they belong.

6.4 THE STUDY

This chapter reports results from a recent study which tested two hypotheses:

1. The level of material welfare of small peripheral island states depends directly on the strength of political ties to their patron economies (thickness of the relevant spokes in Figure 6.1).

2. The level of material welfare of small peripheral island economies, and their rates of growth, depend directly on the level and growth rate of the GDP per capita of the metropolitan state to which each peripheral state is most closely linked.

To test these hypotheses, data were assembled on GDP per capita for 22 small Pacific island economies, and compared with data on the income levels of their principal aid, trade and constitutional partner economies in the global core, to which the islands are hypothesised to have converged. The Pacific islands region is thus envisaged not as a self-contained economic system but as a mosaic of overlapping systems, each tied to a major economy of the core.

Just as atlases of the world in the colonial era colour-coded colonial territories by imperial allegiance (British, French, German, Dutch, Portuguese, etc.) so we provisionally assign each island economy in the post-colonial era to a particular sphere of influence (Poirine, 1995), with a dominant core economy as the 'pace-setter' for real income trends in its small island satellites.

Table 6.1 provides a first look at the importance of political integration. On average across the Pacific islands region, politically integrated units exhibit per capita incomes nine times higher than sovereign island states. Excluding the two large island economies Hawaii (integrated) and Papua New Guinea (sovereign), which weigh heavily in the results for the first two columns, the ratio comes down to nearly three times.

The direction of causality lying behind Table 6.1 is obviously an important issue. Former colonial powers might be argued to have been keen to divest themselves of poor territories such as Papua New Guinea or Kiribati while holding on to more 'worthwhile' possessions such as New Caledonia. Even anecdotally, however, this is not a particularly plausible hypothesis. Papua New Guinea contains mineral resources on a par with those of New Caledonia, yet was quickly decolonised. French Polynesia, on the other hand, contains no more economic resources than Kiribati, yet was tightly held by

France and boosted to high income levels by massive government spending (including the nuclear test programme) by the patron economy.

Table 6.1 Per capita GDP by political status, US dollars

	At current exchange rates	In purchasing-power parity (PPP)	PPP excl Papua New Guinea and Hawaii
Sovereign territories	1,229	2,898	4,164
In free association	2,187	2,435	2,435
Politically integrated	22,615	26,095	11,717
Region average	6,351	7,841	6,402

Source: First column from Bertram (1999b), p.338, Table 28.2. PPP data from *CIA World Factbook 2001*. Averages are weighted by population

The pattern of political linkages of Pacific island economies does not seem to have been driven *ex ante* by relative income or resource endowments in the island territories. On the contrary, the linkages have tended to come first and the corresponding income and growth prospects have followed. This is one key implication of the MIRAB model (Bertram and Watters, 1985; Bertram, 1986; Bertram, 1999a).

While the importance of political linkage is clear from Table 6.1, the second hypothesis (that for any given level of political linkage, per capita GDP should correlate positively with that of the respective patron economy) requires further exploration. This is the task undertaken in the remainder of this chapter, beginning with a review of the only major econometric study to date of the convergence issue in the Pacific islands region, by Cashin and Loayza (1995).

6.5 THE CASHIN–LOAYZA RESULTS

Cashin and Loayza (1995) addressed the hypothesis that the Pacific island economies, because of their geographic location within a single region, should tend to converge to a common mean income level. They found, on the contrary, that although each individual economy was converging towards some steady state (which Cashin and Loayza interpreted as a Solow–Swan steady state), regional per capita output had diverged over the period 1971–1993, with official and private transfer payments merely providing a counterbalance sufficient to hold the dispersion of per capita disposable income constant over the two decades. This result held for both their 'PAC9' data set (seven small-island economies plus Australia and New Zealand) and their 'PAC7' (seven-country) and 'PAC5' (five-country) data sets, which contained only small-island economies.

An alternative explanation of their results would be that each island economy has been converging to the income level of a counterpart economy or economies in the global core, and that the constant dispersion of real disposable income levels reflects the fact that those metropolitan counterparts all belong to the OECD 'convergence club' so that island living standards derive their relativities from sources external to the region. The Cashin–Loayza results would then have nothing to do with dynamic market interactions among the island economies themselves.[4]

This suggests a quantitative research strategy addressed to the possibility of convergence of individual periphery units with their respective core counter parties instead of (or as well as) convergence towards each other. Section 6.6 reviews some economic data for the small Pacific island economies, and tests the hypothesis that Pacific island GDP per capita can be explained primarily by linkages between island territories and core patron states.

6.6 ESTIMATING THE CORE–PERIPHERY MODEL

6.6.1 Data

To obtain data on per capita GDP for the Pacific islands, a variety of sources have been used. The most reliable and consistent data are those produced by the major international agencies in standard formats, but these databases often exclude very small islands, along with fully politically integrated island territories such as Hawaii.[5] For the present study, 1999 cross-section data have been taken from the *CIA World Factbook*, which provides PPP estimates of GDP per capita in US dollars. For time-series data the main source is the Asian Development Bank's *Key Indicators 2001*, supplemented by information from island-specific sources where available.

Table 6.2 reproduces PPP data from the *CIA World Factbook 2001* covering 21 Pacific island territories, to which have been added figures for Hawaii from the US Department of Commerce. The CIA data re-weight each island economy's GDP to US relative prices and convert it to US dollars to give consistent estimates of the purchasing power of GDP per capita across countries at about 1999.

Table 6.2 Basic data from CIA World Factbook 2001

Island	Population	Area (km²)	GDP (US$m PPP)	GDP per capita	Exports (US$m)	Imports (US$m)	Currency in use
American Samoa	67,084	199	500	8,000	500	471	US $
Cook Islands	20,611	240	100	5,000	3	85	NZ $
Fiji	844,330	18,270	5,900	7,300	537	653	Fiji $
French Polynesia	253,506	4,167	2,600	10,800	205	749	CPF
Guam	157,557	549	3,200	21,000	76	203	US $
Kiribati	94,149	717	76	850	6	44	Aust $
Marshall Islands	70,822	181	105	1,670	28	58	US $
Micronesia	134,597	702	263	2,000	73	168	US $
New Caledonia	204,863	19,060	3,000	15,000	411	843	CPF
Niue	2,124	260	5	2,800	0.12	4	NZ $
Nauru	12,088	21	59	5,000	25	21	Aust $
Northern Marianas	74,612	477	900	12,500	n.a.	n.a.	US $
Palau	19,092	458	129	7,100	14	126	US $
Papua New Guinea	5,049,055	462,840	12,200	2,500	2,100	1,000	Kina
Samoa	179,058	2,860	571	3,200	17	90	Tala
Solomon Islands	480,442	28,450	900	2,000	165	152	Sol. Is $
Tokelau	1,445	10	2	1,000	0.10	0.32	NZ $
Tonga	104,227	748	225	2,200	8	69	Pa'anga
Tuvalu	10,991	26	12	1,100	0	4	Aust $
Vanuatu	192,910	12,200	245	1,300	25	77	Vatu
Wallis and Futuna	15,435	274	30	2,000	0	0	CPF
Hawaii*	1,185,497	16,641	40,914	34,512	1,531	12,629	US $

*US Department of Commerce data

Table 6.3 matches up each island economy with a metropolitan patron and shows the degree of constitutional linkage between the two in terms of the three categories 'integrated', 'associated' and 'independent'. 'Patron' economies were identified from data on each island's leading source of imports, currency used and political linkages. The data are plotted in Figure 6.2.

Table 6.3 Island–patron pairs at 1999

	GDP per capita, PPP (US$)	Patron economy	Patron economy's GDP per capita (PPP estimates)	Political status of the island territory
American Samoa	8,000	USA	36,200	Integrated
Cook Islands	5,000	New Zealand	17,700	Associated
Fiji	7,300	Australia	23,200	Independent
French Polynesia	10,800	France	24,400	Integrated
Guam	21,000	USA	36,200	Integrated
Hawaii	34,512	USA	36,200	Integrated
Kiribati	850	Australia	23,200	Independent
Marshall Islands	1,670	USA	36,200	Associated
Micronesia	2,000	USA	36,200	Associated
New Caledonia	15,000	France	24,400	Integrated
Niue	2,800	New Zealand	17,700	Associated
Nauru	5,000	Australia	23,200	Independent
Northern Marianas	12,500	USA	36,200	Integrated
Palau	7,100	USA	36,200	Associated
Papua New Guinea	2,500	Australia	23,200	Independent
Samoa	3,200	New Zealand	17,700	Independent
Solomon Islands	2,000	Australia	23,200	Independent
Tokelau	1,000	New Zealand	17,700	Integrated
Tonga	2,200	New Zealand	17,700	Independent
Tuvalu	1,100	Australia	23,200	Independent
Vanuatu	1,300	Japan	24,900	Independent
Wallis and Futuna	2,000	France	24,400	Integrated

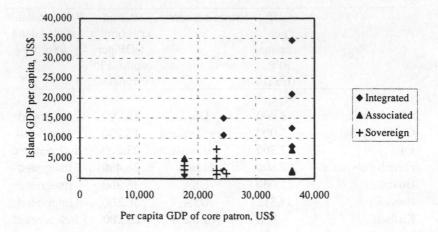

*Figure 6.2   GDP per capita in 22 Pacific island economies and their
metropolitan patrons, by political status, 1999*

6.6.2 Cross-Section Regressions

Table 6.4 shows the results from regressing island per capita GDP on
metropolitan per capita GDP and constitutional status, using data from Table
6.3. The model is:

$$Y_i = \alpha_0 + \alpha_1 INT_i + \alpha_2 ASSOC_i + \alpha_3 METY_i + \varepsilon_i \qquad (6.1)$$

where Y_i is per capita GDP of island economy i in PPP terms; INT_i is a binary
dummy variable for full constitutional integration between the island
territory and the relevant metropolitan patron state; $ASSOC_i$ is a dummy
variable for territories classified as 'self-governing in free association';
$METY_i$ is the per capita PPP GDP of the major 'patron' economy to which
island i is linked and ε_i is the error term. Three regressions are reported, all
calculated using OLS with White's heteroscedasticity-consistent standard
errors, which successfully corrected for the heteroscedasticity in the data,
which is apparent in Figure 6.2.[6]

The results provide some support for both hypotheses tested. The
coefficient on *INT* in the first two equations is significant at 5 percent, and in
the third at 10 percent. It indicates that politically integrated territories have

per capita incomes nearly $8,000 higher than other island economies. The intermediate political status *ASSOC* was not significant in the cross-section study, and was dropped from the preferred result, regression (1). Metropolitan GDP per capita, *METY*, is significant at the 10 percent level and positive; its coefficient in equation (1) indicates that each additional dollar of per capita GDP in a patron economy is associated with an additional 37 cents of per capita GDP in its related island economies. The log regression in equation (3) shows the corresponding elasticity as 1.15 (i.e., a 1 percent increase in *METY* raises *Y* by 1.15 percent).

Table 6.4 Cross-section regression results

Regression number	Constant	*INT*	*ASSOC*	*METY*	R^2	Adjusted R^2
(1)	−5,920	8,137		0.369	0.462	0.405
	(−1.12)	(2.47)		(1.69)		
(2)	−6,220	7,296	−1,821	0.408	0.468	0.380
	(−1.10)	(2.23)	(−0.61)	(1.61)		
Equation 1 re−estimated in logs of Y *and* METY						
(3)	−3.777	0.969		1.154	0.392	0.328
	(−0.46)	(2.01)		(1.41)		

Note: All regressions are ordinary least squares with White heteroscedasticity-consistent standard errors. *t*-statistics are in brackets

6.6.3 A Panel Model

This section presents results from use of a panel data set to test further the hypothesis that the income of small island economies in the Pacific region is mainly determined by (i) the degree of political integration with a metropolitan economy and (ii) the income of the patron economy. The database (available from the authors on request) is a panel of per capita GDP, population and political linkage for the 22 Pacific island economies and their metropolitan patron economies at intervals of five years over the period 1971–1999. Data were taken mostly from the Asian Development Bank's *Key Indicators 2001* and the IMF's *International Financial Statistics*.

Fourteen island economies have at least four entries in the panel and four (Fiji, French Polynesia, Hawaii and the Solomon Islands) have data going back to 1971.

To construct the GDP data, nominal GDP per capita for each island and patron economy at each date was converted to US dollars using the current nominal exchange rate, and deflated to the 1996 US price level using the US GDP deflator. Each island economy was paired with a metropolitan patron at each date, with binary dummy variables to distinguish between politically integrated territories, associated territories and island states which were independent at the date of the observation. Figure 6.3 plots the data in logs.

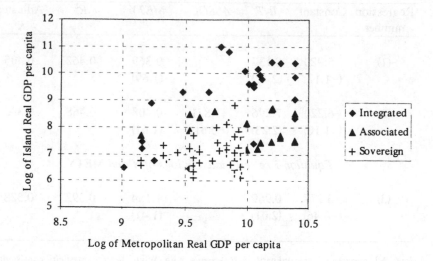

Figure 6.3 Plot of the panel data, 1971–1999

The panel data were checked for unconditional beta convergence (Barro and Sala-i-Martin, 1995) among the island economies in the study. No evidence was found for any tendency towards mean regression – that is, the Pacific islands exhibit no tendency over time to move towards any common regional steady state.

The core–periphery model was estimated using the equation

$$\log Y_{it} = \alpha_0 + \alpha_1 INT_{it} + \alpha_2 ASSOC_{it} + \alpha_3 \log METY_{it} + \varepsilon_{it} \qquad (6.2)$$

Table 6.5 Panel regression results

	Constant	INT	ASSOC	Log METY	1975	1980	1985	1990	1995	1999	R^2	Adjusted R^2
(1)	-2.932 (-0.961)	1.776 (6.680)	0.478 (2.144)	1.032 (3.267)							0.536	0.519
With island fixed effects												
(2)	0.861 (3.604)		*	0.734 (4.632)							0.920	0.896
With time dummies												
(3)	-6.329 (-1.894)	1.613 (6.616)	0.503 (1.866)	1.403 (3.939)	0.072 (0.146)	0.138 (0.246)	0.043 (0.085)	-0.198 (-0.367)	-0.123 (-0.221)	-0.291 (-0.499)	0.528	0.480
(4)	-3.855 (-0.947)	1.815 (6.226)		1.127 (2.576)	-0.010 (-0.019)	0.282 (0.483)	0.052 (0.098)	-0.089 (-0.161)	0.008 (0.013)	-0.200 (-0.332)	0.550	0.497
With time dummies and island fixed effects												
(5)	0.742 (2.863)		*	0.270 (0.778)	0.388 (2.974)	0.736 (2.328)	0.288 (1.765)	0.414 (1.792)	0.586 (2.328)	0.452 (1.747)	0.937	0.905

Notes: * With fixed effects included, one of the political status variables had to be excluded (near-singular matrix). t statistics in brackets

Table 6.5 reports the regression results for this model. All equations were estimated with White heteroscedasticity-consistent standard errors. *INT* and *METY* are statistically significant, and both have positive coefficients as predicted. *ASSOC* is also significant at 5 percent, and positive in the two regressions that included it. None of the time dummies is significant.

Adding fixed effects to the analysis (regressions (2) and (5)) raises the R^2s while reducing the significance of *INT* and *METY*. However, the fixed-effect results in Table 6.5 are suspect because of collinearity between island fixed effects and political status, and were set aside in drawing conclusions from the analysis.

Equations (1) and (4) in Table 6.5 are the preferred regressions. The coefficients in equation (4) indicate an ascending hierarchy of per capita GDP from independent to associated to integrated political status, while across the whole sample a 1 percent increase in metropolitan income is associated with a 1.1 percent increase in income in the corresponding island satellite economies.

These regressions are consistent with the proposition that the real per capita GDPs of Pacific island economies depends on (i) the real income of the linked metropolitan countries and (ii) the closeness of political integration of each island with its patron.

6.7 CONCLUSION

Structuralist world-systems historians (e.g., Senghaas, 1985), and proponents of centre–periphery models such as those suggested by Myrdal (1958) and Sunkel (1973), have portrayed global economic history as a dynamic interplay between centrifugal and centripetal forces in the world economy. The analysis presented in this chapter characterises the small Pacific island economies as units in the global economic periphery – units that are related bilaterally to countries in the global core rather than to other similarly located peripheral economies. The economic forces promoting global income convergence in the long run (labour and capital migration, commodity trade, diffusion of technology and tastes) link these small island units to the outside world, not to each other. Economic forces which act centripetally at global level have divergent effects within the Pacific region, sustaining and continually reproducing wide differences in per capita GDP, and hence in material welfare, among the economies of the region. The popular concept of a 'Pacific way' in the cultural and political realms has no apparent economic counterpart.

NOTES

1. Low-saving economies would end up with lower per capita income because of their inability to provide for the depreciation to maintain a capital stock as large as that sustained by high-saving economies.
2. There had, of course, been numerous earlier studies of the international distribution of income across nations over time, following the pioneering work of Kuznets, but accurate measurement of relative growth trends in real per capita incomes over long timespans of the 20th century became possible only with the development of purchasing-power parity series which compared like with like across economies at all levels of development.
3. Within island groups, however, there are significant informal capital markets operating.
4. This obviously has to be qualified somewhat for the obvious existence of migration links between some islands – for example, Samoa and American Samoa; Samoa and Hawaii; Guam and the rest of Micronesia.
5. World Bank *World Development Report*, International Monetary Fund *International Financial Statistics* and *Staff Country Reports*, Asian Development Bank *Key Statistical Indicators of Member Countries* and the United Nations *Statistical Yearbook*.
6. Two checks were made for remaining heteroscedasticity in the regression results in Tables 6.4 and 6.5. First the residuals were plotted against island income and inspected. Second, White's general heteroscedasticity test was used, involving auxiliary regression of the residuals against the dependent variables, their squares and cubes, obtaining the result that no significant correlations were found.

REFERENCES

Asian Development Bank (2001), *Key Indicators 2001: Growth and Change in Asia and the Pacific*, www.adb.org/Documents/Books/Key_Indicators/2001.

Barro, R. J. (1991), 'Economic growth in a cross-section of countries', *Quarterly Journal of Economics*, 106, 407–443.

Barro, R. J. and V. Grilli (1994), *European Macroeconomics*, London: Macmillan.

Barro, R. J. and X. Sala-i-Martin (1991), 'Convergence across states and regions', *Brookings Papers on Economic Activity*, 1, 107-182.

Barro, R. J. and X. Sala-i-Martin (1992), 'Convergence', *Journal of Political Economy*, 100, 223-251.

Barro, R. J. and X. Sala-i-Martin (1995), *Economic Growth*, New York: McGraw-Hill.

Bertram, G. (1986), 'Sustainable development in pacific micro-economies', *World Development*, 14, 809-822.

Bertram, G. (1999a), 'The MIRAB model twelve years on', *The Contemporary Pacific*, 11, 105-138.

Bertram, G. (1999b), 'Economy', Chapter 28 in Rapaport, Moshe (ed.) *The Pacific Islands: Environment and Society*, Honolulu: Bess Press.

Bertram, G. and R. F. Watters (1985), 'The MIRAB economy in South Pacific microstates', *Pacific Viewpoint*, 26, 497-519.

Brander, J. A. (1992), 'Comparative economic growth: evidence and interpretation', *Canadian Journal of Economics*, 15, 792-818.

Cashin, P. (1995), 'Economic growth and convergence across the seven colonies of Australasia: 1861–1991', *The Economic Record*, 71, 132-144.

Cashin, P. (1998), 'Disparities in Australian regional incomes: are they narrowing?', *Australian Economic Review*, 31, 3-26.

Cashin, P. and N. Loayza (1995), 'Paradise Lost? Growth, Convergence and Migration in the South Pacific', *IMF Staff Papers*, 42, 608-641.

Dowrick, S., and D. Nguyen (1989), 'OECD comparative economic Growth 1950–1985', *American Economic Review*, 79, 1010-1030.

McGregor, A.M., Sturton, M. and S. Halapua (1992), *Private Sector Development: Policies and Programs for the Pacific Islands*, Honolulu: East–West Center, University of Hawaii.

Maddison, A. (1994), 'Explaining the economic performance of nations 1820–1989', in Baumol, W.J. and R.R. Nelson, (eds), *Convergence of Productivity*, New York: Oxford University Press.

Maddison, A. (2001), *The World Economy: A Millennial Perspective*, Paris: OECD Development Centre.

Marx, K. (1848) *Manifesto of the Communist Party*, reprinted in D. Fernbach (ed.)(1973), *Marx: The Revolutions of 1848*, Harmondsworth: Penguin.

Myrdal, G. (1958), *Economic Theory and the Underdeveloped Regions*, London: Duckworth.

Poirine, B. (1995), *Les Petites Économies Insulaires: Théories et Stratégies de Développement*, Paris: Editions L'Harmattan.

Pritchett, L. (1996), 'Forget convergence: divergence past, present and future', *Finance and Development*, 33, 40-43.

Romer, P. (1994), 'The origins of endogenous growth', *Journal of Economic Perspectives*, 8, 3-22.

Rostow, W. W. (1960), *The Stages of Economic Growth: A Non-Communist Manifesto*, Cambridge: Cambridge University Press.

Senghaas, D. (1985), *The European Experience: A Historical Critique of Development Theory*, Leamington Spa: Berg.

Summers, R. and A. Heston (1991), 'The Penn World Table (Mark 5): an expanded set of international comparisons, 1950–1988', *Quarterly Journal of Economics*, 106, 327-368.

Sunkel, O. (1973), 'Transnational capitalism and national disintegration in Latin America', *Social and Economic Studies*, 22, 132-176.

7. The Impact of Scale and Remoteness on New Zealand's Industrial Structure and Firm Performance

Geoff Simmons

7.1 INTRODUCTION

As already noted in Chapter 1, the case of New Zealand would appear to be particularly relevant for a study of the impact of geographical features on the economic performance of countries. Except for some island microstates, New Zealand could arguably be considered the most remote economy in the world. With a population of only 4 million spread over a land mass of between that of Britain and Japan, and a distance of 2,150 km between Auckland and the nearest major city Sydney, it is clear that if scale, density and location do not influence New Zealand's economic performance, such factors would have little significance elsewhere. The common perception is that New Zealand's isolation and smallness have had a dampening effect on the gains that have been achieved since economic reform commenced in 1984. This perception has undoubtedly contributed to rather widespread pessimism about the country's ability to catch up with its OECD peers. The pessimistic mood is reflected in this statement of a well-known local commentator who remarked, 'We have an archipelago economy, with lots of little islands poking up from a continental shelf that is gently subsiding' (James, 2001).

This chapter looks at New Zealand's firm size and performance to check for evidence on the importance of location and scale in the New Zealand economy, as suggested by Skilling (2001a).[1] Skilling argued that New Zealand's small market size and isolation might help to explain its relatively poor economic performance in recent times. He postulated that the small domestic market size and, often large, fixed costs involved in moving into exporting limits the growth of New Zealand businesses. This may impact on performance by preventing firms from achieving minimum efficient scale, and may cause productivity and innovation losses as firms are not closely located to competitors, suppliers and markets.

Table 7.1 Possible effects of scale and location on economic performance

Causes	The New Zealand economy has both a small domestic market and is distant from the majority of its trading partners. Since New Zealand is an outlier in the OECD with respect to both features, we can expect these to be particularly important for the New Zealand economy.
Transmission mechanisms	• The small economy requires an early shift to exporting among firms that wish to expand. • There are barriers to exporting, including a substantial fixed cost investment, that make the transition to exporting difficult, especially for small firms. • Capital market imperfections also make it difficult for small firms to finance substantial expansions. • Inability to expand causes many firms to be trapped below minimum efficient scale, leaving them with poor returns and unable to compete internationally. • Distance from markets and suppliers hinders the dissemination of marketing information and reduces innovation. • Small size and distance from trading partners make it unprofitable to invest in producing highly specialised goods, because of the difficulty of developing the complex forward and backward linkages that are typically needed to produce high-value-added goods.
Effects on New Zealand	• An abundance of small firms. • A dependence on a small number of firms to generate export revenue. • Poor productivity, especially among small firms. • A lack of high-value-added products. • Individual firms producing a diversified product range.

The small market may also force firms to diversify to a greater degree and sooner than they would do otherwise in order to increase their sales. Hence a small market will also make it less likely that New Zealand firms will specialise and produce high-value-added products. Similar concepts can be applied to the labour market, as the absence of specialised firms will discourage the accumulation of specialised skills.

A first attempt at testing the impact of size and distance on New Zealand firm size, behaviour and performance was made by Skilling (2001b), using readily available data, mostly from the OECD. The purpose of the present chapter is to deepen this analysis of firm behaviour and performance, mainly using New Zealand-specific Annual Enterprise Survey (AES) data. This is the first time that AES data have been used for this purpose.

Using the ideas proposed by Skilling (2001a), a summary of the causes, transmission mechanisms and effects of New Zealand's economic geography is given in Table 7.1. The claims made in Table 7.1 give rise to a plethora of hypotheses, most of which cannot be tested with the data currently available. This chapter does not aim to establish causality, but will instead check for consistencies or inconsistencies with some of the hypotheses.

The data used in this chapter come from three main sources, which are set out and described below:

• AES data from Statistics New Zealand for the period 1994–1999. The AES is an annual survey of most industries in the New Zealand economy. The 1998 sample covered 250,000 businesses. The survey covers employment, wages, revenue, assets and profit of firms. The coverage of firms has increased over time. Being a sample survey, the results are subject to sampling errors. These can particularly affect the data on smaller firms where the sampling rate is lower. Some industrial activities are entirely excluded and others are under-represented with regard to smaller business units, particularly those that fall below the threshold for compulsory goods and services tax (GST) registration.
• Business demographics data from Statistics New Zealand. The data coverage has changed over time. From 1987 until 1993 the data are based on GST Compulsory Survey Coverage and from 1994 until 2000 on 1994 Economically Significant Enterprises Survey Coverage (which excludes all of the A01 Agriculture ANZSIC Code). The data cover employment and the number of firms for all New Zealand businesses that meet the above criteria.
• Customs data from Tradenz and Statistics New Zealand. These data trace the export values and the number of firms involved in exporting by the value of their exports from 1994 onwards. They also provide a limited breakdown of the composition of exports and some dynamics in terms of firm movement between export revenue categories.

7.2 DOES NEW ZEALAND HAVE A COMPARATIVE ABUNDANCE OF SMALL FIRMS?

Skilling (2001b) demonstrated that New Zealand has a firm distribution heavily skewed towards small firms. This section analyses recent data on New Zealand firm sizes and then compares the results with the available OECD data.

Table 7.2 shows data on the distribution of firm sizes from the Statistics New Zealand section on business demographics, and allows us to track changes in total firm numbers through time.

Table 7.2 Change in the size distribution of New Zealand firms, 1987–2001

Number of employees	0–5	6–9	10–49	50–99	100+	Total
Average annual growth in number of firms 1987–2001 (%)	4	3	3	1	0	4
Average annual growth in number of firms 1987–1992 (%)	5	0	1	–1	–2	4
Average annual growth in number of firms 1993–2001 (%)	4	4	4	2	2	4
Number of firms 1987	111,000	12,000	11,000	1,279	1,210	137,000
1987 firm distribution (%)	81.02	8.76	8.03	0.93	0.88	100.00
Number of firms 2001	197,000	17,000	17,000	1,404	1,282	234,000
2001 firm distribution (%)	84.19	7.26	7.26	0.60	0.55	100.00
1987–2001 growth (%)	77	42	50	10	6	71

Source: Statistics New Zealand, Business Demographics Data, Enterprise Level

The majority of New Zealand firms (84.19 percent) had 5 or fewer employees in 2001 and almost all (98.71 percent) had fewer than 50 employees. The number of small businesses increased over the 1987 to 2001 period, while the absolute number of large firms initially fell and then recovered over the same period. Overall, this has led to proportionally fewer large firms and the distribution of New Zealand firms is increasingly skewed towards small firms. AES data provide a more detailed distribution of firm sizes, as measured by Full Time Equivalent employees (FTEs). This shows that only 0.08 percent of New Zealand firms have more than 500 employees.

Internationally, manufacturing firms tend to be larger, and Table 7.3 shows that this is also the case in New Zealand. However, manufacturing is one sector in New Zealand where a trend of falling average firm size is particularly noticeable and has been evident since 1978. Carlsson (1996) used the Census of Manufactures to show that the average establishment size in manufacturing fell from 30.9 employees in 1978 to 21.1 in 1983 and 14.2 in 1988. This trend has continued, as is evident in Table 7.3. The changes in this sector have been absolute as well as relative: by 1999 there were fewer large and medium–sized manufacturing firms and more small manufacturing firms.

Consistent with other countries, the proportion of small firms is even higher in the services sector. In 1999 97.5 percent of firms in the service sector had less than 20 employees.

Table 7.3 Average number of employees per firm, New Zealand, 1994–2001

Average number of employees per firm	Primary	Manufacturing	Services	Total
1994	4.31	12.83	6.33	6.68
1995	3.89	14.04	5.92	7.36
1996	3.92	13.23	5.87	6.74
1997	3.23	12.91	5.79	6.66
1998	2.99	12.63	5.53	6.40
1999	3.00	11.63	5.59	5.99
2000	2.91	12.01	5.28	6.22
2001	3.02	11.29	5.49	5.69

Source: Statistics New Zealand Business Demographics Data

Average firm size appears to have been falling also across all firm size groups. The biggest falls have occurred among the largest businesses (with more than 100 employees), where the average size of businesses has fallen by over 20 percent since 1987.

Consistent with the AES data, Business Demographics statistics show that almost 55 percent of employees are employed in businesses with less than 50 employees. These data also show that the share of employment in large businesses has fallen dramatically over the past 14 years, whereas the growth in employment has largely come from businesses employing less than 50 people.

The variation across industries in the distribution of employment across firm size groups is also interesting. Services and agriculture have in general larger concentrations of employment at small firm sizes, while manufacturing employment is more evenly spread. Only a few industries stand out in terms of large concentrations of employment in large companies. They are: Food, Beverage and Tobacco Manufacturing, Electricity, Gas and Water Supply, Communication Services, and Finance and Insurance.

Comparisons with some OECD countries are possible, using data from OECD (2001). For example, New Zealand has a larger proportion of manufacturing firms with less than 20 employees than most other OECD countries. The New Zealand percentage was 90.6 percent in 1994 and increased to 91.7 percent in 2001. The differences with other countries are quite marked, with only Italy (89.7 percent in 1992), Iceland (90.8 percent in 1992) and the Czech Republic (94.9 percent in 1995) displaying similar concentrations of firms employing less than 20 people.

The data can also be split into manufacturing and services. The New Zealand data are more recent, but show relatively high proportions of firms with less than 20 employees in all sectors of the economy (97.5 percent in services and 91.7 percent in manufacturing in 1999).

Table 7.4 permits similar comparisons based on average firm size. New Zealand has the smallest average firm size and average manufacturing firm size in the table. The data show that the average number of employees per firm is larger in manufacturing across all countries. Only Italy (14.4 employees per firm in manufacturing and 8.1 employees per firm in services) and The Netherlands (18.0 employees per firm in manufacturing and 5.3 employees per firm in services) have comparable firm sizes to New Zealand in terms of employees per firm.

In conclusion, New Zealand certainly has one of the largest proportions of small firms across the board, in both manufacturing and services. However, New Zealand is not alone in its skew towards small firms. Italy, Iceland and the Czech Republic also share similar distributions. While New Zealand is certainly not an outlier in terms of having a preponderance of small firms, it is certainly different from the norm and is also different from typical comparator countries.

Table 7.4 Average number of employees per firm in selected countries

Country	Total	Non-agricultural business sector	Manufacturing	Services
United States[a]	24.0	23.5	75.0	22.2
West Germany[a]	17.2	17.9	45.0	13.1
France[a]	23.8	23.6	24.0	25.3
Italy[a]	9.7	9.2	14.4	8.1
UK[a]	n.a.	n.a.	53.0	n.a.
Canada[a]	12.7	15.2	40.5	12.0
Denmark[a]	13.2	15.2	30.0	12.8
Finland[a]	14.3	14.3	28.7	10.3
Netherlands[a]	6.2	5.8	18.0	5.3
Portugal[a]	18.4	18.8	33.1	12.5
New Zealand[b]	6.7	7.1	12.8	6.3
New Zealand[c]	5.7	6.1	11.3	5.5

[a] Average 1989–1994
[b] 1994
[c] 2001

Source: OECD (2001), Table 5; Statistics New Zealand

7.3 SMALL FIRM PREVALENCE, MARKET SIZE AND REMOTENESS

The only way to explore the possible correlation between small firm prevalence with market size and relative remoteness is by means of international comparison. There are very few countries, with similar sized domestic markets and geographic peripherality, for which data on the size distribution of firms are available. Ideally the effects of distance and size should be considered separately, as well as combined. However, this is difficult to do. There are only a few OECD countries with populations similar to that of New Zealand for which we have firm size data. Atlantic Canada (an area of Canada including the provinces of New Brunswick, Nova Scotia, Newfoundland and Prince Edward Island) may be a possible comparator. Atlantic Canada is of a similar size and is somewhat isolated from its main foreign markets, although not to the same degree as New Zealand. Manufacturing firm size data for selected small OECD countries and Atlantic Canada are set out in Table 7.5.

Table 7.5 Manufacturing firm size distributions in New Zealand and similar countries/territories

Country/ Territory	Year	Popn. (000s)	Number of Employees			
			1–19	20–99	100– 499	500+
			Percentages			
New Zealand	**1994**	**3,761**	**90.6**	**7.7**	**1.5**	**0.3**
Denmark	1993	5,284	82.0	14.6	3.1	0.3
Finland	1992	5,140	50.8	36.1	11.6	1.5
Iceland	1992	282	90.8	6.7	2.5	0.0
Luxembourg	1992	424	79.4	15.0	4.7	0.9
Norway	1994	4,393	40.2	47.4	7.5	4.9
Atlantic Canada	1995	2,381	89.5	5.6	2.7	2.2

Source: OECD (1997), New Zealand Annual Enterprise Survey, Atlantic Canada Opportunities Agency (1998)

Table 7.5 shows that Finland and Norway have very low concentrations of small firms, Denmark and Luxembourg are somewhere in the middle, and New Zealand, Iceland and Atlantic Canada are at the top end. Interestingly, New Zealand, Iceland and Atlantic Canada are the relatively more remote territories. Atlantic Canada seems largely similar to New Zealand in firm distribution, especially given that Canada as a whole has a very low proportion of small firms in manufacturing (OECD, 1997). However, Atlantic Canada has a proportion of large firms many times New Zealand's.

The difficulty with this analysis is finding countries of similar size and distance from markets to compare with New Zealand. Size of the domestic market in itself seems to have little relationship with firm distributions. One might think that Iceland's small population of 234,000 might be a cause of its huge proportion of small firms. However, Luxembourg provides an interesting counter–example: it has a population of only 424,000 yet sustains quite a high proportion of large firms.

The combination of small market size and distance from markets, rather than either factor alone, may create a preponderance of small firms. The hypothesis seems to fit at least the cases of Iceland, New Zealand and Atlantic Canada. If data could be obtained, it might be useful to formulate a 'reduced form' model of the distribution of firm sizes in terms of population and distance from markets.

However, a great difficulty with these comparisons is isolating cultural and institutional aspects, which may have a large impact on firm sizes across the world. For instance, the Nordic countries seem to have above average proportions of large firms despite their small domestic populations. Frame (2000) notes the marked difference between New Zealand and Finnish industrial structure, and attributes this to large government involvement in the Finnish economy that has created (through public ownership) or favoured (through institutions) large firms. Such institutional and cultural differences make cross–country comparisons notoriously difficult.

The Italian firm structure is puzzling. While New Zealand and Italy have several similarities in the distribution of firm sizes, Italy is a country of 60 million people that is part of the core of the European economy. How does this reconcile with the size and distance hypothesis?

However, the Italian experience is unique in ways that may make it difficult to compare with New Zealand. There are strong regulatory and tax incentives for small businesses that may encourage fragmentation of larger Italian business units into smaller units with superficial administrative walls between them. North Italian firms are also noted for their considerable use of clustering and alliances to leverage external scale economies while still allowing small firm sizes. One classic example is the large clothing company Benetton that contracts manufacturing to a plethora of small firms.

The message from this is that firm size is not the perfect measure of industrial structure. New Zealand has its own example of this: many small farmers obtain scale through cooperative structures. Therefore, while domestic market size and isolation of a nation could well have some impact on industrial structure, firm alliances and cooperative arrangements, policy distortions and culture also have potent effects on firm sizes. This makes comparisons or judgements difficult.

7.4 DOMESTIC MARKET SIZE, INTERNATIONAL REMOTENESS AND FIRM GROWTH

Do a small domestic market and distance from other markets inhibit firm growth? Ideally this question ought to be embedded in a complete analysis of the dynamics of firm growth and decline. At present longitudinal analysis of firm growth in New Zealand is limited, although more is planned.

To date, Johnson (1999) and Carroll et al. (2002) have produced papers on firm dynamics in the New Zealand economy. Both of these studies have focused on firm and employment creation and destruction. Detailed analysis of firm growth is yet to be done. Johnson showed that New Zealand had increasing firm turnover over the period 1987–1999. This was due to an increasing number of small firms (which have higher entry and exit rates on average) and also due to an increasing rate of firm births and deaths among New Zealand's small firms. Johnson found that, over the 1996–1999 period, large firms had on average a greater chance of increasing their size.

Carroll et al. (2002) showed that New Zealand had higher rates of turnover of both firms and employment than many other OECD countries. Comparisons with the UK and USA are made in Table 7.6. Carroll et al. note that the high degree of turnover in New Zealand can largely be attributed to the high population of very small firms, which naturally have higher failure rates. The turnover of firms in New Zealand also appears to be increasing over time.

Table 7.6 Comparisons of job turnover studies

	Job creation rate	Fraction due to firm entry (%)	Job destruction rate	Fraction due to firm exit (%)
1. NZ – 1995–2001	17.5	39.8	15.3	40.4
2. NZ – 1989	14.1	52.2	16.0	48.4
3. NZ – 1987–1992	15.7	47.1	19.8	42.9
4. US – 1984–1991	13.0	65.0	10.4	70.0
5. UK – 1985–1991	8.7	31.0	6.6	59.0

Source: Carroll et al. (2002)

The research by Johnson (1999) suggests that it is more difficult for a small firm to grow in New Zealand than for a large firm. However, Johnson could not calculate the growth of firms that do survive from the data available at the time. It is therefore impossible to state if the firms that do grow expand very rapidly, although research is taking place on this question.

Clearly, New Zealand has by international standards high rates of creation and destruction, both in terms of firms and jobs. While New Zealand seems to have little difficulty in creating new firms, the high rate of firm exits suggests that New Zealand firms also find it difficult to survive and grow. There appears to be no lack of raw entrepreneurial talent, but it seems difficult to grow businesses to a size at which they can begin to benefit from economies of scale.

Economic theory suggests that this sort of turnover in firms and jobs is a natural part of market adjustments and should be viewed as positive (Foster et al., 1998). The concept of creative destruction is central to the idea of innovation and improving productivity. As poorly performing firms exit, capital is reallocated more efficiently elsewhere. However, too much creative destruction could also have a negative effect (Caves, 1998). Perhaps too much upheaval leads to the benefits of resource reallocation being outweighed by lower productivity resulting from excessive change. This productivity loss may come from uncertainty that demoralises workers (or entrepreneurs) or from longer spells of unemployment while searching for new employment.

In conclusion, New Zealand has experienced a period of upheaval, followed by a rapid increase in firm numbers. There seem to be two ways to interpret the data on turnover. From a positive perspective, it could be argued that small firms are more dynamic, so that we would expect to see higher rates of turnover for some time. Gradually, however, a growing proportion of these new firms would expand, and rates of turnover would fall. The alternative, negative, perspective is that barriers to firm growth will lock New Zealand into a cycle of high firm turnover and low growth. If this excessive churn continues without the growth of some firms, it is possible that the effects of a small domestic market and a large distance from overseas markets are restricting the growth of New Zealand firms.

Clearly, further work on firm dynamics is warranted to determine whether New Zealand has unusual barriers to firm growth.

7.5 ARE THERE BARRIERS TO EXPORTING?

The propensity to export appears to be closely linked to firm size (Skilling, 2001a). The bulk of New Zealand exporting is conducted by a handful of firms. In 2001 9,306 firms exported, out of a total of 234,000 economically significant enterprises, where significant is defined as an annual turnover of

30,000 New Zealand dollars or more. Thus, only about 4 percent of New Zealand firms are exporters. Of those exporting firms, 921 firms (9.9 percent) export over 95 percent of the value of exports, and 151 firms (1.6 percent) export over 78 percent of the total.[2] This means that 0.06 percent of New Zealand firms generated 78 percent of export earnings.

Many of the firms that export do so on a small scale and fleetingly. Just under 64 percent of exporting firms exported less than $100,000 worth of goods in 2001. The majority of these firms (around 85 percent) were either not exporting the previous year or would not be exporting the following year.

Since 1994, the absolute number of exporters exporting less than $100,000 has decreased, while the number of exporters exporting more than this has risen. Overall, however, the number of exporters has been without trend since 1994. Contrast this with a rapid increase in firms over the same period and it is clear that the proportion of firms exporting has fallen since 1994. Even when controlling for the growth in numbers of very small businesses (fewer than 10 employees), the proportion of exporters has fallen over the entire period 1994–2001. This suggests that the new crop of New Zealand firms – even those of moderate size – may be slow to move into exporting.

However, there are a growing number of exporters who export in relatively large volumes. As a result of this, New Zealand's reliance on a few companies for the bulk of exports may be slowly starting to reduce.

Figure 7.1 displays the composition of New Zealand's total merchandise exports in 2001. Figure 7.2 depicts the average value of exports per exporting firm in that industry. Together, these figures suggest that New Zealand's biggest export industries also exhibit the largest scale in terms of exports per firm (with the exception of Forestry). Consistent with the analysis of firm performance below, these large-scale exporting firms can be found in the Food Manufacturing industries.

Contrast this experience with that of Australia.[3] Australia has a similar number of exporting firms (4 percent) but the input into exporting is more evenly spread. Some 3.9 percent of exporting firms export 76 percent of Australia's exports, while 1.6 percent of New Zealand exporters export a similar proportion of New Zealand's exports. Interestingly, the Australian data suggest that the growth in Australian exports has come from firms with less than 20 employees, while exports of the very large companies have fallen.

In terms of the number of firms exporting, New Zealand's exporting base appears to be narrow, especially compared with Australia's. Most of New Zealand's export sales are made by a very small proportion of its firms. Most of the recent growth in New Zealand's exports has come from large exporters. Looking at the static data it seems that New Zealand's small firms struggle to engage in exporting on a continual basis, something that small Australian firms seem to find somewhat easier (given the growth of small–scale exporters).

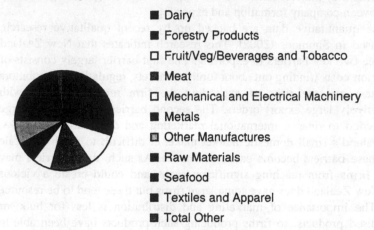

- ■ Dairy
- ■ Forestry Products
- □ Fruit/Veg/Beverages and Tobacco
- ▨ Meat
- □ Mechanical and Electrical Machinery
- ■ Metals
- ▨ Other Manufactures
- ■ Raw Materials
- ■ Seafood
- ■ Textiles and Apparel
- ■ Total Other

Figure 7.1 The composition of New Zealand merchandise exports, 2001

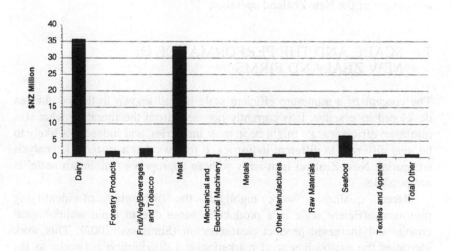

Figure 7.2 Average value of exports per firm by industry, New Zealand, 2001

As noted earlier, the proportion of New Zealand firms exporting has also fallen over the last few years. This indicates that, despite a large increase in firm numbers, this has not translated into a greater number of exporting firms. This may indicate barriers to moving into exporting or a lag that may exist between company formation and exporting.

These quantitative data are backed up by recent qualitative research, summarised in Simmons (2002). This research indicates that New Zealand firms face two key barriers to exporting. The first barrier largely consists of information costs (finding out about foreign markets, regulations, distributors and tastes) and the risks of expanding the firm rapidly to cope with comparatively large export orders. The second barrier relates to the large scale needed to finance international marketing and distribution networks. New Zealand's small domestic market makes it difficult to reach the scale where these barriers become easier to finance. As such, these barriers may prevent firms from reaching significant scale, and could create a vicious circle. New Zealand does have some large firms but these tend to be resource based. The importance of marketing and distribution is less for bulk, or standardised products, so firms producing such products have been able to by–pass the second barrier. This second barrier could also explain the high rate of foreign ownership among emerging New Zealand firms; the parent company has the scale in marketing and distribution to fully exploit the advantages of the New Zealand operation.

7.6 SCALE AND THE PERFORMANCE OF NEW ZEALAND FIRMS

The concept of a minimum efficient scale is well known in theory but less developed in practice. It is currently not clear from the literature what size minimum efficient scale might be in most industries, and indeed it is likely to be very different in different industries. It follows that a systematic analysis comparing New Zealand firm sizes with an appropriate 'minimum scale' is not possible.

Recent qualitative work highlights the difficulties of identifying minimum efficient scale in a production sense due to rapid technological change and increased product customisation (Simmons, 2002). This work identified the establishment of marketing and distribution networks as the key area where scale is important for New Zealand exporting firms. Scale enables firms to finance the large set–up costs of entering new markets, then marketing and distributing their products directly to customers, thereby capturing all of the margin. Smaller companies instead must rely on distributors – the extra costs this poses force these firms into niche industries.

Clearly, a production–focused term such as 'minimum efficient scale' may be of limited usefulness. Instead, the concept of exploiting economies of scale is probably more useful.

One way to consider the possible importance of scale is to look at those sectors in New Zealand that seem to possess it. There are two industries that stand out in New Zealand in terms of a scale comparable with that of those industries in other countries. These industries are Food, Beverage and Tobacco Manufacturing (48.8 FTEs per firm in 1999) and Electricity, Gas and Water Supply Services (35.8 FTEs per firm in 1999).

Without food manufacturing, average employment in manufacturing would be only 9.6 FTEs. This is far below average manufacturing firm size overseas, which may help explain the poor performance of the rest of the manufacturing sector. The Food Manufacturing sector produces almost 50 percent of New Zealand goods exports, suggesting that the country is competitive on the world stage in this sector. It is likely that a good deal of the production scale in food manufacturing is achieved in the dairy and meat processing industries.

Another way to approach scale is by looking at those sectors with significant concentrations of employment in large businesses. These sectors have been defined here as having greater than 60 percent of employment in enterprises with one hundred or more employees. Table 7.7 lists these sectors and reports their average annual productivity growth. This table shows that total factor productivity growth varies widely across industries with employment concentrated in large firms.

New Zealand firms are clearly smaller than their international counterparts in manufacturing. This lack of scale is a candidate for explaining the sector's poor performance over recent years. In contrast, the competitiveness of the food manufacturing industry may follow from its ability to reach sufficient scale.

However, the total factor productivity statistics do not show better annual total factor productivity growth for industries with employment concentrated in large firms. While the productivity improvements of the utilities sector and communication services are impressive, this could have resulted from the removal of past inefficiencies by means of deregulation or technological change rather than from benefits of scale. A similar productivity growth is not evident in food manufacturing or in finance. However, productivity data in finance are inherently unreliable and this may explain the poor performance of this sector.[4]

Even if the performance of industries with larger firms was markedly better, would that show that the rest of the economy is operating below efficient scale? Clearly there are causation issues: because of their productivity growth, some companies have been able to achieve a larger scale of production. For firms that have not achieved a large scale it is difficult to tell whether there are barriers to growth or just that there is no market for their product. Without overseas comparisons it is difficult to establish which of these forces is the chief driver behind scale concentration in these industries.

Table 7.7 Productivity growth in sectors where large firms dominate,
New Zealand, 1978–1998

ANZSIC code	Description	% employment in firms with more than 100 employees	% annual total factor productivity growth 1978–1998
C21	Food, Beverage and Tobacco Manufacturing	78.59	0.68
D	Electricity, Gas and Water Supply	81.75	3.50
J	Communication Services	72.98[a]	6.77
K	Finance and Insurance	75.71	−2.11

Note: [a] % employment in firms with more than 200 employees

Source: Statistics New Zealand AES data; Diewert and Lawrence (1999). Note that Diewert and Lawrence strongly caveat the reliability of their sectoral data.

What is interesting to note is that almost all the sectors that appear to have achieved scale have done so through atypical means. Food Manufacturing has arguably achieved scale through the producer board structure. Utilities and Communications (in which New Zealand Telecom is the dominant player) gained their scale through past State monopolies, as well as being network industries with a natural push towards concentration. In addition, many other successful medium–sized exporting companies credit their ability to achieve scale to grants and loans from the Development Finance Corporation (DFC) (Simmons, 2002).[5] Finance and Insurance, on the other hand, is the only sector to achieve agglomeration through a market process – albeit foreign–driven mergers and acquisitions. This observation could be consistent with the existence of barriers to growth in other industries.

Overall, these results are consistent with New Zealand manufacturing firms lacking economies of scale, but the evidence is far from conclusive. Those sectors that have achieved scale do seem to be more internationally competitive, but do not seem to show systematically higher productivity growth statistics. Determining minimum efficient scale for industries is difficult to do, as is showing that New Zealand firms have barriers to achieving scale.

To study the possible relationship between scale and firm performance further, the performance of firms will be measured in what follows by two key variables, namely value added per FTE (split into wages and profit) and return on assets (ROA). Conclusions are drawn by means of AES data for the 1994–1999 period.[6]

Revenue per FTE generally increases with the size of the firm. The only clear exceptions to this are in Utilities and Finance and Insurance, where small businesses seem to have a very high revenue per FTE. All other industries show increasing revenue per FTE or at least constant revenue per FTE.

Profit per employee seems to vary greatly over industries; however, in general it seems to fall with firm size. Again, this is especially true for Utilities and Finance and Insurance, where large profits per employee seem to be concentrated in very small businesses. Profit does seem to be related to scale in some (mostly manufacturing) industries, namely Wood and Paper Product Manufacturing, Printing, Publishing and Recorded Media, Non Metallic Mineral Product Manufacturing and also Communication Services. It is also interesting to note that profit per FTE increases with scale for Food, Beverage and Tobacco Manufacturing but then falls away for very large firms.

Wages appear to have an inverse relationship to profit per FTE. In general, larger firms pay higher wages per FTE. If wage per FTE is interpreted as a proxy for the level of human capital per worker, this suggests that the level of human capital per worker is greater in larger firms.

The results for profit and wages give an interesting picture for value added per FTE. For most industries, the value added per FTE has an inverted U–shaped relationship with firm size. The exact parameters vary by industry, but in general value added is the lowest for both the very small firms and the very large firms in an industry. There are two sets of exceptions to this pattern:

- As would be expected, Utilities and Finance and Insurance have heavy concentrations of value added per FTE in their small businesses, as do Health and Community Services.
- Some industries show largely monotonic increases in value added per FTE with firm size, especially Wood and Paper Product Manufacturing, Construction, Wholesale Trade and Transport and Storage.

The results for ROA are somewhat different from those of value added. The data show a lower concentration of assets in small firms, associated with markedly higher ROAs. Conversely, there are high concentrations of assets in large firms, associated with lower ROAs. In general ROA seems to decrease with firm size, although this result is again not true for some sectors. Food Manufacturing, Printing, Publishing and Recorded Media, Accommodation and Restaurants, Property and Business Services and Cultural and Recreational Services all have a relatively constant ROA in relation to size, while in Utilities ROA increases with size.

The clearest signs of the importance of scale are in the value added per FTE figures. In most industries there are, up to a point, increases in value added with firm size. The most obvious explanation for this effect in economic theory is that the larger firms are exploiting economies of scale. Assuming that New Zealand firms were constrained in their growth due to the small size of the domestic market and distance, this analysis suggests that many New Zealand firms could be missing out on scale economies.

These value–added results can probably be explained in part by higher levels of physical and human capital per employee. However, this in turn raises the question of why larger firms can attract these higher–skilled individuals and higher levels of investment.

The data do seem to show that ROA decreases with firm size for the majority of sectors. While there are exceptions to this, only the Utilities sector has an increasing ROA with firm size. These results are contrary to the claim of the importance of scale for firm performance. This raises an alternative possibility that firms may not be expanding in New Zealand because it is not profitable to do so.

The one consistent factor arising from the value added and ROA figures is the poor performance of the larger businesses. This is consistent with Healy (2000), who showed that New Zealand's large firms have consistently destroyed shareholder value over time. These results suggest that any economies of scale may fall away and possibly become diseconomies of scale when firms become large. There are many possible explanations for this phenomenon, but the poor performance of large New Zealand business is a mystery that cannot be fully untangled here. This area deserves further analysis, especially to see if there are common elements causing the poor performance of large firms.

Overall, this section is inconclusive on the role of scale in firm performance. Firms may not expand in New Zealand because there are barriers to them doing so, or quite possibly because there is no market for expansion.

7.7 CONCLUSION

New Zealand has a high proportion of small firms that is relatively unusual in the OECD. However, other countries and territories that have a similar size distribution of firms, such as Iceland and Atlantic Canada, are similar to New Zealand in that they have a small domestic market and are distant from other markets. While comparing firm sizes across countries is made problematic by the influence of strong cultural elements, New Zealand's differences with usual comparator countries such as the UK and Australia indicate that there is more to New Zealand's firm distribution than culture. It is possible that the dual forces of a small domestic market size and a large distance from markets are at work in fashioning New Zealand's unusual firm distribution.

Longitudinal business dynamics data show that New Zealand has internationally high rates of firm creation and destruction. However, there are gaps in the analysis on firm growth patterns. The data on firm growth seem to be supportive of two possible hypotheses: either barriers exist or things are (slowly) coming right. Qualitative analysis seems to support the barrier hypothesis.

The concept of a minimum efficient scale, with its production focus, seems increasingly impractical in today's economy. However, research suggests that scale is still important, especially in establishing marketing and distribution channels. The data show that New Zealand has distinctly smaller firms across the board, which may indicate that New Zealand firms cannot benefit from economies of scale in most industries. However, New Zealand seems to have isolated pockets of scale, notably in Food Manufacturing. New Zealand's international competitiveness in Food Manufacturing may be a signal of the importance of scale. Similarly, the fact that industries of comparatively large scale did not arise naturally may be symptomatic of barriers to growth in other industries.

The performance data show some signs of economies of scale; large companies are more effective at adding value up to a point. However, the arguably most important indicator variable – return on assets – showed a negative relationship with scale. Value added also seems to fall away for many very large businesses. Further work is required to unpick the mysteries of large business performance in New Zealand.

In short, the New Zealand economy is unusual in its prevalence of small businesses, and it is plausible that this is related to New Zealand's domestic market size and its distance from foreign markets. It is similarly plausible, however, that the recent growth in small firms will in due course lead to increases in larger firms and exporters. The key question here relates to the existence of barriers to firm growth and the time it would take for firm growth to take off. The poor performance of large New Zealand firms and the apparent inverse relationship between size and return on assets remain also of interest.

NOTES

1. I would like to acknowledge Geoff Lewis and David Skilling, both of the New Zealand Treasury Economic Transformation Team, for their assistance and guidance in developing this chapter.
2. This information was provided by Tradenz, using Statistics New Zealand data.
3. All Australian data were obtained from the Australian Bureau of Statistics 2000 publication *A Portrait of Australian Exporters*.
4. Finance and Insurance productivity data cannot effectively account for the rapid change in the nature and variety of products in this sector. For details, see Diewert and Lawrence (1999).
5. DFC was a government body. One of its roles was to administer grants and low interest rate loans to exporters to encourage firms to move into exporting.
6. The data are too complicated to be included in this chapter but can be obtained upon request from the author.

REFERENCES

Atlantic Canada Opportunities Agency (1998), 'The state of small business and entrepreneurship', http://www.acoa.ca/e/business/entrepreneurship/state_business /index.shtml.
Buckle, R., Haugh, D. and P. Thomson (2001), 'Calm after the storm? Supply–side contributions to New Zealand's GDP volatility decline', Working Paper 01/33, Wellington: New Zealand Treasury.
Carlsson, B. (1996), 'Differing patterns of industrial dynamics: New Zealand, Ohio and Sweden, 1978–1994', *Small Business Economics*, 8, 219–234.
Carroll, N., Hyslop, D., Mare, D., Timmins, J. and J. Wood (2002), 'The turbulent labour market', Paper presented at the New Zealand Association of Economists' Conference in Wellington, 25–27 June.
Caves, R. (1998), 'Industrial organisation and new findings on the turnover and mobility of firms', *Journal of Economic Literature*, 36, 1947–1982.

Diewert, E. and D. Lawrence (1999), Measuring New Zealand's productivity, Working Paper 1999/5, Wellington: New Zealand Treasury.

Foster, L., Haltiwanger, J. and C. Krizan (1998), 'Aggregate productivity growth: lessons from microeconomic evidence', National Bureau of Economic Research, Working Paper W6803.

Frame, D. (2000), 'Finland and New Zealand: a cross-country comparison of economic performance', NZ Treasury Working Paper 00/1.

Grey, A. (1995), 'Job gains and job losses: recent literature and trends', report OCDE/GD(95)23, Paris: OECD.

Haugh, D. (2001), 'Business activity statistics, 1987–2001', mimeo, Wellington: New Zealand Treasury.

Healy, J. (2000), 'Corporate governance and shareholder value', ANZ presentation to the New Zealand Treasury, 24 March.

James, C. (2001), 'Hard choices – Colin James' summing up at the knowledge wave conference', http://www.synapsis.co.nz/speeches_briefings/Knowledge_Wave_speech_3_Aug.htm.

Johnson, B. (1999), 'Business dynamics 1987–1999', mimeo, Wellington: New Zealand Treasury.

OECD (1997), *Small Businesses, Job Creation and Growth: Facts, Obstacles and Best Practices*, Paris: OECD

OECD (2001), 'Productivity and firm dynamics: evidence from microdata', report ECO/CPE/WP1(2001)8, Paris: OECD.

Pink, B. and C. Jamieson (2000), *A Portrait of Australian Exporters*, Canberra: Australian Bureau of Statistics and Australian Trade Commission.

Simmons, G. (2002), 'Growing pains: New Zealand qualitative evidence on hurdles to exporting growth', Working Paper 02/10, Wellington: New Zealand Treasury.

Skilling, D. (2001a), 'The importance of being enormous: towards an understanding of the New Zealand economy', Treasury discussion paper, Wellington: New Zealand Treasury, http://www.treasury.govt.nz/et/.

Skilling, D. (2001b), 'The behaviour and performance of New Zealand firms: some preliminary findings', Treasury discussion paper, Wellington: New Zealand Treasury http://www.treasury.govt.nz/et/.

8. Currency Unions and Gravity Models Revisited

Christie Smith

8.1 INTRODUCTION

Newton's theory of gravity asserts that the force exerted by two objects is a function of their respective masses and the square of the distance between them. Analogues of this theory have been applied in a number of different contexts, primarily to explain economic interactions with spatial dimensions, such as trade or migration. Gravity models represent trade between two economies as a function of their respective economic masses, the distance between the two economies and a variety of other factors. Gravity models of bilateral trade were originally developed by Pöyhönen (1963) and Tinbergen (1962) but with little in the way of theoretical justification.[1]

Gravity models have been used to investigate a number of empirical regularities. One avenue of this empirical research has been to investigate whether borders inhibit trade. For example, Helliwell (1996, 1998) finds that trade between Canadian provinces far outweighs trade between the provinces and US states, taking into account distance and economic mass. McCallum's (1995) initial investigation suggested that intra-Canada trade was approximately 22 times larger than trade between Canadian provinces and US states; Helliwell's (1998) estimate was similar in magnitude.[2]

Fitzsimons et al. (1999) use a gravity model to investigate the border effect between Ulster and the Republic of Ireland. They find that Ulster and the Republic trade together more than would be predicted by their gravity model, taking into account the Republic and Ulster's common language and common land border. This is an interesting result, given that Ulster and the Republic use different currencies (though up until March 1979 they were exchanged costlessly at par).[3]

Following on from the border-effects literature, Andrew Rose and a number of co-authors in, for example, Rose (2000), Frankel and Rose (2002), Rose and van Wincoop (2001), and Glick and Rose (2002) have attempted to show the impact that currency arrangements have on bilateral trade. To be more specific, Rose and his co-authors conclude that two countries sharing the same currency trade roughly three times as much as they would if they used different currencies. In order to capture the partial impact of currency arrangements, Rose (2000) also takes into account structural and institutional features – common language, common colonial history, the presence of trade agreements, and so on – that might also be correlated with a 'common currency' dummy variable. The impact of currency union is also found to be distinct from that of currency volatility.

The above claims about the benefits of currency union are fairly sanguine. If these claims are correct, currency union could offset some of the negative consequences of peripherality. According to Aghion and Howitt (1998), the benefits of trade liberalisation for growth are theoretically ambiguous. However, Aghion and Howitt go on to conclude that the *empirical* literature broadly suggests that openness is growth promoting. If this empirical conclusion is correct, and if Rose and his co-authors are correct about currency union, then currency union is a policy variable that may be used to offset peripherality.

The main goal of this chapter is to examine some of the claims that are made with respect to currency union by elaborating on the numerous robustness checks undertaken by Rose (2000). It is desirable to use the original data that underpinned the earlier results: contrary results based upon the same data are more compelling than contrary results from an entirely different data set (unless of course the alternative data set is of demonstrably superior quality). Andrew Rose has accumulated a large panel data set on bilateral trade flows, and has made these data available on the Internet.[4] This chapter uses the data from Rose and van Wincoop (2001), a closely related variant of the data used by Rose (2000).

The empirical literature also provides information about the impact that other variables have on trade. Geographical variables, both human and physical, do influence trade outcomes. Rose, however, does not pay much attention to the 'control variables' that enter his currency union regressions. For him such variables simply yield nuisance parameters that must be accounted for to obtain appropriate estimates of the currency union effect. And yet human geography and history – colonial relationships, languages and so forth – have effects that are potentially as important as currency union. Understanding such effects is important since trade contributes to economic development. However, although the 'extra' geographical variables included in Rose's (2000) analysis are statistically significant, they make a fairly marginal contribution to explaining variation in trade, unlike the income and distance variables.

Distance and income are the most important explanatory variables. If the coefficients for these two variables are not estimated correctly, there must be considerable doubt over the coefficient estimates obtained for any of the other explanatory variables. The empirical analysis of this chapter raises such doubt in two ways: first, by suggesting that some of the regressors may be endogenous and, second, by looking for spatial variation in the parameter estimates.

In the Rose and van Wincoop data there are two main geographical areas that have currency unions – the Caribbean and West Africa – with a number of other currency union observations scattered around the rest of the world. Rather curiously, the currency union countries seem to be less affected by distance than the average country in the data set. Taking this effect into account by interacting the currency union dummy with the distance variable, the impact of the currency union dummy is reversed.

This does not necessarily indicate that currency union is materially related to distance. Rather, the general implication is that there is important heterogeneity in the data that may not be captured in the regressions usually run to detect the effect of currency unions. The heterogeneity is likely to relate, at least in part, to the spatial characteristics of the global economy.

Rose and his co-authors have tried very hard to resolve the econometric issues with respect to currency union. However, since the coefficient estimates for income and distance do not appear to be stable for different regions, it is not clear that the coefficient estimates for the other variables – including the currency union dummy – are reliably estimated. Still, some of the empirical results presented in this chapter are also not above econometric reproach. Consequently, the reader may wish to draw his or her own conclusion from the available evidence. The rest of this chapter discusses these issues in greater depth.

8.2 ANALYTICAL FRAMEWORK

The basic gravity equation for trade analysed in this chapter is:

$$trade_{ijt} = A_t \, . d_{ij}^{\beta_1} \left(y_{it} \, . y_{jt} \right)^{\beta_2} \qquad (8.1)$$

In equation (8.1) trade is the sum of exports and imports between countries i and j. Trade at time t is a function of the distance between the two countries, d_{ij},[5] and the product of the incomes of countries i and j (y_{it} and y_{jt} respectively). At various times below, this log of the product of GDPs will be referred to as the 'GDP', 'income' or 'output' regressor. A_t is a proportionality factor that can be a function of many variables. β_1 and β_2 are coefficients; β_1 is assumed to be negative and β_2 is assumed to be positive.[6] This functional form is fairly ubiquitous as an analytical starting point; Deardorff (1998) refers to this function as the 'basic' gravity equation.

It is generally more convenient to deal with this equation in logs,[7]

$$\ln(trade_{ijt}) = \ln A_t + \beta_1 \ln(d_{ij}) + \beta_2 \ln\left(y_{it} \cdot y_{jt}\right) \tag{8.2}$$

Replacing A_t by a multiplicative function of additional variables that are included in the specification to investigate issues such as currency union, and allowing for a disturbance term, yields

$$\ln(trade_{ijt}) = \beta_0 + \beta_1 \ln(d_{ij}) + \beta_2 \ln(y_{it} \cdot y_{jt}) + \beta_3' X_{ijt} + u_{ijt} \tag{8.3}$$

In this equation X_{ijt} is a column vector of the additional variables (all vectors are column vectors unless otherwise specified); β_3 represents a vector of coefficients; and u_{ijt} is a stochastic error term. The parameters for the log variables above can be interpreted as elasticities.

The 'additional variables' that have been considered include: time dummies to account for possible institutional changes that may have affected trade (time dummies can also be interpreted as a time trend), common currency dummies and regional trade agreements. Various physical geographical characteristics have also been accounted for: trading partners with contiguous borders, that are island nations, or that are landlocked. A number of variables describing human geographical characteristics have also been included; for example, common colonisers, common language, common countries and the like.

The same basic elements (income and distance) are expected to apply equally to exports and imports, and hence also to their sum (bilateral trade). Among the regressors, incomes enter as a product, so that they are restricted to having a common elasticity.[8] It is not easy to test this empirical restriction with the available data, as it involves some rather tedious data manipulation, since the product of incomes is the variable recorded in the data set.[9]

8.3 VISUALISING THE DATA

Before considering the econometric issues, it is helpful to visualise the data in several different ways. Using the Loess algorithm, for example, one can plot log trade against log income and distance non-parametrically (e.g., Cleveland, 1993). As can be seen in Figure 8.1, trade is increasing in income and decreasing in distance, as expected. There is some non-linearity evident in Figure 8.1.

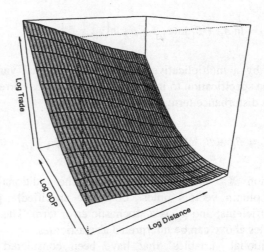

Figure 8.1 Non-parametric log trade surface

Another way to visualise the data is to use a 'co-plot' of trade against a currency union dummy conditioning on the two most important regressors (distance and income). Currency union is a dummy variable and only assumes two values, zero and one. In Figure 8.2, the ranges of log income and log distance have been broken up into six distinct subsets (indicated above and to the right of the main graph), and then a scatterplot is performed for log trade against the currency union dummy variable in each of these subsets. This figure indicates that the currency union observations are heavily represented in the low-distance/low-income group of countries. One also gets a sense of the variation in trade values for the trade outcomes associated with currency union and non-currency union countries. However, this co-plot does not take into account the other geographical conditioning variables.

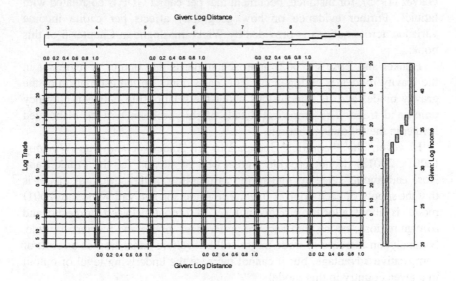

Figure 8.2 Co-plot of trade and currency union

8.4 ECONOMETRIC ISSUES

8.4.1 The Endogeneity of Income

Frankel and Rose (2002) are not simply trying to establish that currency unions improve trade. Rather, their research agenda is to establish that currency unions would be a welfare-improving monetary framework – see also Rose and van Wincoop (2001). The line of argument is approximately that currency unions increase trade, and trade increases output, and thus welfare.

This line of reasoning highlights that the income regressor in equation (8.3) is endogenous. In assessing trade's impact on output, Frankel and Rose (2002) use the exogenous regressors of the gravity model to form a predicted trade variable, which is then used as an instrument for a regression where the dependent variable is income. In essence, the income regressor has shifted across to the left-hand side of the equation, and an instrumented version of trade has shifted to the right-hand side. Frankel and Rose (2002) interpret this exercise as suggesting that trade does facilitate growth. In contrast,

Rodrik suggests that the causality might not necessarily be so straightforward – geography might affect both trade and output simultaneously.[10] Theil and Galvez (1995), for instance, document that per capita GDP is correlated with latitude. Further evidence on how geography affects per capita income variation across nations is provided by Wickramasinghe in Chapter 5 of this book.

Frankel and Rose's (2002) approach suggests that output, a regressor in the gravity model, is endogenous. This casts doubt on the estimation of the gravity model and its conclusions about the relationship between currency union and trade. The empirical details of this problem will be elaborated further in the following sections.

However, the theoretical foundations of Anderson and van Wincoop (2001a, 2001b) do not provide a great deal of support for the Frankel and Rose endeavour, since an underlying assumption of the structural model is that the supply of each good is fixed. The Anderson and van Wincoop (2001) model is about allocating a given level of output between domestic and foreign regions, taking into account preferences, prices and barriers to trade. Naturally, an increase in trade might still be welfare enhancing as a result of comparative advantage, but it cannot increase the underlying level of output in a given country in this model.

8.4.2 The Endogeneity of Currency Union

The previous section argued that income is an endogenous variable in the gravity models that are used to assess the impact of currency union. This problem may be compounded by the fact that forming a currency union – or staying within a currency union – is also an endogenous choice.[11] Rose and van Wincoop (2001, p.387) argue that:

> Reverse causality also does not explain away the findings [that currency union affects trade]; there is little evidence in the political science literature that countries join currency unions to increase trade, and instrumental variables only increase the impact of currency unions on trade.

To make this endogeneity issue concrete, consider the case of Ecuador. There are certain elementary issues that Ecuador had to address in 2000 when choosing to adopt a foreign currency. Obviously Ecuador was not going to adopt a currency that had an unstable internal value, since it already had its own unstable, high-inflation currency. There are, of course, quite a few currencies that have stable internal values (as opposed to stable external prices/exchange rates, which may be another story). Countries such as

Canada, the United Kingdom, the Eurozone countries, Sweden, Switzerland, New Zealand, Australia and the United States, all have currencies that could have been adopted as Ecuadorian legal tender.

How, then, to discriminate between the currencies of these different countries? Given that the United States is Ecuador's biggest export market, taking 38 percent of Ecuadorian exports in 1997, it is perhaps not particularly surprising that Ecuador decided to US-dollarise, since dollarising would also minimise trade transaction costs with the United States. Europe, by way of comparison, received 19 percent of Ecuador's trade, while 'other' unspecified countries accounted for 28 percent, making other currencies less desirable than the US dollar. The US market is also one of the largest in the world, and the Ecuadorians probably felt confident that there was scope for their trade with the United States to continue to grow. It is hard to believe that Ecuador's decision to US-dollarise did not take trade considerations into account.[12]

Rose (2000) discusses another currency union transition – Ireland's abandonment of the peg against the pound sterling. He argues that reverse causality – trade causing currency union – does not explain Ireland's entrance into the Exchange Rate Mechanism (ERM) in 1979. Indeed, Thom and Walsh (2002) note that political and inflation concerns were the major motivations for the change in the exchange rate regime. Nevertheless, it is worth noting that Ireland's trade with the European mainland had increased substantially during the years prior to joining the ERM. And, at least initially, there was some expectation that the United Kingdom would also enter the ERM (the United Kingdom eventually joined the ERM in 1990).

Thom and Walsh (2002) investigate Irish-Anglo trade in some detail. If currency union is trade enhancing then breaking a currency union should be trade retarding (this is a natural consequence of the linear models used here). In their case study, Thom and Walsh find that Ireland's entry into the ERM did not retard Irish-Anglo trade. They suggest that Rose's (2000) results for Ireland reflect the measurement of Irish trade in US dollars deflated by US price indices.[13]

The Bahamas provide another explicit example where trade patterns have affected the exchange rate regime. Up until 1968 the (Bahamian) Commissioners of Currency acted as a currency board, exchanging local currency for pounds sterling at parity. However, as noted by DaCosta et al. (1999, p.6):

> In light of the shift in the country's trading pattern in favour of the United States, and the increasing reliance of the Bahamian economy on the United States for tourism revenue and investment, in 1967 the government decided to switch the currency peg to the U.S. dollar at the rate of B$1 to US$1.

Similarly, Hargreaves and McDermott (1999) explicitly considered New Zealand's trading pattern and the lack of concentration in New Zealand's trade in their discussion of currency union issues for New Zealand. In other words, notwithstanding the earlier quote from Rose and van Wincoop (2001), trade concentration does appear to influence both the discussion and decision regarding the benefits of currency union (or its cousin, currency-board arrangements).[14] Together, these examples cast some doubt as to whether currency unions can be treated as exogenous to trade.

In a direct parallel, Baier and Bergstrand (2002) suggest that dummy variables used to identify the effects of trade agreements also suffer from endogeneity problems. This casts doubt on yet another parameter used in the standard currency union regressions.

The usual approach to dealing with this simultaneous equations problem is to use instrumental variables (IVs). But it is difficult to find a good instrument for the binary currency union variable. Rose (2000) uses various functions of inflation rates as instruments for the variance of exchange rates, and for the currency union parameter, but of course inflation has quite a different scale from a binary variable. One of the key requirements for an instrument is that it should be correlated with the endogenous regressor. What one finds is that the inflation measures that Rose (2000) uses are poorly correlated with the currency union dummy variable.

Unfortunately, it seems unlikely that a good instrument actually exists for currency union. Thus, the endogeneity problem for currency union may not be solvable.

8.4.3 The Endogeneity of Income Revisited

As noted above, distance and income provide most of the explanatory power in all of the regressions. The various dummy variables and other variables provide little additional explanatory power. If these so-called 'nuisance factors' are uncorrelated with the currency union variable then omitting them from the regression would not bias the estimate of the currency union coefficient. Table 8.1 records the correlations between trade, currency union, distance, GDP and the other regressors. The table makes it fairly clear that the currency union variable is at most moderately correlated with the other regressors.

It is interesting to consider what happens when a stripped-down regression is estimated, with trade as the dependent variable and distance, GDP and the currency union variables as regressors. What one finds using ordinary least squares (see Table 8.2) is that the distance and GDP coefficients are much as expected, and the currency union coefficient is large and positive (much as in the more elaborate regressions).

Table 8.1 Correlations

	Log trade	Currency union	Log distance	Log GDP
Log trade	1	−0.02	−0.19	0.65
Currency union	−0.02	1	−0.21	−0.20
Log distance	−0.19	−0.21	1	0.18
Log GDP	0.65	−0.20	0.18	1
Language	0.01	0.19	−0.22	−0.21
Common border	0.15	0.05	−0.38	0.03
Trade agreement	0.10	0.19	−0.30	−0.11
Common coloniser	−0.15	0.22	−0.15	−0.32
Colony	0.12	0.01	0	0.04
Same country	−0.01	0.27	−0.04	−0.10
Log GDP per capita	0.45	−0.07	0.04	0.36
Landlocked	−0.07	0.00	−0.07	−0.03
Land area	0.24	−0.12	0.16	0.63

Suppose that the currency union variable is treated as exogenous, as in Rose (2000). It is reasonable to assume that the distance variable is also exogenous.[15] However, even in a stripped-down regression this still leaves questions about the income variable – which should not be regarded as exogenous, since trade increases income. What, then, can be used to instrument for income? Rose (2000) provides a suitable instrument: the log product of land areas. The correlation between this variable and income is approximately 0.63. Unfortunately, this variable fails to capture the growth of income over time, which means one abandons the advantages of having a panel data set. However, one can still examine each of the cross-sections to gauge the impact of the currency variable. The regression results obtained from the different cross-sections prove to be fairly similar (see Table 8.5).

Table 8.2 Stripped-down regressions

Year	Parameters					
	1970	1975	1980	1985	1990	All
OLS regressions						
Constant	−10.04	−9.92	−10.67	−10.77	−11.67	−9.91
	(0.60)	(0.54)	(0.46)	(0.47)	(0.47)	(0.23)
Currency	1.63	2.23	1.56	2.34	2.34	1.81
union	(0.43)	(0.40)	(0.28)	(0.29)	(0.28)	(0.14)
Log	−1.17	−1.25	−1.21	−1.22	−1.31	−1.24
distance	(0.04)	(0.04)	(0.03)	(0.03)	(0.03)	(0.02)
Log	0.86	0.87	0.88	0.86	0.91	0.86
GDP	(0.01)	(0.01)	(0.01)	(0.01)	(0.01)	(0.01)
IV regressions						
Constant	1.74	−1.15	−0.37	−1.13	−0.48	−0.65
	(0.84)	(0.72)	(0.66)	(0.63)	(0.68)	(0.31)
Currency	0.51	0.92	−0.09	0.69	0.40	0.38
union	(0.51)	(0.43)	(0.31)	(0.33)	(0.31)	(0.16)
Log	−1.04	−1.11	−1.02	−1.07	−1.16	−1.09
distance	(0.05)	(0.04)	(0.04)	(0.04)	(0.04)	(0.02)
Log	0.48	0.58	0.53	0.55	0.55	0.55
GDP	(0.02)	(0.02)	(0.02)	(0.02)	(0.02)	(0.01)

Notes:
a Standard errors in parentheses
b Variable definitions in note 16
c *AREAPROD* is used as an instrument for GDP in the IV regressions

The impact of using an instrumental variable for income is fairly large. The estimated coefficient for income drops away dramatically, nearly halving in size, to a level closer to that obtained from the Caribbean sub-sample (see Table 8.5). Similarly, the coefficients estimated for the currency union dummy variable also drop substantially. By way of contrast, the overall distance elasticity remains roughly the same (give or take a 15 percent change in the coefficient). The reasonably substantial change in the income coefficient apparently differs from Frankel's (1997) findings, as cited by Baier and Bergstrand (2002). Frankel, using labour and capital stocks as instruments for GDP, finds that 'the endogeneity of income makes little difference' to the coefficient estimates in gravity equations.

The estimate of the income coefficient is material in determining the magnitude of the currency union effect. One can establish this quite easily by conducting a grid-search over 'plausible' income elasticities, and looking at the currency union parameter estimates that arise given the restriction on the income elasticity. There is quite clearly a positive relationship – a higher income elasticity implies a larger currency union effect. The estimates of the income elasticity obtained from instrumental variables are much lower, and thus imply a much lower currency union effect.

The reason for this result is obvious once one plots the income–trade data, highlighting the observations involving the currency union countries. Most currency union pairs have comparatively low incomes. Thus, by reducing the income coefficient one raises the predicted values for low-income country pairs in an ex-currency union regression (since the regression hyper-plane still passes through the vector of data corresponding to the sample means). Consequently, the regressions errors for the currency union countries are correspondingly smaller – since the currency union effect is simply a dummy variable, the coefficient value is determined by the average regression error for the currency union countries. The impact of this effect is illustrated in Figure 8.3 (abstracting from the other regressors). The magnitude of the errors for the currency union trade observations – the distance from the solid dots to the two hypothetical regression lines – clearly depends on the magnitude of the income elasticity.

One might question whether these lower parameter values are plausible. Naturally, there are theoretical reasons that predispose us to believe that the coefficient on GDP is close to one, for example if utility can be represented by constant elasticity of substitution functions. However, it seems possible that for some countries, those that produce agricultural products for example, an increase in foreign income might not translate into a one-for-one increase in demand.

Of course, there is an inherent econometric tension in what has been done here. The land area variable was already included in the regression. By excluding land area (which is necessary to be able to use it as an instrument) and by excluding log per capita GDP, for which there is no second instrumental variable, the regression may suffer from an omitted variable bias. Pre-testing of the exclusion restrictions (e.g., using an F-test based on the R^2 from the two regressions) indicates that the restrictions are not valid.

This result is driven by the fact that the sample size, $n = 26{,}608$, is very large, blowing up the denominator of the statistic.

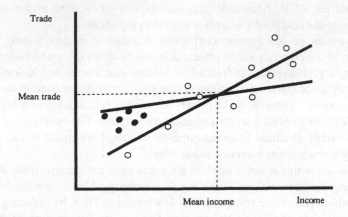

Figure 8.3 The impact of a lower income elasticity

8.4.4 Omitted Variables

Many currency unions, though not all, reflect a historical relationship, such as colonisation. Suppose for a moment that the currency union variable, *CU*, and other regressors in the gravity model are exogenous. Rose (2000) and his co-authors seek to ensure that the coefficient estimated for the *CU* variable is appropriate by including controls that might be correlated with both the *CU* dummy variable and trade. To be confident that the coefficient estimated for the *CU* variable is appropriate, one would have to assume that the selection of controls adequately encompasses all of the other factors that positively affect trade. One would also have to assume that the relationship between trade and the control variables has been appropriately specified.

Consider the Ecuadorian case once more. Ecuador is a beneficiary of the Generalised System of Preferences (GSP) with respect to the United States, as well as the European Union and Japan. Potentially, then, the GSP may increase Ecuadorian exports to the United States, at least relative to the 'expected' exports derived from a gravity model estimated on the 'world' (or some similarly large group of countries). In other words, there is a variable that helps to explain high Ecuadorian–US trade and, in turn, this higher-than-predicted trade is likely to have affected the choice to US-dollarise.

The 'world', of course, includes countries that are not beneficiaries of the GSP, countries such as Australia and New Zealand. To the extent that it is countries like Ecuador – countries whose weak economic institutions encourage them to dollarise or adopt the currency of some other area – the currency union dummy may also be capturing the impact of the Generalised System of Preferences. Grether and Olarreaga (1998) note that preferential trade represents approximately 40 per cent of world trade. Failing to account for these agreements may thus have a noticeable impact on the estimate of the currency union coefficient. Furthermore, even if currency union does improve trade, extrapolating the behaviour of the GSP-advantaged countries to countries such as New Zealand and Australia may be inappropriate. Rose (2000) makes a similar point when he notes that the outcomes from the EMU might not be generalisable to other countries.

To deal with the omitted variable problem, Glick and Rose (2002) use time-series evidence in the post-World War II era to examine the effect of transitions into and out of currency unions. They argue that a substantial loss of trade is associated with exiting a currency union. However, as Honohan (2001) notes in his discussion of Persson (2001) and Rose (2001), and as reiterated by Thom and Walsh (2002), many of these transitions represent the break-up of colonial relationships, the adoption of autarkic policies in the wake of colonialism, and oftentimes civil war. In these circumstances it is not surprising that one subsequently witnesses a decline in trade. Thus, even the time-series evidence based on exchange rate regime transitions can be contested.

8.4.5 Cleaning the Data

The variety of 'countries' that are included in the Rose data set may cause sceptics to be concerned about the validity of the empirical results. To some degree, scepticism about the empirical results can be allayed by using diagnostics to search the data set for influential observations; that is, observations that have a material effect on the parameter estimates.

Krasker et al. (1983) provide econometric tools that can be used to identify observations that have a material effect on parameters. Krasker et al. show that one cannot identify influential observations simply by looking at the magnitude of the residuals; one also has to take account of the 'leverage' that such residuals have, which is a function of the regressors. They show that the difference between $\hat{\beta}$ and $\hat{\beta}(i)$, where $\hat{\beta}(i)$ is the parameter estimate one obtains from deleting the ith row in the data, can be represented as:

$$\hat{\beta} - \hat{\beta}(i) = \frac{(X'X)^{-1}x_i e_i}{1 - h_i} \qquad (8.4)$$

where x_i is the ith row of the regressor matrix, and $h_i = x_i (X'X)^{-1}x'_i$. If X is perfectly balanced then $h_i / \Sigma h_i = 1/T$.

Krasker et al. (1983) argue that observations that have leverage greater than $3\Sigma h_i /T$ are potentially influential. A conservative approach is adopted here: leverage points are examined when they are greater than $5\Sigma h_i /T$. Using this metric on the full Rose data set (for the five-yearly data from 1970 to 1990) yields 523 influential rows, from a data set with 26,608 rows of data. In the terminology of Krasker et al. (1983), these rows can be examined for 'gross errors', numbers that may have been mis-identified or mis-entered. This enables one to establish observations that have been mis-coded (e.g., Surinam was formerly part of The Netherlands and never part of Portugal), as well as identifying other rows of data that might also be rather questionable.

The techniques used to identify influential observations also show how difficult it is to represent geographical characteristics using dummy variables. For example, the Indonesia–Malaysia observation is identified as being influential. If one looks at these data one finds that Indonesia and Malaysia are regarded as having a common border but not a common language (though Malay and Bahasa Indonesia are generally considered to be mutually intelligible). However, taking greater care with the language variable also does not appear to make a great deal of difference.[17]

The common border dummy for Indonesia–Malaysia is also perhaps an overstatement, since the common land border is in Borneo, between Kalimantan (Indonesia) and Sabah and Sarawak (Malaysia). Borneo is of course one of the more remote regions of the world – having a common land border in Borneo is unlikely to greatly facilitate trade. Similarly, the common Indonesia–Papua New Guinea border in New Guinea is unlikely to do much for trade, given that it connects two remote areas with low population density and poor transportation infrastructure.

The South Pacific Regional Trade Agreement (Sparteca) is also revealed as another data inconsistency. Sparteca opens Australian and New Zealand markets to small South Pacific countries but does not imply free trade among the Pacific island countries themselves. Thus, the regional trade agreement dummy variable for Tonga–Kiribati, Kiribati–Samoa, Niue–Samoa, and Niue–Fiji, and so on, appears to be mis-coded.

As one can see from equation (8.4), the effect that a residual has on the parameters depends on the regressors. When the CU and the same-country dummy variables are included in the regression, *all* currency union and same-country pairs are considered to be influential. This is not surprising given that there are very few currency union observations, at least relative to the sample size as a whole.

Nevertheless, bar removing all such observations, one finds that influential observations have an approximately neutral effect on the estimate of the currency union parameter – there are as many positive adjustments as there are negative. The influential observations analysis is particularly useful in this regard. It makes it clear that there is no single observation, and no small sub-sample of currency union observations, that drives the currency union estimate. The next section demonstrates that this does not necessarily imply that the estimate of the currency union effect is robust. The impact of the currency union effect depends crucially on the parameters that one estimates for income and distance.

8.4.6 Sub-sample Variations

It is instructive to consider the data from the currency union and non-currency union countries respectively. Table 8.3 records the means of the data from currency union and non-currency union sub-samples of data, and also provides standard errors for the means of the currency union sample. The standard errors for the data means have been constructed by treating the full sample of data as the population of interest.[18] One can then assess whether the sub-sample means are statistically similar to the expected values of the whole population (the full sample means).

This is an important comparison to make if one wants to generalise the impact of currency union to those countries that have independent currencies. What one finds in Table 8.1 is that currency union country pairs tend to have lower incomes and they tend to be closer. This feature of the data was also revealed in Figure 8.2. The currency union countries are also much more likely to have a common border, are more likely to have a regional trade agreement, and are much more likely to have historical ties, such as language, the same coloniser, or indeed are much more likely to be part of the same country (such as France and its overseas dependencies).

In short, the currency union pairs of countries may not be representative of the wider sample. Rose (2001) performs a similar exercise on the IMF data set that Glick and Rose (2002) later used and suggests that the means of variables for currency union and non-currency union countries are the same in that data set, with the exception of the common language dummy. Still, this does not address the issue presented by the data set used here and by Rose and van Wincoop (2001) and by Rose (2000).

Table 8.3 Means of trade and regressors for currency union/non-currency union sub-samples

Variables	Full sample	Sub-sample CU=0	Sub-sample CU=1
Log distance	8.18	8.20	6.47* (0.052)
Log GDP	34.38	34.43	28.87* (0.173)
Language	0.15	0.19	0.98* (0.022)
Border	0.03	0.03	0.11* (0.010)
Trade agreement	0.02	0.02	0.30* (0.009)
Common coloniser	0.09	0.08	0.71* (0.018)
Colony	0.01	0.01	0.03 (0.007)
Same country	0.00	0.00	0.14* (0.003)
Log GDP/capita	16.23	16.24	15.25* (0.086)
Landlocked	0.18	0.18	0.16 (0.025)
Land area	24.08	24.12	20.01* (0.211)
Number of observations	26,608	26,356	252

Notes:

a   The standard errors in parentheses in the last column are calculated by resampling 30,000 times from the full sample

b   An asterisk indicates that the mean of the regressor for the sub-sample where *CU*=1 is more than three standard deviations from the full sample mean

c   *CU* is an abbreviation for the currency union dummy

d   See note 19 for details of the data

Table 8.4 reports parameter estimates from regressions on data where the country pairs are in currency unions (a sample with 252 observations) and on data where the countries are not in currency unions (26,356 observations). The specification of the regression is as close as is possible to that in Rose and van Wincoop (2001). There are sizable differences in the point estimates of the parameter values from the two sub-samples, though for the most part the parameter estimates obtained from the currency union data (*CU*=1) are not significantly different from the parameters estimated on the whole population of countries. The exception appears to be the distance parameter, which is noticeably smaller for the currency union countries.

Table 8.4 Regression for currency union/non-currency union sub-samples

Variables	Full sample		Sub-sample *CU*=0		Sub-sample *CU*=1	
Constant	−19.07	(0.26)	−18.99	(0.26)	−13.55	(2.20)
Currency union	1.37	(0.14)	—		—	
Log distance	−1.04	(0.02)	−1.05	(0.02)	−0.63	(0.17)
Log GDP	0.92	(0.01)	0.92	(0.01)	0.82	(0.12)
Language	0.54	(0.04)	0.54	(0.04)	1.01	(1.16)
Border	0.61	(0.08)	0.56	(0.08)	0.98	(0.44)
Trade agreement	1.02	(0.07)	1.11	(0.07)	1.48	(0.54)
Common coloniser	0.37	(0.06)	0.38	(0.06)	−0.54	(0.47)
Colony	2.10	(0.07)	2.07	(0.07)	2.11	(0.45)
Same country	0.95	(0.32)	1.43	(0.57)	0.54	(0.42)
Log GDP/capita	0.48	(0.01)	0.48	(0.01)	0.13	(0.15)
Landlocked	−0.25	(0.03)	−0.26	(0.03)	−0.66	(0.39)
Land area	−0.14	(0.01)	−0.14	(0.01)	−0.07	(0.10)
Dummy 1970	1.66	(0.04)	1.66	(0.04)	1.42	(0.49)
Dummy 1975	1.40	(0.04)	1.40	(0.04)	1.37	(0.42)
Dummy 1980	1.02	(0.04)	1.02	(0.04)	0.84	(0.28)
Dummy 1985	0.25	(0.04)	0.24	(0.04)	0.40	(0.27)
No. of observations	26,608		26,356		252	

Notes:
a The first column records parameters for a regression on all of the trade pairs
b The second column records parameters from a regression on countries *not* in a currency union
c The third column records parameters from a regression on data only from country pairs in a currency union
d Standard errors in parentheses

Persson (2001) attempts to cope with the problems raised by Table 8.3 (and to a lesser extent Table 8.4) by using a treatment effect approach adopted from health and labour economics (see also Kenen (2002)). The essence of this approach is to find a control group that has similar characteristics to the 'treated' group (i.e., the group of countries that has been 'treated' with a currency union). One then compares the mean trade of the treated group with the mean trade of the appropriately similar control group. Persson (2001) finds that the effect of currency union is much reduced in this comparison, and is not statistically significant. Of course, questions remain about the degree of comparability between the control group and the treated group.

8.4.7 Regional Subsets

One of the sensitivity checks that Rose (2000) has performed is an examination of various sub-groups of countries. For example, he has examined the results on purely intra-Less Developed Country trade. He has also considered parameter estimates when Australia, France, New Zealand and the United States are excluded from the sample. In a third experiment Rose (2000) excludes African countries; a fourth experiment excludes Europe and countries in the Pacific. A fifth experiment excludes countries from the Caribbean and the Americas.

This section takes a slightly different tack from Rose. Rather than excluding subsets of countries, this section focuses on regional subsets (see Table 8.5). In general, one finds that many of the influential observations arise from trade between African countries, as well as Belize, Panama, Kiribati and a number of Caribbean countries. Since the CFA Franc area (that is, the franc of the African Financial Community) and the member countries of the Eastern Caribbean Central Bank provide many of the currency union observations (approximately 100 observations in each), it seems sensible to consider Africa, the Caribbean and 'the rest of the world' separately, to examine whether the parameters of the equation are in fact stable over different geographical areas. These samples overlap, since a data point is included if one of the two countries is from a particular region. Thus, for example, Bahamas–Liberia trade affects both the Caribbean and African regressions.

Table 8.5 presents the regression parameters associated with regressions run on these geographical sub-samples. The results indicate that the effect of currency union varies sharply across the different regions. Most notably, the point estimate of the currency union parameter for the Caribbean is actually negative, though it is not statistically significantly different from zero

Many of the other regressors are also quite different across the various geographical regions. Interestingly, the parameter estimates on the income variable are markedly lower for the Caribbean in comparison to the world as a whole.

Table 8.5 *Geographical sub-region regressions*

	All countries	Not Caribbean	Not Africa	Caribbean	Africa
Constant	-19.07	-19.14	-21.91	-15.07	-18.51
	(0.26)	(0.28)	(0.34)	(0.82)	(0.53)
Currency	1.37	1.79	0.90	-0.13	1.81
Union	(0.14)	(0.16)	(0.21)	(0.28)	(0.19)
Log distance	-1.04	-0.99	-0.99	-0.92	-1.10
	(0.02)	(0.02)	(0.02)	(0.05)	(0.04)
Log GDP	0.92	0.94	0.91	0.56	1.03
	(0.01)	(0.01)	(0.01)	(0.03)	(0.02)
Language	0.54	0.56	0.74	0.75	0.27
	(0.04)	(0.04)	(0.04)	(0.11)	(0.06)
Border	0.61	0.70	0.32	0.37	1.74
	(0.08)	(0.08)	(0.08)	(0.43)	(0.17)
Trade	1.02	0.63	1.16	1.96	
Agreement	(0.07)	(0.07)	(0.07)	(0.22)	
Common	0.37	0.33	0.44	-0.11	0.17
coloniser	(0.06)	(0.06)	(0.08)	(0.17)	(0.08)
Colony	2.10	2.07	1.63	2.41	2.25
	(0.07)	(0.08)	(0.10)	(0.25)	(0.12)
Same country	0.95	1.22	1.19	0.65	3.77
	(0.32)	(0.40)	(0.35)	(0.45)	(0.34)
Log GDP per	0.48	0.47	0.63	0.68	0.37
capita	(0.01)	(0.01)	(0.02)	(0.05)	(0.03)
Landlocked	-0.25	-0.28	-0.37	-0.76	-0.14
	(0.03)	(0.03)	(0.04)	(0.15)	(0.05)
Land area	-0.14	-0.18	-0.14	-0.01	-0.23
	(0.01)	(0.01)	(0.01)	(0.02)	(0.01)
No. of obs	26,608	23,543	16,671	3,065	9,937
Adjusted R^2	0.63	0.64	0.68	0.41	0.48

Notes:
a   Not Caribbean and Not Africa: regression on data where neither member of a country pair is in the Caribbean or Africa (as appropriate)
b   Caribbean and Africa: regression on data where one (or more) of the two countries is from the Caribbean or Africa (as appropriate)
c   Time dummies were included in all regressions
d   Standard errors in parentheses

Similar estimates of the currency union effect are obtained if one estimates the currency union regression on low-income/low-distance countries (e.g., on countries in the bottom left hand quadrant of Figure 8.2). There are 1,294 country pairs in this quadrant compared with the full sample of 26,608. Of these country pairs, 172 are in a currency union.

Border effects appear to be much more important for African countries than for the rest of the world. Interestingly, language does not appear to be a very important determinant of trade in Africa, when compared with its impact on trade elsewhere in the world, perhaps because multi-lingualism is more prevalent (meaning that the dummy variable does not accurately reflect the language barrier in Africa). The constants in these regressions also differ fairly substantially and this suggests that a fixed effects model might be appropriate.

It can be concluded that there are substantial differences in the parameter estimates for regional sub-groups, which is suggestive of important heterogeneity. One can illustrate this by considering regional regressions once more. Is it, for example, legitimate to assume that the coefficient on the currency union dummy is the same across the Caribbean and across the rest of the world? This can be tested by interacting the currency union dummy variable with a dummy variable indicating whether a country pair has a member in the Caribbean, and testing whether this interacted variable has a zero coefficient. The answer is that such a restriction does not hold. The F-statistic is 16.0, which is far in excess of the critical value (which is approximately 3.84). The data also reject the restriction that the GDP regressor is the same across the two groups of countries.

Performing similar experiments on the currency union sub-sample yields similar results. If one interacts the currency union dummy variable with income or distance (or indeed both), the interaction variable is significantly different from zero. The sign of the interacted distance term is consistent with the results from the regional regressions: the coefficient is negative and very large (–0.53). This indicates that the overall distance coefficient for the currency union countries is –0.74, much lower than usual but consistent with the African and Caribbean regressions. Perhaps more importantly, when the interaction terms are included the currency union coefficient becomes negative.

8.4.8 What About Distance?

Much of the analysis has emphasised that income and distance are by far the most important variables. The regional regressions discussed in the previous section demonstrate that the impact of distance varies considerably depending on the region being considered. This result may reflect the heterogeneous distribution of income and hence transportation networks. Anderson and van Wincoop's work (2001a, 2001b) suggests that there is an important omitted variable, which is 'multilateral trade resistance' – essentially a measure of the average difficulty associated with exporting from a given country. This term may be correlated with individual distances (e.g., because of spatial location) and may thus affect the magnitude of the distance coefficient.

Other indicators of trade costs support the view that geographical differences are important. South Pacific countries, for example, appear to be more severely affected by distance than developed countries in general. Table 8.6 illustrates that developing countries' transportation costs are much higher than those experienced in developed countries. The coefficient on log distance in gravity regressions can be interpreted as an elasticity. Thus, a coefficient of, say, –1 implies that a 1 percent increase in distance reduces trade by 1 percent. A comparison of Ireland and New Zealand provides an indication of the trade consequence of peripherality. Ireland's average trade-weighted distance is around the 3,200 kilometre mark. New Zealand's average trade-weighted distance is 7,700 kilometres or more for the years in the data set. If New Zealand's average distance could be reduced to the Irish average distance this would increase New Zealand's trade by about 140 per cent. The situation is much worse if one uses a 'Pacific' distance coefficient, since the distance coefficient for the Pacific appears to be about –2.5, rather than –1. New Zealand trade would increase approximately eightfold if this larger coefficient were used.[20]

8.5 CONCLUSION

This chapter has emphasised that the examination of currency union using gravity models is primarily an econometric exercise without an explicit theoretical foundation. Consequently, this chapter has focused on some of the empirical and econometric issues that arise with respect to estimating currency union effects.

Using econometric techniques it has been established here that the empirical estimates of the currency union effect, as typically calculated, are not driven by a single trade relationship or a small number of trade relationships. These techniques also help identify influential data observations, some of which have been affected by coding errors. While these techniques support the importance of the currency union effect, some of the other econometric issues cannot be resolved so easily.

Table 8.6 Aggregate freight costs as a percentage of import value

Country group	1980	1991
World	6.64	5.24
Developed countries	5.49	4.35
of which:		
New Zealand	8.60	9.39
Developing countries	10.44	8.48
of which:		
Africa	13.42	11.10
Americas	8.85	8.08
Asia	10.41	8.12
Europe	8.23	8.99
Oceania	12.84	12.26

Note: UNCTAD estimates based on US dollar import data, NZ estimate based on NZ dollar data

Source: UNCTAD, except for the author's New Zealand estimate

The first of these issues is that the currency union dummy variable and income regressor are likely to be endogenous. Endogeneity raises serious questions about the possibility of inference. Instrumental variables estimation can be used to take account of income's endogenous character. The IV estimates of the income elasticity and the currency union coefficient are substantially smaller than the corresponding OLS estimates. It turns out that the currency union effect is closely related to the magnitude of both the income and distance coefficients; the IV results raise questions about the income estimates that are usually obtained.

The second problem is that the currency union country pairs may not be representative of the rest of the sample. Extrapolating the impact of currency union from those countries to the rest of the sample may lead to inappropriate conclusions. The currency union and other parameters vary substantially across regional sub-samples. Furthermore, when income and distance are interacted with the currency union dummy, the positive currency union effect disappears.

The econometric problems may mean that the currency union parameter estimates are not robust. In any case, currency union is no panacea for the problems of location.

Although it would be desirable to place more emphasis on the 'extra' geographical variables that are sometimes included in gravity model regressions – language, trade policy and so on – the preceding analysis suggests that the parameter estimates for these variables may be fragile, unless the income and distance coefficients are correctly estimated. An important direction for future research would be to try to understand how spatial location, rather than simply distance, affects these parameters. Given that large data sets are available for trade, it may be possible to make more extensive use of non-parametric methods to consider these spatial effects.

NOTES

1. The views contained in this chapter are those of the author and should not be attributed to the Reserve Bank of New Zealand or its employees. The author wishes to thank, without implicating, Michelle Barnes, Nils Bjorksten, Sean Collins, Peter Kenen, Jacques Poot, Andrew Rose, Dean Scrimgeour and an anonymous referee for valuable comments and discussion.
2. Wei (1996) studies the magnitude of 'home bias' for a variety of OECD countries: he estimates that the average magnitude is much smaller than is identified for North America. OECD home bias also declined over the 1982–1994 sample period.
3. Over half of the data sample used by Fitzsimons et al. (1999) is post-1979, during which time Ireland was part of the European Exchange Rate Mechanism and the United Kingdom was not.
4. See http://www.haas.berkeley.edu/~arose/.
5. The subscript t indicates that the cost of bridging distance can change over time.
6. Such a specification can be derived from constant elasticity of substitution utility functions.
7. Coe and Hoffmaister (1999) argue that using logarithms is inappropriate in considering African data, since it results in censoring a large number of zero-trade observations (since the log of zero is undefined).
8. This restriction has also been justified by noting that if one of the countries has zero income it has nothing to trade (e.g., Deardorff, 1998), though this is less apparent if the regression equation is in logs or has additional variables.
9. Kenen (2002) has noted that it is possible to extract most of the individual income data by identifying US GDP in the corresponding years. The remaining income data can usually be found by taking one intermediate step – finding the income of a country that trades with the United States and thence the income for the country that does not trade directly with the United States. A similar approach could be used to divide trade into its export and import components.
10. See http://ksghome.harvard.edu/~.drodrik.academic.ksg/shortpieces.html.
11. See Hayashi (2000) or any advanced econometrics textbook for a discussion of simultaneity bias.
12. Rose (personal communication) identifies financial considerations as being important too.
13. Rose's response to the Thom and Walsh paper is Glick and Rose (2002); see http://haas.berkeley.edu/~arose/RecRes.htm. Glick and Rose's response is subject to problems that are discussed in the text.
14. In the Rose data set the Bahamian currency board arrangement is treated as being equivalent to a currency union.

15. The location of firms – and hence their distance from other countries – responds to trade agreements (consider the development of Northern Mexico post-NAFTA), but typical measures of distance will not capture such developments.
16. Log trade is the natural log of the sum of exports and imports between two countries. Currency union is a binary variable assuming a value of one when two countries use the same currency, and is zero otherwise. Log distance is measured in the logarithm of kilometres. Log GDP is the log of the product of the GDPs of the two countries. Land area is the log product of the areas of the two countries. See Rose (2000) and Rose and van Wincoop (2001) for more extensive descriptions of the data. All logs are natural logs. The sample consists of data from 1970, 1975, 1980, 1985 and 1990. (The 1995 data were not used due to the rebasing of the 1995 income data.) The standard errors are those obtained using OLS, except for the IV standard errors which were calculated using the IV analogue. This is not entirely desirable, since group-wise heterogeneity in the errors may also affect inference. However, the 'natural' cross-sectional group seems to be trade between countries *i* and *j*, which implies that there are more than 6,000 groups.
17. There are quite a few data errors associated with French as a lingua franca. Nevertheless, replacing the CIA language data with a more authoritative source, such as www.ethnologue.net, does not make a material difference to the analysis.
18. A sample of 252 is actually quite large, so the central limit theorem implies the means of the currency union sub-sample are, to a reasonable approximation, normally distributed. The variances of the means were also calculated by repeatedly re-sampling from the population (the full sample) with replacement. This exercise confirmed that the variance implied by the normal distribution was appropriate.
19. See note 16 for some data definitions. Log GDP per capita is the log of the product of per capita GDPs. Same country is a binary variable taking the value one if the two regions are part of the same country, zero otherwise. Common coloniser is one if the two countries were colonies after 1945 and had a common coloniser, zero otherwise. Language is one if the two countries have a language in common and is zero otherwise. The language variable has been modified from the original Rose data set. A language is held in common if it is commonly understood or is an official language (English, for example, is an official language in both Nauru and Kiribati). Colony is one if a country pair represents a colony and a coloniser, zero otherwise. Landlocked is a trinary variable with values zero, one and two that counts the number of countries in the pair that are landlocked. Border is one if the two countries share a common land border and is zero otherwise. See Rose (2000) and Rose and van Wincoop (2001) for more extensive descriptions of the data.
20. The starting point matters in these calculations. If one starts from the hypothetical Irish distance the effects are a 60 and 89 per cent decline in trade respectively by moving to New Zealand's average distance.

REFERENCES

Aghion, P. and P. Howitt (1998), *Endogenous Growth Theory*, Cambridge, Massachusetts and London: The MIT Press.

Anderson, J.E. and E. van Wincoop (2001a), 'Gravity with gravitas: a solution to the border puzzle', *NBER Working Paper*, 8079.

Anderson, J.E. and E. van Wincoop (2001b), 'Borders, trade and welfare', *NBER Working Paper*, 8515.

Baier, S.L. and J.H. Bergstrand (2002), 'On the endogeneity of international trade flows and free trade agreements', Mimeo, University of Notre Dame. See http://www.nd.edu/~jbergstr/working_papers.html.

Cleveland, W.S. (1993), *Visualizing Data*, Summit, NJ: Hobart Press.
Coe, D.T. and A.W. Hoffmaister (1999), 'North-South trade: is Africa unusual?', *Journal of Financial Research*, 8, 228-256.
DaCosta, M., A. Gómez-Oliver, S. Itam, C. Piñerúa and S. Shah (1999), 'The Bahamas: selected issues and statistical appendix', *IMF Staff Country Report*, 99(106).
Deardorff, A.V. (1998), 'Determinants of bilateral trade: does gravity work in a neoclassical world?', in Frankel, J. (ed.), *'The Regionalization of the World Economy'*, Chicago: University of Chicago Press.
Fitzsimons, E., V. Hogan and P.J. Neary (1999), 'Explaining the volume of North-South trade in Ireland: A gravity model approach', *Economic and Social Review*, 30, 381-401.
Frankel, J.A. (1997), *Regional Trading Blocs*, Washington, DC: Institute for International Economics.
Frankel, J.A. and A.K. Rose (2002), 'An estimate of the effect of common currencies on trade and income', *Quarterly Journal of Economics*, 117, 437-466.
Glick, R. and A.K. Rose (2002), 'Does a currency union affect trade? The time series evidence', *European Economic Review*, 46, 1125-1151.
Grether, J.-M. and M. Olarreaga (1998), 'Preferential and non-preferential trade flows in world trade', *WTO Staff Working Paper*, 98-10, 98-110.
Hargreaves, D. and C.J. McDermott (1999), 'Issues relating to optimal currency areas: theory and implications for New Zealand', *Reserve Bank of New Zealand Bulletin*, 62, 16-29.
Hayashi, F. (2000), *Econometrics*, Princeton and Oxford: Princeton University Press.
Helliwell, J.F. (1996), 'Do national borders matter for Quebec's trade?', *Canadian Journal of Economics*, 29, 507-522.
Helliwell, J.F. (1998), *How Much Do National Borders Matter?*, Washington, DC: The Brookings Institution.
Honohan, P. (2001), 'Discussion', *Economic Policy: A European Forum*, 0(33), 457-459.
Kenen, P.B. (2002), 'Currency unions and trade: variations on themes by Rose and Persson', Mimeo. Princeton. See http://www.princeton.edu/~pbkenen/.
Krasker, W.S., E. Kuh and R.E. Welsch (1983), 'Estimation for dirty data and flawed models', in Griliches, Z. and M.D. Intriligator (eds), *Handbook of Econometrics*, Amsterdam: North-Holland Publishing Co., pp. 651-698.
McCallum, J. (1995), 'National borders matter: Canada-U.S. regional trade patterns', *American Economic Review*, 85, 615-623.
Persson, T. (2001), 'Currency unions and trade: how large is the treatment effect?', *Economic Policy: A European Forum*, 0(33), 433-448.
Pöyhönen, P. (1963), 'A tentative model for the volume of trade between countries', *Weltwirtschaftliches Archiv*, 90, 93-99.
Rose, A.K. (2000), 'One money, one market: estimating the effect of common currencies on trade', *Economic Policy: A European Forum*, 0(30), 7-33.
Rose, A.K. (2001), 'Currency unions and trade: the effect is large', *Economic Policy: A European Forum*, 0(33), 449-457.
Rose, A.K. and E. van Wincoop (2001), 'National money as a barrier to international trade: the real case for currency union', *American Economic Review*, 91, 386-390.
Theil, H. and J. Galvez (1995), 'On latitude and affluence: the equatorial canyon', *Empirical Economics*, 20, 163-166.

Thom, R. and B. Walsh (2002), 'The effect of a currency union on trade: lessons from the Irish experience', *European Economic Review*, 46, 1111-1123.

Tinbergen, J. (1962), *Shaping the World Economy: Suggestions for an International Economic Policy*, New York: Periodicals Service Co.

Wei, S.-J. (1996), 'Intra-national versus international trade: how stubborn are nations in global integration?', NBER Working Paper, 5531.

9. Australia–New Zealand Border Effects and Trans-Tasman Integration

Tim Hazledine and Sara Lipanovic

9.1 INTRODUCTION

About 100 million people live in the seven provinces and thirteen states that abut the 49th parallel dividing Canada from the United States. Suppose these people were evenly spread along the border. Then, in the absence of 'border costs' (such as tariffs), would we not expect that a typical Canadian would naturally carry through just one out of every four transactions with other Canadians, given that Canadians make up about one-quarter of the 100 million? That is, Canadian exports to the United States would be at least three times larger than domestic shipments, if not even more, given the additional attractors of higher US per capita incomes and the further opportunities of doing business with the 200 million other Americans who live south of the border states.

Yet the actual ratio is the inverse – Canadians ship nearly three times as much to other Canadians as they do to Americans. That is, the predicted and actual trade ratios differ by almost an order of magnitude. There is far 'too little trade' between these two countries whose bilateral trade flows are actually the largest in the world.

Until the mid-1990s, the sensible-sounding response from those (few) who had noticed this apparent anomaly would have been to query the simplification of the geography. The 100 million people in fact live in a broad band, not dotted along a line, and location and distance in the band do matter. Most people do not drive 100 miles, or even 10, to find a convenience store. If they live in Vancouver, they don't phone Seattle for a plumber. So, the chances of a Canadian doing business with another Canadian are actually much higher than the ratios of total populations.

This idea can be formalised in the 'gravity model', already discussed extensively in the previous chapter. Shipments from one region to another are expected to be directly proportional to the product of the two regions' GDPs and inversely proportional to the squared distance between them. Gravity models do a pretty good job at matching observed international trade flows: in particular, they identify a strong role for distance – too strong, actually (a point to which we shall return below).

However, there was an empirical hole at the centre of the gravity model literature. It used the readily available data on shipments of goods between countries, but actually omitted the much larger internal shipment flows, which are much less conveniently measured. Still, probably very few economists – certainly not those surveyed by Helliwell (1996) – expected that filling this hole in the data would change the results significantly.

This changed when McCallum (1995) analysed an unusual Statistics Canada database, which tracked shipments of merchandise goods (so no plumbing or retail services are included in the data) between Canadian provinces and between provinces and US states in 1988. Estimating the gravity model on these shipments data, McCallum found that he needed an enormous dummy variable to enable it to encompass the two types of shipment flows. Basically, for given values of incomes and distance, trade between the provinces is much more likely than trade across the border. For example, a business in British Columbia was more than *twenty times* more likely to import goods from Ontario than a business in Washington State, even though both are about the same distance from Ontario. So, there really is 'too little trade' – it is not (just) a matter of distances between economic agents.

Helliwell (1998) extended the estimation period to 1996, well into the Canada/US free trade era (which began in 1989) and found that 40 per cent of the estimated border effect evaporated in just four years, dropping from about 20 in 1990 to around 12 in 1993 and thereafter – rather more than Helliwell (1996) had predicted. Recent work by Head and Ries (2001) seems to imply that more than half of the decline is due to the tariff cuts, with the remainder coming from some shrinkage of non-tariff border effects. The latter remain substantial, however, with tariff-equivalent values in 1995 ranging from 27 per cent to 45 per cent, depending on method of estimation.

Wei (1996) added estimates of the distances between people *within* regions, and came up with much smaller border effects for OECD economies. But his method appears to underestimate true internal distances, and other measures (Nitsch, 2000) result in higher numbers.[1] Even using the Wei procedure, Helliwell (1998) estimates OECD border effects of around ten. Some other studies (e.g., Frankel and Rose, 2000) find even larger effects, while Anderson and van Wincoop (2001) and Anderson and Smith (2001) find lower, but still large, estimates.

Thus, the border effect appears to be substantial. It cannot be explained away: it must be explained. What generates it? Is it good or bad? These are questions still not adequately addressed in the literature, despite their evident importance. This chapter offers a discussion of the possible causes of the border effect, along with some estimates of the economic size of the 'border' between Australia and New Zealand, and the implications of this for closer economic integration between the two economies.[2] Following the theme of the previous chapter, we will also consider some other integration issues, including those of possible monetary union.

9.2 INTERPRETING BORDER EFFECTS

To explore the meaning of 'borders', we begin by drawing attention to another rather large number, which has been around for a long time without, apparently, upsetting anyone. This is the exponent on distance in gravity models of trade, which, as a stylised fact, is between −1 and −2 (see the previous chapter), which is not far from the value predicted by the actual gravity model used to account for the physical attraction between two masses. Probably this is why no one paid much attention to it, but even −1 seems far too big a number to be explained conventionally in economics. Distance may be a big deal in physics but it is not in economics – not at least, as far as transportation costs are concerned. As Grossman (1998) may have been the first to point out, if average transport costs of exports are around 5 percent of their free on board (f.o.b.) value, and there are some fixed costs of transportation and Cobb–Douglas demand functions, then the predicted coefficient on distance in a gravity trade model is only −0.03 – smaller than one-thirtieth of the estimated number!

We suggest that the two effects – distance and border – should be explained together and that this should be done in terms of the factors introduced by Helliwell (1998) to try to make sense of the border effect, namely transaction costs broadly defined (see also Chapters 2 and 3 in this book). Helliwell puts forward the importance of shared values, institutions, histories and cultures in establishing behavioural norms that build empathy and trust (sometimes called social capital) between agents, which are in turn important for fostering the cooperative behaviour needed to extract potential gains from trade. As Helliwell points out, these norms can differ objectively across cultures. What may be important for transaction costs is that within each culture the prevailing norms are well understood.

It is easy to see how this relativist approach to societies can explain the existence of a border effect, and it may also underpin the distance effect if there are good reasons for empathy and trust to diminish with the distance between agents, so that although the potential gains from exchange increase with the number of potential trading partners, the difficulties in realising such potential go up as well. What all this adds up to could be summarised as follows: nations (and regions) still do matter, even in a world of 'free' trade and globalisation.[3]

But is it good that they do? Are those transaction costs that underpin border and distance effects simply the obsolete legacy of ancient systems of protection and/or the manifestations of xenophobic mistrust and ill will, to be eventually swept aside as nations and regions achieve true integration? Or does the fundamental scarcity of information mean that people really do need to limit the domain over which they search for trading partners, such that overzealous integration policies could actually reduce efficiency, by making it more difficult for agents to form and sustain cooperative relationships?

Most economists contributing to this literature have assumed, without discussion, that the border effect is a bad thing; the manifestation of an unfortunate 'bias' against trade – basically, a non-tariff barrier which reduces welfare just as surely as do tariffs and import restrictions. But this really needs to be examined. Hazledine (1995) sketched out possible alternative interpretations in a comment on a precursor of McCallum's discovery – the finding – termed 'remarkable' – by Frankel et al. (1995) that countries with a common linguistic/colonial tradition tend to trade 65 percent more with each other than they would otherwise. We can expect this to apply to Australia and New Zealand, which of course share (most of) a language and are both former British colonies.

To make the point, we simplify by assuming no trade creation, so that more trans-Tasman trade means less trade with the Rest of the World (RoW). Then we can set up a diagram like Figure 9.1, with New Zealand's trade with Australia measured as a percentage of New Zealand's total trade from left to right and its trade with the rest of the world from right to left. Trade shares are determined by the intersection of the two marginal value curves, with the marginal transaction worth V. With the common Australasian heritage, and so on, the actual trade shares are about 25:75 (Australia/RoW); whereas without these cultural and historical linkages the Frankel et al. (1995) model would predict something like a 15:85 split of the trade cake.

Suppose first that having a common language is purely efficiency enhancing, through the associated reduction in transaction costs. Then, without this bond, the marginal value of New Zealand's trade with Australia would be lower (V'), as would the equilibrium value of the marginal transaction, and a big hunk of economic surplus would be lost. We could call the vertical distance between the curves mv_A and mv'_A a 'common culture' bonus.

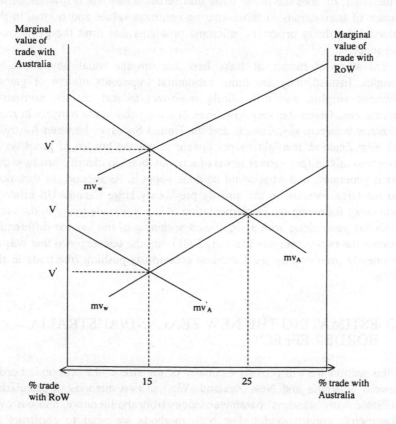

Figure 9.1 Implications of New Zealand–Australia border effects

But now suppose that the common language effect is the result of prejudice and ignorance (possibly reinforced by regulations and barriers against true 'foreigners'), so that New Zealand is actually missing out on profitable opportunities for trading with non-Anglophone, non-Commonwealth countries. Then the efficient outcome would be 15:85, but now with a *higher* marginal value, V″, and higher surplus than the current status quo. In this case, we could dub the vertical distance between mv_w and mv'_w the 'insularity tax'.

Applied to the border effect, this analysis would ask with respect to internal and external trade flows: are the former too large because of barriers to the latter, or does the home trade bias reflect a sensible restriction of the domain of transactions to those sharing common values and norms, in the interests of solving prisoners' dilemma problems that limit the gains from exchange?

The sums of money at stake here are not the usual tiny allocative triangles. Instead, they are quite substantial trapezoids of lost or gained economic surplus, and it is surely important to sort out the normative implications. Given the very low level of observable trade barriers in most industries between, say, Canada and the United States, or between Australia and New Zealand, it might be reasonable to put the burden of proof on to those who talk in (pejorative) terms of a home 'bias' to identify just how this bias is generated, and what could be done about it. As support for this, note that the large increase in the already previously large Canada–US bilateral trade flows following the implementation of the free trade treaty in the early 1990s has gone along with a significant widening of the income differential between the two economies (Trefler, 2001), not the convergence that was so confidently promised by the Canadian economists pushing free trade in the 1980s.

9.3 ESTIMATING THE NEW ZEALAND/AUSTRALIA BORDER EFFECT

In this section we will provide estimates of the size of the economic border between Australia and New Zealand. We use two methods: a calculation calibrated with 'standard' parameter values from the literature, and our own econometric gravity model. For both methods we need to construct an estimate of the internal distances in the two countries. That is, we need to know how far apart a randomly chosen New Zealander is likely to be from another randomly chosen New Zealander, and for the calibration exercise we need the same number for Australians.

Clearly, the Wei procedure of taking one-quarter of the distance between neighbouring capitals is not suitable for island regions, whatever its appropriateness to, say, European economies. But there is in any case a better method, namely to disaggregate each country into its own set of regions and then use census or other population data, along with data on air-mile distances between the major city or town within each region, to calculate a weighted average distance between the inhabitants. In essence, this method, which was first used by Helliwell and Verdier (2001), replicates the standard gravity model procedure for calculating distances between nations, at the sub-national level. As such it does not deal with the problem of inferring the distance between people living in the 'same' place, but it does move this problem down a level.

In calculating the average internal distance for New Zealand we first divided the country into regions and allocated to each of these the relevant population figures, in terms of population of the main urban centre, population of rural areas within that region and total regional population. We then selected a main centre for each region and used road distance tables to determine the distance in kilometres between each combination of main centres. This approximates the distance between regions. We then multiplied the distance between each centre and every other centre (including itself) by the proportion of the total population living in the destination region. To approximate the average distance for each rural and urban area respectively within each region we used Nitsch's (2000) method applied on a smaller scale. Average distance for the whole region then is the sum of the average rural distance times the proportion of the region's population living in rural areas plus the average urban distance multiplied by the proportion of the region's population living in the urban area. On summation of these distances for each region we then multiplied by the proportion of the total population living in that region. Finally, we added up the end figures for each region to get an average internal distance for New Zealand. That is, we derived an estimate of the expected distance between any two randomly selected residents of the country.

This number is 551 kilometres, which is perhaps surprisingly large. It can be taken as about one-quarter of the distance between the average New Zealand resident and the average Australian, given that the distance between any of the three largest New Zealand cities (Auckland, Wellington, Christchurch) and any of the three largest Australian cities (Sydney, Melbourne, Brisbane) is between 2,100 and 2,600 kilometres.[4]

For Australia the calculation involved distances between six states and two territories, and the capital cities of those regions. Most Australians live along the eastern and south eastern freeboard of their continent, but this is a very long freeboard, and the average distance between Australians comes out as 1,158 kilometres, which we will round up to 1,200 kilometres.

Now we need figures for the internal and external flows of goods. The most recent New Zealand input–output study is for the 1995/96 year, in which GDP totalled $91.7 billion. Total gross shipments of goods and services, before taxes, were $214.1 billion, of which $134.6 billion (nearly 63 percent) came from what we could call the tradables sector, accounting for about 98 percent of all exports (excluding re-exports of imports). Of those tradable shipments about $26 billion were exported, and imports of goods and services in the same industry categories were almost the same size, in that year. About 22 percent, or $12 billion in total exports plus imports, of New Zealand's trade was with Australia.

9.3.1 Calibration Exercise

First, we carry out a 'back of the envelope' border effect calculation, assuming that bilateral trade shipments between two economies fall 1 percent for every one percentage increase in the distance between them. There were about 3.8 million people in New Zealand (in 2000) and 19 million in Australia (in 1999) – a ratio of one to five. Domestic shipments between New Zealanders within New Zealand are equal to about $109 billion, so that we would expect trans-Tasman trade to be about five times this based on the 'attraction' of the five-times greater population in Australia, divided by four, for the attenuating effect of distance, which comes to $136 billion. Actual trade flows were about one-eleventh of this, implying a border effect of eleven – similar to the figures typically thrown up in the econometric studies of the Northern Hemisphere economies.

How does it look from the other side of the Tasman Sea? The total shipments of the Australian tradables sector in 1995/96 were $800 billion (in NZ dollars), of which about $100 billion was exported and (of course) $12 billion exported and imported to/from New Zealand. With the estimated internal distance between Australians equal to about one-half of the distance between Australia and New Zealand, and using the same gravity model coefficient, and $700 billion for total internal shipments, we would expect transactions of Australians with New Zealanders to total about 700 × 0.2 × 0.5 = $70 billion – which is about six times as large as the actual flows – implying a smaller border effect to that derived from the New Zealand perspective. If we allowed 10 percent or so each way for the difference in mutual attraction of Australians and New Zealanders due to the lower per capita incomes of the latter, then the New Zealand border effect would be increased and the Australian reduced.[5]

The large trans-Tasman border effect is quite unexpected. The $12 billion gross trans-Tasman trade flow is a much larger fraction of New Zealand's total trade than of Australia's, and there would be significant gains for New Zealand from a reduction in the border effect.

9.3.2 Econometric Gravity Equation

The calibration exercise above took numbers for the exponents on economic mass and distance in the gravity equation from the empirical econometric literature. But what if those exponents do not in fact apply to New Zealand? We now estimate our own gravity equation, using data on New Zealand's trade with its main trading partners. We do not estimate the same equation for Australia or any other of the partners.

Econometric border effects are calculated from augmented gravity models of trade estimated on cross sections of country data. The standard model has the volume of trade between two countries, i and j, being related to the economic size of the countries (Y) and the geographic distance between them ($DIST$), along with a dummy variable ($DOMESTIC$) taking the value 1 for $j = i$ – that is, for when the trade is internal to the country:

$$TRADE_{ij} = \alpha + \beta_0 Y_i + \beta_1 Y_j + \beta_2 DIST_{ij} + \beta_3 DOMESTIC + u_{ij} \qquad (9.1)$$

Apart from the dummy variable, the data are entered in logarithmic form. The coefficient on the domestic dummy indicates the size of the border effect – it tells by what factor internal trade exceeds the level we would expect for this country based on its trading behaviour with other countries in the case of no difference between external and internal propensities to transact.

We collected data for New Zealand's top 40 export destinations for the year 1999. Together these countries account for approximately 90 percent of New Zealand's trade exports. The year 1999 is the most recent year for which data for all series are available. Bilateral export and import data were collected from the New Zealand Ministry of Foreign Affairs and Trade, while GDP data were sourced from the *World Development Indicators* database compiled by the World Bank. Bilateral distances between countries are approximated using great circle distances between the trading partners – generally from capital to capital but alternatively principal trading city when more appropriate. A great circle path represents the shortest path on the surface of the Earth between two given points, and can be acquired by inputting the relevant map coordinates into an appropriate formula. Although this is only an approximation of actual trade routes, it is a generally accepted methodology for obtaining the relevant distance variables. In particular, it is asserted that in the case of faraway regions such as New Zealand, the difference between actual trade routes and great circle routes will be minimal and have a negligible effect on results.

We estimated equation (9.1) and some of the usual variants of it, including substituting measures of population for GDP as the mass variable and supplementing the model with measures of per capita GDP, as a proxy for levels of development, which might affect trade. The results are reported in Table 9.1. None of our refinements or experiments added significantly to the explanatory power of our model, and they will not be reported here.

Table 9.1 Estimates of the coefficients of equation (9.1)

Independent variable	Coefficient	Standard error
lnY_i	0.86	0.11
lnY_j	0.63	0.11
ln$DIST_{ij}$	−1.37	0.33
DOMESTIC	2.91	1.63

The R^2 of this regression was 0.55, or 0.53 adjusted for degrees of freedom (the number of observations was 81), which is not low by the usual standards of cross-sectional econometrics, though lower than achieved by many other econometric gravity equations, which are usually estimated on larger multilateral databases that allow additional explanatory and dummy variables to be included to account for factors such as remoteness, cultural and language links, and whether the trading partners are geographically adjacent to each other (see also the previous chapter).

Our coefficients imply that economic mass is a weaker attractor for New Zealand, and distance is more important than is implied by the numbers culled from the literature and used in the calibration exercise. The net result is a border effect estimated at 18 (the exponent of 2.91) – even larger than that emerging from the calibration exercise and close to McCallum's original estimates for Canada. A worrying feature of the results is the rather large standard error on the *DOMESTIC* dummy variable. We would expect that given the huge over-prediction of internal New Zealand trade by the non-augmented gravity model (i.e., the quantitatively large border effect), then the dummy variable needed to correct for this would come in with a very small standard error.

9.4 WHITTLING AWAY THE BORDER EFFECT

Although we cannot be precise about its size, our calculations and estimates in Section 9.3 strongly suggest that there is a substantial economic 'border' between Australia and New Zealand. In this section, we focus on the possibilities for changes in policies to promote further economic integration between Australia and New Zealand. Plater and Claridge (2000) provide a useful list:

- Tariffs and non-tariff barriers
- Immigration policy
- Investment rules
- Fiscal policy
- International treaties and agreements
- Regulations (e.g., standards, competition policy, capital markets, legal, transport, telecoms, postal, trade in services)
- Monetary policy
- Political arrangements

Of these, the first is already quite well covered by the Closer Economic Relations free trade agreement, and the last we will rule out of consideration in this chapter. Immigration policies are nominally independent, but in fact are *de facto* integrated, with a lag, by the ease of labour mobility of the citizens of the two countries.

Investment rules are not integrated, and it is a moot question whether they need to be at a national level, since much of the 'action' in attracting both domestic and foreign investment occurs at a lower level – the state or the municipality. Fiscal policies are of course not integrated, but then they are not fully integrated within Australia, either – the state governments collect and spend taxes. International treaties are not, on the whole, integrated and there is scope for working together here; for example, in negotiating trade agreements with third countries.

The list of policies covered by the rubric 'regulations' is long and important and probably maps out the most promising territory for harmonisation and integration – though always bearing in mind the caveat that we will stress in the concluding section, namely that we should always ask why in a mature democracy the particular institutions of policy have evolved differently from those in other countries.

We will here just elaborate on competition policy.[6] It does seem quite reasonable that the jurisdiction of Australian and New Zealand competition policy be integrated, so that the interests of citizens of both countries can enter into consideration. An example of this not happening is the case of the small trans-Tasman airline Kiwi International that was in 1996 successfully predated out of the market by the incumbent carriers, Air New Zealand and Qantas. Kiwi International appealed to the New Zealand Commerce

Commission, but under the national jurisdiction of competition policy the airline could only complain about Air New Zealand, whereupon the Commission immediately ruled that it could not even investigate the alleged predation, since Air New Zealand was not 'dominant' in the market, which of course it shared with the Australian airline. Were the policy written to encompass both countries' firms – and to consider the interests of both countries' consumers – the case could at least have been heard.[7]

Most arguments for harmonisation of regulations turn out to be more solidly based on transaction cost considerations than on those disappointingly tiny efficiency triangles generated in theory by the reallocation of resources. This is not inconsistent with evidence on the importance in the economy as a whole of inputs devoted to handling and (presumably) economising on transaction costs – these being the costs of coordinating, monitoring, controlling and measuring economic activity. For example, Hazledine (2001) finds that a large share of GDP (around 40–50 percent in Australia and New Zealand) is not concerned with producing things but transacting them – moving them from producer to consumer; determining the conditions under which such exchange occurs; and safe-guarding the property rights that are always at risk, but especially when title is transferred.

Transaction costs issues are probably particularly relevant to the issue of harmonisation of monetary policy, going as far as the actual choice of currency. Two countries might each want their own independent currency so that their exchange rates can deliver the 'correct' relative consumption prices, based on production costs. But the savings in transaction costs if they shared a common currency might easily outweigh the 'deadweight triangles' of consumption/production inefficiency from having the 'wrong' level of the exchange rate, bearing in mind the evidence of the general puniness of such efficiency costs.

On top of this, Grimes and Holmes (2000) claim that in New Zealand's case the actual results of the floating independent currency do not seem to have delivered allocative efficiency in the sense of acting to compensate for exogenous movements in the terms of trade. Short- and long-term capital movements may play a larger role in determining exchange rate activity, perhaps especially in a very small and very open economy such as New Zealand.

Frankel and Rose (2000) find econometrically that countries share a currency trade about three times more with each other than would be predicted by other factors in the gravity model, such as distance and relative size. Smith provides in the previous chapter of this book a careful critique of the data and methods behind this result, one aspect of which is the possible endogeneity of existing currency areas. It seems that we should not expect anything like a three-fold increase in trans-Tasman trade from monetary union, but these results do quite powerfully support the idea that sharing a currency can put a big dent in the border effect through making transactions easier and the size of resources devoted to transaction activities points fairly clearly to why this could be so. Economising on transaction costs is not just about, say, savings in trips to the bank to convert one currency into another. It seems to be much bigger than that: shared financial and regulatory institutions lead to a shared business and consumer culture which gives businesses the confidence to look further afield for partners to invest and deal with.

Plater and Claridge's (2000) list given at the beginning of this section is not, of course, exhaustive. There is more to policy than just economics and politics, narrowly defined. Thus, we could consider the possible integration of:

*   Social policies (benefits, pensions, etc.)
*   Policies relating to ethnicity and bi- or multi-culturalism
*   'Big-C' cultural policies (e.g., in broadcasting)[8]
*   Sporting integration
*   Environmental and genetic engineering policies

Naturally, these ideas give rise to some complicated issues.

9.5 CONCLUSION

Enthusiastic boosters of 'free' trade and globalisation – including most American-trained economists and all governments of New Zealand since 1984 – should worry about the border effect. The made-in-Washington, one-size-fits-all, 'McModel' (Hazledine, 1998) is an awkward fit with the pervasively strong national preferences implied by the own-country dummy variables in gravity trade models. There just does not seem to be enough left, after four decades of serious trade liberalisation that have reduced readily identifiable trade barriers to just a few percentage points, to account for the 20 or 30 percent tariff equivalents implied by border effects of ten or more. And we do not know whether the relatively low border effects between Australia and New Zealand calculated in this chapter represent good or bad news in terms of their implications for further integration.

It is true that border effects can be accommodated in models with 'Armington' national preferences (Head and Ries, 2001), but this just moves the question along to asking what could be the source of the non-replicable advantage domestic firms have in satisfying the tastes of their domestic customers. This chapter has not answered this question, but it does offer a suggestion in terms of transaction costs: people prefer, on the whole, to deal with others of the same ilk, because they can trust them. Then, they can escape from inferior prisoners' dilemma-type Nash equilibria and generate greater prosperity. The sources of this trust include opportunities to enforce cooperative behaviour through repeated interactions, as stressed – almost obsessively – by game theorists, which are clearly likely to decrease with distance. But perhaps even more important is the trust between strangers – between people who do not know each other and may not expect ever to meet again – which Fukuyama (1995) proposed as a prime source of the wealth of nations in his book on social capital. Such trust probably depends on people being similar enough in their tastes and values to be empathetic and sympathetic with each other, and it may be that modern nation states are most usefully seen from an economic perspective as voluntary grouping of like-minded souls into convenient aggregations or cultures.[9]

If so, then a determined programme to obliterate nations as serious economic entities – also known as globalisation – could be seriously misconceived. In terms of the banal but powerful metaphor of the 'level playing field', it is not just that nations want to tilt the playing field in favour of their national industries. They all do that (with a few exceptions, such as New Zealand), and not one more aggressively than the United States – indeed, globalisation would more accurately be termed Americanisation. The real point is that they may have sound *economic* reasons for doing so: that it is *efficient* for countries to play their own games with their own rules most (though not all) of the time. Perhaps the injunction to *laissez-faire* needs to be extended to *laissez-jouer*!

NOTES

1. Wei (1996) assumes that the average distance between people within an economy is equal to one-quarter the distance between the capital city of that region and the capital city of the closest neighbouring region.
2. Financial support from the Auckland University Research Committee is gratefully acknowledged. We also thank participants at the 2001 *Off the Map* Symposium in Wellington and an anonymous referee for his or her comments.
3. See Leamer and Storper (2001) for an interesting perspective on the role of geography on the location of economic activity.
4. Refinements could add to the trans-Tasman distances an allowance for the internal travel needed for the average person to access the nearest airports at departure and destination. Using the figure of 100 km at each end of the journey gives a typical New Zealand–Australia distance of about 2,500 km, which is six times the New Zealand internal distance.

5. Another source of bias operating in the same direction would be the 'remoteness' effect – the effect on any bilateral trade flow of the availability of alternative trading partners, as proxied by distance from these. New Zealand is probably the most remote country in the world; Australia might be next, but it is closer than New Zealand to all significant trading partners apart from those in the Americas. Greater remoteness should make New Zealand relatively keener to trade with its closest partner, Australia. However, note that Nitsch (2000) gets the wrong sign on the remoteness variable in his gravity model estimated for European economies.
6. For a useful survey of the issues on harmonisation of regulations, see Guerin (2001).
7. The New Zealand government has since weakened the requirement that a firm be adjudged 'dominant' in a market before it can be assumed capable of abusing market power, to the international (including Australia) standard of holding 'substantial' market power. But even under this standard we have the problem of the jurisdiction of competition policies being limited nationally, and of the policies not being required to take into account the interests of consumers and firms in the other country.
8. Big-C, or 'high' culture, refers to tangible cultural assets such as churches and historical sites, and intangible assets such as common values and identity. Such cultural assets can contribute to country competitiveness.
9. We can ask what might be the cultural differences between Australians and New Zealanders. Just to motivate this, look at differences in the characteristics of those who choose and succeed in immigrating to the two countries. It may be a large but not extreme simplification to apply the political scientist Seymour Martin Lipset's distinction between Canada and the United States to New Zealand and Australia (Lipset, 1996). Lipset noted that immigrants to Canada tend to be 'escaping from' (persecution, insecurity), whereas the USA attracts people 'escaping to' the American Dream. As support for this in the Anzac context, note Hazledine and Siegfried's (1997) finding that first-generation immigrants to New Zealand are no more likely than native-born Kiwis to show up on that country's 'Rich List', whereas in Australia immigrants are twice as likely as natives to amass large fortunes.

REFERENCES

Anderson, J.E. and E. van Wincoop (2001), 'Gravity with gravitas: a solution to the border puzzle', NBER Working Paper 8079.

Anderson, M.A. and S.L.S. Smith (2001), 'Information networks, hysteresis, and the border effect in international trade', paper presented to the American Economics Association meetings, New Orleans, January.

Frankel, J.A., Wei S.-J. and E. Stein (1995), 'APEC and regional trading arrangements in the Pacific', in W. Dobson and F. Flatters (eds), *Pacific Trade and Investment: Options for the 90s*, Kingston, Ontario: John Deutsch Institute, pp. 289-312.

Frankel, J.A. and A.K. Rose (2000), 'Estimating the effect of currency unions on trade and output', NBER Working Paper 7857.

Fukuyama, F. (1995), *Trust: The Social Virtues and the Creation of Prosperity*, London: Hamish Hamilton Ltd.

Grimes, A. and F. Holmes with R. Bowden (2000), *An ANZAC Dollar? Currency Union and Business Development*, Wellington: Victoria University of Wellington Institute of Policy Studies.

Grossman, G.M. (1998), 'Comment on Alan V. Deardoff "Determinants of bilateral trade: does gravity work in a neoclassical world?", in J.A. Frankel (ed.), *The Regionalization of the World Economy*, Chicago and London: University of Chicago Press.

Guerin, K. (2001), 'Regulatory harmonisation: issues for New Zealand', Wellington, NZ Treasury, Working Paper 01/01.

Hazledine, T. (1995), 'Comments on papers on formal and informal barriers to trade and investment', in W. Dobson and F. Flatters (eds), *Pacific Trade and Investment: Options for the 90s*, Kingston, Ontario: John Deutsch Institute, pp. 313-321.

Hazledine, T. (1998), *Taking New Zealand Seriously: The Economics of Decency*, Auckland: HarperCollins.

Hazledine, T. (2001), 'Measuring the New Zealand transaction sector, 1956–1998, with an Australian comparison', *New Zealand Economic Papers*, 35, 77-100.

Hazledine, T. and J. Siegfried (1997), 'How did the wealthiest New Zealanders get so rich?', *New Zealand Economic Papers*, 31, 35-47.

Head, K. and J. Ries (2001), 'Increasing returns versus national product differentiation as an explanation for the pattern of U.S.–Canada trade', *American Economic Review*, 91, 858-876.

Helliwell, J.F. (1996), 'Do national borders matter for Quebec's trade?', *Canadian Journal of Economics*, 29, 507-522.

Helliwell, J.F. (1998), *How Much Do National Borders Matter?*, Washington, DC: Brookings Institution Press.

Helliwell, J.F. and G. Verdier (2001), 'Measuring internal trade distances: a new method applied to estimate provincial border effects in Canada', *Canadian Journal of Economics*, 34, 1024-1041.

Leamer, E.E. and M. Storper (2001), 'The economic geography of the Internet Age', *Journal of International Business Studies*, 32(4), 641-665.

Lipset, S. M. (1996), *Continental Divide: The Values and Institutions of the United States and Canada*, New York: Routledge.

McCallum, J. (1995), 'National borders matter: Canada–US regional trade patterns', *American Economic Review*, 85, 615-623.

Nitsch, V. (2000), 'National borders and international trade: evidence from the European Union', *Canadian Journal of Economics*, 33, 1091-1105.

Plater, V. and M. Claridge (2000), 'Facts about economic integration: How integrated is New Zealand with the rest of the world?', Wellington, NZ Treasury, Working Paper 00/21.

Trefler, D. (2001), 'Recent developments in international economics', paper presented at the 2001 Canadian Economics Association Annual Conference, Montreal, 1 June.

Wei, S.-J. (1996), 'Intra-national versus international trade: how stubborn are nations in global integration?' NBER Working Paper 5531.

PART C

Strategies

10. Small States and Island States: Implications of Size, Location and Isolation for Prosperity

Harvey W. Armstrong and Robert Read

10.1 INTRODUCTION

This chapter considers issues relating to the economic performance of small states, sometimes referred to as 'micro-states', and islands.[1] Both of these types of economy have in the past been relatively neglected by academic research in spite of their prevalence in Western Europe, the Caribbean and Oceania. A significant proportion of all sovereign nations, however, can be regarded as being small and many of these small states are also islands or archipelagos. In addition, the data sets assembled by the authors also include a number of other small entities that, while not sovereign, possess an unusually high degree of political and/or economic autonomy. All told, the authors have identified a total of 109 such entities with populations less than 3 million and 105 for which data were available. Nevertheless, there are substantially more individual islands than this in the Pacific alone.

These substantial data sets have facilitated extensive empirical research into the determinants of the economic performance of small states (see, for example, Armstrong and Read, 1995, 2000; Armstrong et al., 1998). More recently, the focus of this research has been increasingly concerned with the nature of island economies and how 'islandness' affects the economic performance of small states. This includes a consideration of whether those islands that are sovereign small states have specific economic advantages that other islands lacking such sovereignty do not have. Examples of the latter are regions within large countries, such as Hokkaido in Japan. This chapter first examines the principal theoretical arguments that have been proposed in the past to explain why the economies of islands and small states face particular challenges (Section 10.2). This is followed in Section 10.3 by a review of some of the authors' main findings from their previous research on the determinants of growth in small states. This includes a discussion of the growth impact of small size and the contributions of industrial structure, islandness, sovereignty, location and aid to economic performance. Section 10.4 focuses specifically on the economic performance of islands. Some conclusions are drawn in Section 10.5

10.2 THEORETICAL ISSUES IN THE ECONOMIC PERFORMANCE OF SMALL STATES AND ISLANDS

It has long been recognised that small states face a distinctive mixture of challenges and opportunities in stimulating and sustaining the process of growth and economic development. As such, they have tended to be treated as a rather unusual set of economic entities in the research literature. Intriguingly, the analytical perspective of much of this literature is that the challenges and opportunities facing islands are virtually identical to those of small states. Indeed, although small island states might be regarded as a special and distinct subset of small states, the research literature often analyses islands to the exclusion of non-island small states. This apparent over-emphasis is partly a consequence of so many small states also being islands; some 67 of the 105 small entities in the author's own global data sets are either islands or archipelagos (see Table 10.1). It is also, however, almost certainly a reflection of a widespread view that islands, as small open economies, face many of the same challenges as small states generally.

10.2.1 Conceptual Issues

Before beginning the theoretical overview, it is useful to deal with several conceptual issues relating to the definition of size, what is meant by economic performance and the justification for including politically dependent entities in the data sets. Throughout this chapter, the term 'small states' is used to refer to those states with populations below 3 million. There is a general consensus in the research literature that population size is the most appropriate proxy measure of small size although the choice of threshold has been the source of a long-running and vigorous debate. Given that population size is effectively a continuous variable, any choice of threshold is essentially arbitrary, such that this debate is unlikely to be resolved in the near future. The authors' choice of a population threshold of 3 million is based solely on the existence of a natural break in the size distribution of small states and the resultant set of small states being sufficiently large to be amenable to robust statistical analysis. Most international institutions, including the UN and UNCTAD, use a threshold of 1 million although the Commonwealth uses one of 1.5 million. Other researchers refer to 'mini-states' as having a population of less than 5 million and 'micro-states' as having a population of less than 100,000 while for many political scientists, small states have populations of 10 million or less. This debate is summarised elsewhere (see Hein, 1985; Armstrong et al., 1996; Read, 2002).

Table 10.1 The global data set of small states and small island states[a]

Small island states (30 + 38)

Antigua & Barbuda	Bahamas	Barbados
Cape Verde	Comoros	Dominica
Fed. States Micronesia	Fiji	Grenada
Iceland	Jamaica	Kiribati
Marshall Islands	Maldives Malta	
Mauritius	Nauru	Palau
St. Kitts & Nevis	St. Lucia	St. Vincent &
Grenadines	Samoa	Singapore
Sao Tome & Principe		
Seychelles	Solomon Islands	Tonga
Trinidad & Tobago	Tuvalu	Vanuatu

Åland Islands (Fin)[b]	Am. Samoa (USA)	Anguilla (UK)
Aruba (NL)	Azores (P)	Bermuda (UK)
British Indian Ocean	British Virgin Islands	
Territory (UK)	(UK)	Canary Islands (E)
Cayman Islands (UK)	Christmas Islands (Aus)	Cocos Islands (Aus)
Cook Islands (NZ)	Falkland Islands (UK)	Faroe Islands (DK)
French Polynesia (F)	Greenland (DK)	Guadeloupe (F)
Guam (USA)	Guernsey (UK)	Isle of Man (UK)
Jersey (UK)	Madeira (P)	Martinique (F)
Mayotte (F)	Montserrat (UK)	Neth. Antilles (NL)
New Caledonia (F)	Niue (NZ)	Norfolk Island (Aus)

Table 10.1 (continued)

Northern Marianas (USA)	Reunion (F)	St. Helena & Dependencies (UK)
St. Pierre & Miquelon (F)	Tokelau (NZ)	Turks & Caicos Islands (UK)
US Virgin Islands (USA)	Wallis & Futuna (F)	

Small land-locked states (9 + 0)

Andorra	Bhutan	Botswana
Lesotho	Liechtenstein	Luxembourg
Mongolia	San Marino	Swaziland

Small littoral states (24 + 4)

Bahrain	Belize	Brunei
Congo, Republic	Djibouti	Estonia
Gabon	Gambia	Guinea-Bissau
Guyana	Kuwait	Latvia
Liberia	Macedonia, F.Y.R.	Mauritania
Monaco	Namibia	Oman
Panama	Qatar	Slovenia
Surinam	United Arab Emirates	West Bank & Gaza[b]
Ceuta & Melilla (E)	Gibraltar (UK)	Guiane (F)
Macao (P)		

Divided islands (3 + 0)

Cyprus, Republic	East Timor[b]	Turkish Republic of Northern Cyprus[b]

Other small (island & mainland) states (1 + 0)
Equatorial Guinea

Notes:
[a] The maximum size threshold is a population of 3 million. Politically sovereign small states are included separately from territories and other entities. Figures in parentheses indicate the number of sovereign states and territories respectively in each group
[b] These four states are additional to the original 105 included in the authors' global data set referred to in the text

Source: Based upon Armstrong and Read (2004).

'Economic performance' here refers to aggregate and per capita GDP/GNP values and their growth rates as well as, in some cases, unemployment rates. Although this is a very limited range of economic indicators, there are severe data limitations associated with empirical research in this subject area, whether at a regional or a global level, because the available data sets for many economic and other variables are neither comprehensive nor harmonised. Further, the smallest states and islands are the least likely to collect and publish such data because of resource constraints. Their omission from statistical analyses, however, introduces additional problems relating to truncated data sets and sample selection bias. Therefore, the better the coverage of small states and islands in the sample, the fewer the indicators available for statistical analysis.

It should also be noted that the data sets utilised by the authors include, along with fully sovereign small states, a number of other entities that possess an unusually high degree of political and economic autonomy even though they are strictly parts of larger states. These entities include the Faroe Islands in Europe (a dependency of Denmark) and the dependent territories of the former colonial powers such as France and the UK, including French Polynesia and St. Helena. These dependent territories are not sovereign states according to the UN definition but they do have their own elected political assemblies and, typically, also have greater economic policy discretion than the regions of larger states.

10.2.2 Small Size and Economic Performance

Until relatively recently, the general impression given by much of the theoretical literature was that small states, and islands in particular, encounter almost insuperable adverse economic conditions which inhibit their growth processes. In this case, small states and islands could be regarded as representing a group of states that are failing in some sense. On the contrary, however, the global set of small states contains within it some of the most successful countries with very high per capita income levels, such as Luxembourg and Singapore. Further, in some regions of the world where small states are abundant, such as Western Europe, there is evidence to indicate that most of these states outperform their larger state neighbours in economic terms (Armstrong and Read, 1994, 1995). Even at the global level, disproportionately fewer small states, including islands, are to be found in the World Bank's lowest income categories, Groups 1 and 2 (Armstrong et al., 1996, 1998). This suggests that small (population) size does not appear to be an insurmountable constraint on growth.

These findings are borne out by studies of growth rates as well as comparative levels of economic performance. Several studies reveal that the role of country size is generally insignificant (Chenery and Taylor, 1968; Kuznets, 1971; Chenery and Syrquin, 1975; Chenery et al., 1986), even when size variables are incorporated into formal growth models (Blazic-Metner and Hughes, 1982; Milner and Westaway, 1993; Armstrong et al., 1996, 1998; Milner and Weyman-Jones, 1998). These findings do not preclude the adverse effect of small size on growth but rather suggest that any such effects are insufficiently systematic to be significant. In this context, it is also noteworthy that the economic performance of many larger comparator states has been relatively poor, particularly that of other less developed countries and least developed countries. Nevertheless, these latter groups of states can be said to face broadly similar challenges to small states in terms of their low aggregate levels of domestic economic activity (Read, 2002).

In spite of the evidence of successful economic performance of many small states, it has long been recognised that they face formidable challenges. Their small size and high degree of openness make them particularly vulnerable to external forces of many kinds. The political and strategic vulnerability of small states has long been recognised (Blair, 1967; Vital, 1967; Wood, 1967; de Smith, 1970; Commonwealth Consultative Group, 1985; Harden, 1985; Clarke and Payne, 1987). In addition, small states are exposed to an array of external economic fluctuations that are usually beyond their control (Holmes, 1976; Bune, 1987; Pollard, 1987). Together with environmental and topographical factors, these may cause sudden and highly disruptive shock effects in a small land area (Briguglio, 1995; Atkins et al., 2000). The devastating effect of the 1997 volcanic eruption on the Caribbean island of Montserrat, the severe impact of the hurricanes in St. Lucia, St. Vincent and Vanuatu, and the evacuation of some islands in Tuvalu as a consequence of rising sea levels are recent examples of vulnerability.

10.2.3 The Economic Challenges of Small Size

The remainder of this chapter focuses exclusively on the economic challenges facing small states, including islands. The analytical literature highlights a number of different issues (summarised in Armstrong and Read, 1998, 2002a). Of particular importance is the challenge posed by the small size of the domestic market, especially for small island states or those located in geographically remote areas of the world (Knox, 1967). This causes problems for local manufacturers faced with levels of domestic demand lying below the minimum efficient scale of production as well as higher costs of inputs in the production process. R&D is also likely to be adversely affected by a small domestic market and so hinders both the development of indigenous technologies and the emergence of fast growth sectors (Kuznets, 1960; Selwyn, 1975; Thomas, 1982; Briguglio, 1995).

Small states with a small geographic area face additional challenges arising from their limited natural resource base, often coupled with an absolute scarcity of domestic capital. Those small states fortunate to be in possession of valuable natural resources might be expected to perform uniformly well. Caution needs to be exercised here, however, since a significant number of resource-rich countries, particularly those with 'point-source' resources, do not perform well – the 'resource curse' thesis (Auty, 1993). Further, other countries lacking a natural resource base can still perform spectacularly well, such as Singapore. Nevertheless, even among those small states with abundant natural resources, there may be difficulties associated with the undiversified nature of the available resources.

It is sometimes argued that a small geographic area also means that the agricultural sector 'crowds out' alternative economic activities because it absorbs such a high proportion of the available land area (Commonwealth Secretariat, 1996). The extent to which this is a problem is unclear, especially given that some small states have been able to rely upon imported agricultural products while simultaneously devoting their limited land area to higher-value added manufacturing and services. This has enabled small states, such as Malta and Singapore, to overcome successfully the problems associated with a limited land area.

It is clear that small states possess only a small domestic labour force, often in combination with a limited land area. This means that the standard role of the agricultural sector in structural transition, as the supplier of substantial quantities of low-productivity labour to a nascent technology-intensive larger-scale manufacturing sector, is not applicable (Lewis, 1955). A small population severely constrains the general feasibility of large-scale labour-intensive manufacturing, although it also implies the absence of a large and backward agricultural sector hindering the growth process. The scarcity of domestic labour imposes a critical constraint on the growth potential of low-cost labour-intensive industrialisation (Read, 2002) such that activities intensive in human capital, skills and physical capital are more likely to be the source of growth success in small states (Bhaduri et al., 1982).

In less developed small states, the scarcity of domestic employment opportunities has tended to result in out-migration and subsequent inflows of worker remittances – migration, remittances, aid and bureaucracy (MIRAB) economies (Bertram, 1986; see also Chapter 6 of this book). In more successful small states, the scarcity of particular specialist skills and of relatively unskilled labour has been resolved through significant (temporary) in-migration of labour. Nevertheless, the thinness of local labour markets means that even the most successful small states are highly susceptible to the effects of the brain drain on the availability of essential specialist skills.

The various constraints on small states, particularly islands, give rise to a tendency to focus on a narrow array of niche market products for export. Inevitably, the range of export products is likely to be very small, as will be the number of markets at which these exports can be targeted; both effects reinforce the vulnerability of small states to exogenous shocks. The instability of export prices and foreign exchange earnings are a particular problem and 'Dutch Disease' issues are an ever-present threat (Corden and Neary, 1982; MacBean and Nguyen, 1987). While the standard solution to such problems is diversification, the potential for this in small states is severely limited by the size of their domestic markets and the presence of scale economies.

The narrow range of goods and services, which can feasibly be sourced domestically in small states, gives rise to significant asymmetries between the patterns of production and consumption (Kuznets, 1960). This implies that small states have high levels of import dependence and that their domestic markets cannot be a major source of autonomous self-sustaining growth. Import-substituting industrialisation is unlikely to be an appropriate general development strategy for small states given its impacts on the domestic price level and the competitiveness of exporters through higher input prices. Small states must therefore out of necessity pursue highly open trade regimes and so are more likely to favour export-led growth strategies that entail a high degree of interaction with the international economy (Armstrong et al., 1998). There are substantial potential gains from trade for small states because of the large magnitude of their trade multipliers (Ashoff, 1989).

The structural openness of small states, however, greatly restricts their domestic macroeconomic policy options (Kuznets, 1960; Marcy, 1960; Scitovsky, 1960; Triffin, 1960). The risk asymmetry between import prices and export earnings has important implications for the balance of payments and growth (Erbo and Schiavo-Campo, 1969; Lloyd and Sundrum, 1982; Thirlwall, 1991). Further, the significance of foreign currency transactions also implies a high degree of international monetisation, severely constraining domestic monetary autonomy (Ally, 1975; Helleiner, 1982). Exchange rate variations are rarely successful under such circumstances and many small states therefore have either a fixed exchange rate link to a hard currency (e.g., Barbados, Cape Verde, Comoros, Lesotho) or are part of a hard currency area (e.g., Kiribati, Panama, Tuvalu) (Armstrong and Read, 1998, 2002b; Chadha, 2002). This provides insulation against external volatility at the cost of the loss of control of domestic interest rates and inflation, except if capital controls are used (Khatkhate and Short, 1980). Fiscal policy is also of limited value given the low multiplier effects of any spending and the risks associated with the flight of businesses and residents if domestic taxes are too high.

So far, the discussion has focused on the array of economic challenges faced by small states generally. The literature also identifies specific additional problems associated with small island states, although many are equally applicable to small land-locked states (Read, 2002). Islands are argued to experience greater transport costs, diseconomies in loads, routings and return shipments, and problems relating to competition and reliability in transport links (Armstrong et al., 1993). These problems are likely to be compounded where an island is part of a wider archipelago and also where there is a heavy dependency upon neighbouring larger states for access to export markets. The impact of these problems on island production, consumption and welfare is similar to that of a tariff; it may be less costly to produce certain additional goods and services locally, albeit at higher prices. However, the magnitude of this 'tariff' effect should be declining given rapidly falling sea and air transport costs.

This discussion of the challenges faced by small states and islands raises the question as to how so many of them have been able to prosper. Part of the explanation may lie in the fact that they have simply had no choice but to pursue an open, highly competitive trade regime. In this way, they have therefore avoided the protectionist trap of indiscriminate import substitution that has hindered the growth of many larger developing countries (Chai, 1998). Uncompetitive firms disappear rapidly and only the most successful niche market businesses are able to survive.

A distinctive feature of many small states and islands, as well as highly autonomous regions, has been their ability to utilise their smallness advantageously; the 'importance of being unimportant' (Demas, 1965). This applies to many aspects of the growth strategies of small states, including their engagement in international political economy and the pursuit of niche markets based upon innovative regulatory regimes and unique or distinctive assets (Kakazu, 1994; Armstrong and Read, 2002b). Many small states have developed offshore financial services centres, aided by a flexible framework of domestic financial, environmental and commercial registration regulations (see Hampton and Abbott, 1999; Cobb, 2001) and successful international tourism industries, based upon their distinctive environmental and cultural assets.

There is a growing debate as to whether there are advantages in economic management associated with being small. Arguably, governments can respond more quickly to economic change and particular strengths may arise from the accumulation of social capital within small states and on islands. These would resemble the networks of trust and norms of reciprocity that are found in some successful sub-national regions (Putnam et al., 1993). Nevertheless, the frequency of direct contact between decision makers and their constituents may encourage nepotism and clientelism. In small states and islands, the clash of personalities, combined with limited opportunities to dilute them, may also impede policy making.

In the face of the evident challenges constraining the growth and development of small states and islands, particular concern was expressed during the decolonisation process that many dependent territories were too small to be viable as independent states. The preferred solution, for the UK at least, was that the smaller dependent territories should therefore be incorporated into larger entities or federations prior to independence being granted (Labour Party, 1957; Blood, 1958; Benedict, 1967). The result was the creation, and subsequent disintegration, of the West Indian Federation, the Malay Federation, from which Singapore subsequently withdrew, and more recently St. Kitts & Nevis, from which the latter has recently attempted to extricate itself. The size bias in the decolonisation process has been such that many of the very smallest and most remote dependent territories still await independence (e.g., the Cayman Islands, St. Helena and the Turks & Caicos Islands). It is perhaps revealing that no small states have voluntarily chosen absorption or confederation within larger entities; for many, economic viability was a non-issue compared with the desire for their own separate identity, independence and self-determination (Abbott, 1975). The pessimism of the 1950s and 1960s concerning the economic viability of small states has, subsequently, been superseded post-independence by the sustained growth success of many of them.

10.3 THE DETERMINANTS OF THE ECONOMIC PERFORMANCE OF SMALL STATES

The preceding discussion raises important issues concerning the impact of the size constraints outlined on the actual growth performance of small states. This section reviews some of the critical growth issues and the empirical evidence relating to the principal determinants of economic growth in small states.

10.3.1 Data and Methodological Issues

Substantial data and methodological problems are involved in seeking to undertake a systematic analysis of the economic performance of small states and small islands:

- The collection of relatively simple economic indicators, such as GNP per capita, is severely hampered by the exclusion of the smallest states from the main international data sets, such as the World Bank data, resulting in truncated data sets. The tendency to exclude the smallest states, those likely to face the most severe challenges of small size, also introduces potential systematic bias.
- The need for comprehensive data sets to overcome the problems of truncation often means that the additional information is unsuitable for the creation of continuous data sets, particularly given that many of the statistics are not harmonised. One way around this problem is to develop ordinal or binary data sets along the lines of the World Bank's use of four categories to classify annual GNP per capita for many small states.
- It is not always possible to develop a data set in which all of the indicators refer to the same year, such that data for the nearest available year have to be used instead.

The research by the authors reported in this chapter is based upon the collection of data for a set of some 105 small states and territories, many of which are islands. These are listed, together with four recent additions, in Table 10.1. The data sets have been assembled from a variety of sources, including the United Nations *Statistical Yearbook*, World Bank *World Development Reports*, IMF *International Financial Statistics*, International Labour Organisation statistics and the Commonwealth Secretariat's *Small States: Economic Review & Basic Statistics*. In addition, considerable amounts of information were collected directly from the individual states, especially the smallest ones.

The following strategies have been adopted to deal with the unusually difficult nature of the data available for small states and islands:

- Information has been collected directly from small states where necessary.
- Checks for robustness of the research results have been undertaken wherever possible by re-running analyses with alternative data sets where data are more reliable and continuous in nature.

- Wherever possible, assumptions have been made which are least favourable for the hypotheses being tested, such that the 'dice have been loaded' against the principal hypotheses.
- Techniques appropriate for grouped, ordinal and binary data sets have been sought and used. These inevitably require classificatory methods rather than causal analysis (e.g., cluster analysis and discriminant analysis) and the use of limited dependent variable techniques.
- When all else has failed, the results have been qualified as carefully as possible to take account of biases introduced by the data limitations.

10.3.2 Is Small Size a Disadvantage?

The appropriate starting point for an investigation of the disadvantages of small size is perhaps to consider the general conclusions of much of the previous research literature on the subject and test the hypothesis that small size has a detrimental effect on the economic performance of countries.

The detrimental effects of small size can be readily examined with respect to per capita income levels by referring initially to data drawn from the World Bank's *World Development Indicators* CD ROM. The World Bank uses a four-fold categorisation of GNP per capita values for all states and the relative frequency of the appearance of small and larger states in the particular income groups, based upon the 3 million population benchmark, can be compared (see Table 10.2). The evidence in Table 10.2 suggests that small size does not appear to have a detrimental effect on economic performance, at least with respect to per capita income levels. In fact, it is clear from the table that a relatively greater proportion of small states than large states are to be found in both the upper middle and high income categories (61 percent in total as opposed to 43.8 percent). Further, it can be seen that the proportion of small island states in the top three income categories is even greater than that of all small states. The table only provides a summary view and the data set itself suffers from truncation owing to the exclusion of many of the smallest states. Nonetheless, the available information runs counter to the preconceptions of the literature.

An important problem with making this type of direct comparison between small and larger states is that the former are not uniformly distributed around the globe. There are a disproportionate number of small states in Western Europe, a relatively prosperous global region, but also in the Caribbean, Pacific and Sub-Saharan Africa, which are relatively less prosperous. The summary results of an attempt to standardise for regional location and concentration are presented in Table 10.3 for those small states in the data set for which harmonised data are available. The table compares the GNP per capita of each small state and the average GNP per capita values of contiguous countries. It is clear that a significant proportion of small states perform very well relative to adjacent countries. Table 10.3 also demonstrates the use of alternative data sets, including GNP in $US and at PPP $US, to examine further the robustness of the principal research findings. These findings reveal that overall comparisons, such as those undertaken in Table 10.2, tend to understate the actual magnitude of the economic performance of small states because so many of them are located in less prosperous global regions.

Turning to the issue of whether the size of a country influences its rate of growth as well as its level of GNP per capita, the empirical evidence again suggests that small size does not appear to be a major impediment. The inadequate data available for the appropriate explanatory variables for small states means that it is only possible to use a Barro-type conditional convergence growth model rather than more sophisticated models, such as those for endogenous growth. The Barro model is very similar to the types of models run for sub-national regions in the United States, the EU and elsewhere (Barro, 1991; Barro and Sala-i-Martin, 1992, 1995). Even so, it is only possible to run these regressions utilising (global) regional dummy variables as proxies for an array of 'conditioning' variables. The striking results of this exercise, drawn from Armstrong et al. (1998, Table 1), show that in spite of these restrictions, the introduction of a country size variable (*'Population'*) barely improves the fit of the model (the R^2 rises from 0.51 to 0.52). Further, the size variable is significant at neither the 95 percent nor the 99 percent levels. Nevertheless, most of the other variables (initial 1980 per capita income levels, economic structure and regional dummies) are highly significant, bearing out the results of other analyses of the influence of country size on growth (e.g., Kuznets, 1971; Chenery and Syrquin, 1975; Milner and Westaway, 1993; Milner and Weyman-Jones, 1998).

10.3.3 The Principal Determinants of the Economic Performance of Small States

In spite of an extensive and often discursive literature on the comparative economic performance of small economies, particularly small island states, and larger ones, very little attention has been paid to the determinants of the differential economic performance between small states. The magnitude of these differences in performance is as substantial, if not greater, than between large states. The empirical investigation of this differential economic performance, however, has been hampered by the lack of clear theoretical models of their growth.

Table 10.2 Classification of large and small states by GNP per capita band, 2000 (current $US)

World Bank per capita income group	Total		Large states		Small states		Small Islands	
	No.	Share (%)	No.	Share (%)	No.	Share (%)	No.	Share (%)
Low income (<$755)	63	30.3	52	49.2	11	13.4	2	4.5
Lower middle income ($756–$2,995)	54	26.0	33	31.1	21	25.6	12	27.3
Upper middle income ($2,996–$9,265)	38	18.3	18	17.0	20	24.4	13	29.5
High income (>$9,266)	53	25.5	23	21.7	30	36.6	17	38.6
All	208	100.0	106	100.0	82	100.0	44	100.0

Note: The 'small islands' group is a sub-group of the 'small states' group. World Bank per capita income group data are only available for 208 states. Four sovereign small states are omitted from the exercise (East Timor, Nauru, TR North Cyprus and Tuvalu), as are 25 small territories

Source: World Bank, *World Development Indicators 2002*, CD ROM

Table 10.3 Small states with higher GNP per capita than adjacent countries, 1991 and 1994[a]

World Bank region[b]	UN PPP 1991 ($US)			WB 1994 ($US)			WB PPP 1994 ($US)		
	Total	No.	Share (%)	Total	No.	Share (%)	Total	No.	Share (%)
Sub-Saharan Africa (20)	16	10	62.5	15	7	46.7	11	6	54.5
South Asia (5)	1	0	0.0	2	1	50.0	1	0	0.0
Middle East & North Africa (8)	5	5	100.0	4	4	100.0	4	3	75.0
Eastern Europe (4)	–	–	–	3	0	0.0	3	0	0.0
Latin America & Caribbean (26)	11	4	36.4	14	5	35.7	6	2	33.3
East Asia & Pacific (26)	6	3	50.0	8	3	37.5	4	2	50.0
Western Europe (13)	4	3	75.0	3	3	100.0	3	3	100.0
North America (3)	1	1	100.0	–	–	–	–	–	–
All small states (105)	44	26	59.1	49	23	46.9	32	16	50.0

Notes: [a] Adjacent country averages are population-weighted GNP per capita values
      [b] Figures in parentheses indicate total number of small states. Column totals for those small states for which data are available
Sources: World Bank, *World Development Reports* and CD ROMs, 1995 and 1996, Tables 1, 1a; United Nations, *39th Statistical Yearbook*, Table 24

The identification of openness to trade and human capital accumulation as being of critical importance to the growth of small states and islands, as discussed in Section 10.2, suggests that the application of endogenous growth theory models might be appropriate (Armstrong and Read, 2002a). However, this potentially rewarding empirical approach is seriously hampered by the problems of data availability and harmonisation mentioned earlier that are a feature of small states.

The severe difficulties associated with applying large-scale growth models to small states have required the use of alternative methodological approaches and the development of a range of variables which are appropriate to the examination of their comparative economic performance in terms of GNP per capita.

Industrial structure

A persistent theme of the existing theoretical and conceptual literature on small states is that, as extremely open economies with tightly constrained indigenous resources (labour, land, etc.), they are forced to develop niche market activities which must be globally, or at least regionally, competitive. This strategy is aided by their ability to tailor legal, fiscal and other regulations to attract and develop niche sectors (e.g., offshore financial services) – that is, 'the importance of being unimportant'. The effect of industrial structure on the economic performance of small states is investigated using general sectoral variables for agriculture, manufacturing, financial services and tourism. This approach resembles the structural typology approach adopted by UNCTAD (1997) and developed further in Armstrong and Read (1998). The broad nature of these variables does not enable the identification of the precise niche markets in individual small states. For example, it would be very useful to be able to distinguish between those small states specialising in cruise tourism, package holidays, cultural tourism, and so on. A similar argument also applies to the types of niche manufacturing, financial services and agriculture. The precise definition of the sectoral variables used in the empirical analyses reported here is discussed in Armstrong et al. (1998). The development of more refined sectoral structure variables is being addressed as part of the authors' ongoing research – *a priori*, agriculture is expected to have a negative relationship with GNP per capita while financial services, manufacturing and tourism are expected to have a positive relationship.

Island status

An island variable is included explicitly in the empirical analysis given the importance that island status is accorded in the literature in terms of the additional economic challenges that they face. The island variable that is used is a simple binary variable – island status is expected *a priori* to have a negative relationship with GNP per capita. The results for the island status variable are discussed in greater detail in Section 10.4.

Global region

Although most small states are highly open to international trade, they are typically heavily dependent upon trade with larger neighbouring states. For those small states for which good trade statistics exist, it is also clear that they are rarely fully globalised. Instead, they tend to have much closer links with other countries within their own particular global region than with the wider international economy – that is, they are 'regionalised' rather than truly 'globalised' economies. The economic performance of a small state is therefore likely to depend crucially upon the economic well being of its own immediate global region. A regional variable, using the World Bank definitions of global regions, is therefore incorporated to pick up any such effects on economic performance – this variable is expected *a priori* to have a positive relationship with GNP per capita.

Political sovereignty

The data set of small states being utilised in the empirical analyses includes both dependent territories and some highly autonomous regions of larger countries. A sovereignty variable is therefore included to differentiate between small states that are politically sovereign, according to the UN definition, and dependent territories and regions. This permits the investigation of whether there is any systematic bias in the economic performance of small states resulting from political sovereignty. *A priori*, the relationship between sovereignty and GNP per capita is unclear.

Natural resource endowment

A resource variable is included to pick up those cases where a small state is fortunate enough to possess a high-value natural resource endowment. In general, this variable is expected *a priori* to exhibit a positive relationship with GNP per capita unless support is found for the 'resource curse' thesis, in which case it could be negative.

Overseas aid inflows

Many small developing states are recipients of significant inflows of overseas aid – as are dependent territories and highly autonomous regions, regardless of their per capita incomes. Using OECD data on the value of overseas development funds per capita (OECD, 1997), aid is expected *a priori* to have a positive relationship with GNP per capita.

10.3.4 Discriminant Analysis Results of the Determinants of Small States' Economic Performance

The results of a discriminant analysis of GNP per capita among small states are summarised in Table 10.4 using the World Bank's four GNP per capita classificatory groups (Armstrong and Read, 2000). Data Set 1 refers to the data set including the highly autonomous regions of larger states and these are excluded in Data Set 2. In each case, the results are presented separately for World Bank GNP per capita data, encompassing 80 of the 105 small states and dependent territories, and for the authors' own classification using the full data set of 105 entities.

The discriminant analysis uses a conventional step-wise Wilks' lambda algorithm to select the independent variables in order of importance in the final discriminant classification. The order in which the variables enter the analysis, and therefore their relative importance, is given in parentheses in the central section of the table. Where a variable fails to meet a minimum F-to-enter criterion, it is excluded from the analysis, indicated by 'Excluded' at appropriate points in Table 10.4. The standardised canonical discriminant coefficients in the top part of the table are the b coefficients in the discriminant function and are similar to partial regression coefficients. The 'Fit of model – Wilks' lambda' coefficients in the central part of Table 10.4 show the significance of each variable in the final discriminant function. The various diagnostics show the overall degree of fit of the discriminant classification. The overall results of the discriminant analysis are generally very good in that the canonical correlations range from 0.81 to 0.86 and the eigenvalue, chi-square and Wilks' lambda tests all suggest that the independent variables are good classifiers of small states into the four GNP per capita groups.

With respect to the roles of each of the individual variables, the standardised canonical discriminant coefficients, shown in the top portion of the table, reveal a distinctive set of relationships. The region variable (*REGION*) is found to have a strongly positive relationship with GNP per capita and generally enters the function at the second or third round of the step-wise process, indicating that it plays a major role in the classification process. This supports the *a priori* view that the global region in which a small state is located has an influential impact on its GNP per capita, in spite of the globalisation process.

In contrast, the island status variable (*ISLAND*) is found to have coefficient that is sometimes negative and sometimes positive. It also enters the function only at a late stage, usually fifth or sixth, and generally has a weak role in explaining per capita GNP in spite of *a priori* reasoning. The tourism variable (*TOURISM*), however, is invariably found to have both an

Table 10.4 *Discriminant analysis results on income per capita for small states, 1994[a]*

Estimated characteristics	Data Set 1		Data Set 2	
	World Bank groups 1994	Authors' groups 1994	World Bank groups 1994	Authors' groups 1994

Standardised canonical discriminant coefficients[b]

REGION	0.38871	0.26286	0.43484	0.35427
ISLAND	0.00405	−0.05292	0.04763	−0.01101
TOURISM	0.64444	0.61704	0.59528	0.57451
AGRIC	−0.58533	−0.56475	−0.60430	−0.54938
RESOUR	0.63925	0.58258	0.61404	0.56179
FINAN	0.18958	0.24905	0.20185	0.29647
MANFG	Excluded	Excluded	Excluded	Excluded
SOVRT	−0.38753	−0.44138	−0.32563	−0.30212

Fit of model – Wilks' lambda

REGION	0.31664 (3)	0.41058 (3)	0.31099 (3)	0.48904 (2)

Table 10.4 (continued)

ISLAND	0.18534 (6)	0.29493 (5)	0.21621 (5)	0.33128 (4)
TOURISM	0.56856 (1)	0.62081 (1)	0.52848 (1)	0.59031 (1)
AGRIC	0.42792 (2)	0.50470 (2)	0.40554 (2)	0.30319 (3)
RESOUR	0.25250 (4)	0.34905 (4)	0.25485 (4)	0.27856 (5)
FINAN	0.15980 (7)	0.22873 (7)	0.18955 (6)	0.24016 (6)
MANFG	Excluded	Excluded	Excluded	Excluded
SOVRT	0.21685 (5)	0.26192 (6)	0.16917 (7)	0.22413 (7)

Eigenvalue[c]	2.8154	1.8813	2.6991	1.8643
Canonical correlation[d]	0.86	0.81	0.85	0.81
Chi-square[e]	36.366	41.069	33.986	41.441
	(p=0.0003)	(p=0.0000)	(p=0.0007)	(p=0.0000)

Table 10.4 (continued)

Wilks' lambda	0.6097	0.6591	0.6258	0.6420
Classification success (%)				
Overall	81.3	73.3	82.3	74.0
Low Income	81.8	92.3	81.8	92.3
Lower middle inc.	80.8	70.6	84.6	67.6
Upper middle inc.	63.6	70.0	77.3	71.4
Upper income	90.5	71.4	85.0	76.0
No. of small states	80	105	79	100

Notes:
a   The analysis is constructed using a step-wise Wilks' lambda method: to a maximum of three functions, results being shown for function 1 (accounting for 83.3% of the variance in the column 2 model and 80.1% in column 3). Variables entering the function must satisfy tolerance level and F-to-enter criteria, where the maximum tolerance level is 0.001 and minimum F-to-enter is 1.00. Selection rule is to maximise Wilks' lambda. Variables not selected are shown in the table as 'excluded'
b   Standardised canonical discriminant coefficients are similar, but not identical, to regression coefficients
c   Eigenvalues measure the ratio of the between-group sums of squares to the total sum of squares. Large eigenvalues therefore imply a 'good' discriminant function
d   In a two-group case, the canonical correlation is equivalent to the value of the Pearson correlation coefficient between the discriminant score and the binary group variable. A value close to 1.00 is therefore to be preferred
e   The chi-square test is derived from Wilks' lambda and tests for the significance (shown in parentheses in the table) of differences between group means

Source: Armstrong and Read (2000), Table 2.

important and a strongly positive relationship with GNP per capita in accord with the *a priori* view.

Agriculture (*AGRIC*) also accords with *a priori* reasoning in that its relationship is found to be strongly negative. Both natural resources and financial services (*RESOUR* and *FINAN*) are also found to have important positive influences on per capita GNP and conform to *a priori* reasoning. For natural resources, this suggests a general rejection of the applicability of the resource curse thesis to the case of small states. Manufacturing (*MANFG*), however, is regularly excluded from the analysis and appears to have no significant effect on GNP per capita. Perhaps surprisingly, political sovereignty (*SOVRT*) has a consistently negative sign in spite of the inclusion in the discriminant function of an array of other key variables known to affect the GNP per capita of small states. Dependent territories appear therefore, *ceteris paribus*, to enjoy higher GNP per capita values than their small politically sovereign counterparts. These results are consistent with those reported by Bertram and Karagedikli in Chapter 6.

10.3.5 Grouped Censored Regression Results of Small States' Economic Performance

Discriminant analysis is a useful exploratory tool but it lacks the explanatory power of regression analysis as a classificatory technique. The grouped nature of the World Bank classification of states by GNP per capita, however, makes causal analysis a difficult task. Since the dependent variable is available in four per capita GNP classes, a censored regression model can be used, of which grouped data regression is an appropriate approach of the range of limited dependent variable models. The dependent variable is GNP per capita while the independent variables are the same as those above. In each run of the model, the column headed 'coefficient' gives the partial regression coefficients, the next column reports the asymptotic t-ratios and 'prob' gives the significance of each coefficient; N refers to the number of observations.

Grouped censored regressions were originally run for the two data sets included in the discriminant analysis (Table 10.4) and were then re-run for those entities for which data on aid flows were available. Comparative data are available on net disbursements of official development assistance from all sources, including bilateral and multilateral aid as well as grants from metropolitan countries, for 76 entities in the global small states data set (for 22 out of 41 dependent territories and 54 out of 64 sovereign states). The regression results for the two original data sets are reported in Table 3 of Armstrong and Read (2000) while the second set of results, which includes the *ODAPC* variable, which measures overseas development assistance per capita, are reproduced here in Table 10.5.

The general results of all of the grouped censored regressions are broadly similar. The signs and t-ratios for the coefficients of most of the various explanatory variables are not greatly changed by the addition of an extra explanatory variable (*ODAPC*) or the use of a 76-entity data set. This again demonstrates the robustness of the model being utilised. In both versions of the model, the political sovereignty variable (*SOVRT*) is again found to have a negative explanatory relationship with GNP per capita, such that dependent territories generally appear to have higher GNP per capita values. This result holds even when the autonomous regions are excluded (Armstrong and Read, 2000, Table 3, Part B) although only at the 90 percent level of significance.

The apparent robustness of the negative coefficient of the political sovereignty variable in the analytical results is an unexpected finding but one confirmed by the more recent results presented in Chapter 6.

Table 10.5   Determinants of GNP per capita in small states: censored (grouped) regression results, incorporating aid flows

Independent variables	Coefficient	t-ratio	prob.
Constant	2,131.00	1.68	0.094
REGION	427.02	2.07	0.039
ISLAND	195.32	0.24	0.814
TOURISM	1,873.60	4.15	0.000
AGRIC	-2,890.70	-3.66	0.000
RESOUR	3,328.70	3.97	0.000
FINAN	1,675.80	2.20	0.028
MANFG	36.98	0.05	0.963
SOVRT	-2,405.80	-3.12	0.002
ODAPC	-0.22	-1.20	0.229
N	76		
Log-likelihood	66.051		

Note: These results were estimated using the LIMDEP7 software package, with grouped data regression being estimated using maximum likelihood procedures. Limits to the groups in this regression are those of the World Bank's GNP per capita classes (i.e., under \$725, \$726–2,895, \$2,896–\$8,955 and \$8,956 and over).

Source: Armstrong and Read (2000), Table 4.

In the first instance, one possibly compelling explanation for this negative relationship is that dependent territories are the recipients of substantially greater transfers of aid on a per capita basis, primarily from their respective metropolitan countries, than are politically sovereign small states. The partial regression coefficient on the aid variable, *ODAPC*, in Table 10.5, however, is found to have a negative sign although its level of significance is low (p = 0.229). Taking into account transfers of aid, particularly with respect to levels of GNP per capita in dependent territories, does not lead to any significant changes in the overall findings of the determinants of the economic performance of small states.

All of the grouped censored regression results indicate once again that the global region within which a small state is located (*REGION*) is of great importance. This finding also applies to the ability of small states to develop a strong domestic economic base founded upon tourism, financial services and/or natural resource exploitation (*TOURISM, FINAN* and *RESOUR*). In contrast, a large agricultural sector (*AGRIC*) is again found to be a clear handicap. All of these explanatory variables are significant at both the 5 and 1 percent levels and are also robust across the various data sets used. The manufacturing variable (*MANFG*) is invariably found to have a weak explanatory impact and, in the initial regression (excluding *ODAPC*), it has a consistently negative sign that is at variance with a priori expectations. With the inclusion of the *ODAPC* variable, its sign becomes positive although its explanatory impact remains insignificant. Island status is also found to have a consistently negative sign in the initial regressions, in accord with *a priori* expectations, although with a weak explanatory impact. Again, its sign changes with the inclusion of the *ODAPC* variable, this time to positive, but it again has weak explanatory power and is insignificant.

10.3.6 Optimal Endogenous Economic Policies and the Strategic Behaviour of Small States

The discussion of sovereignty suggests that explanations of the growth performance of small states should also pay attention to the effectiveness of endogenous policy formulation, particularly in the context of how these policies may, at least partially, offset some of the constraints imposed by their size. While the implementation of some such policies may be easily observable, they are not readily measurable although Lal's political sovereignty typology of states offers some insights (Lal, 1995). Further insights into the endogenous growth strategies of small states can also be derived from consideration of economic as opposed to political sovereignty. This refers specifically to small states' effective jurisdiction over domestic economic policy formulation and implementation and, as such, should therefore be regarded as being distinct from and possibly independent of political sovereignty.

The international political economy dimension of this discussion relates to the scope for states to engage in opportunistic behaviour driven by national self-interest. The potential for small states to engage in such strategic free-riding and rent-seeking behaviour internationally arises primarily as a consequence of their relative global insignificance. This may give rise to significant benefits and/or earn substantial rents at relatively low cost (see Kakazu, 1994; Armstrong and Read, 2002b).

10.3.7 Vulnerability and the Growth of Small States

There has, until recently, been relatively little empirical analysis of the impact of vulnerability on the growth of small states. The primary hypothesis of the vulnerability literature is that the growth of small states experiences disproportionately greater instability than that of larger states, such that they have lower long-run trend rates of growth together with greater short-run volatility around this trend than larger states. The impact of any exogenous shocks will be exacerbated if domestic resources are insufficient to assuage any deleterious effects.

Vulnerability as a concept is relatively simple but its measurement and the analysis of its impact on growth are fraught with difficulty. Although the principal sources of vulnerability are political and environmental as well as economic, data limitations mean that the principal measures tend to be economic variables. Several measures of vulnerability, however, have been developed in the form of composite indices, following Briguglio (1995), including those for the Commonwealth Secretariat (Easter, 1999; Atkins et al., 2000) and the United Nations (2000). A critique of these approaches can be found in Read (2000). Initial empirical analysis of the relationship between vulnerability and growth in small states finds a significantly positive relationship (Armstrong and Read, 2002c). This can be explained primarily because openness to trade, as measured by the share of trade in GDP or GNP, is used as a proxy for economic vulnerability and assigned a significant weight in the index being utilised (that of Briguglio). Given the critical importance of the vulnerability issue to small developing states, particularly islands, and its incorporation into discussions being undertaken by the UN and WTO, further rigorous and more comprehensive analysis of its impact on growth is necessary.

10.3.8 The Regional Location of Small States Revisited

It is useful to report some additional empirical findings with respect to the comparative analysis of the growth performance of small states in Sub-Saharan Africa and the Asia/Pacific region utilising both the discriminant analysis and censored regression techniques summarised earlier. This investigation finds strong evidence to support the view that the growth of these small states has similar determinants and is in accord with those used in the empirical work reported earlier in this section (Armstrong and Read, 2001). Further, the relatively low GNP per capita levels of the small states in Sub-Saharan Africa are found to be primarily the result of their location within a broader region characterised by low incomes and sluggish growth;

in other words, there is no support for a distinct 'Africa effect' (see Sachs and Warner, 1997; Collier and Gunning, 1999).

10.4 'ISLANDNESS' AS A DETERMINANT OF ECONOMIC PERFORMANCE

Much of the literature on small states, reviewed in Section 10.2, focuses primarily on small island states; this is not particularly surprising given that most small states are either islands or archipelagos. The general tenor of this literature is that the specific topography of islandness is an additional challenge over and above those relating to the problems of small size, notably the effects of remoteness and isolation on transport and communications. Given the pessimism of the traditional literature with respect to the economic challenges faced by small states in general, it is perhaps unsurprising that this view is further compounded with respect to island status.

Empirical research on small states, both by the authors and others, suggests that their response to the economic challenges they face is much stronger than that hypothesised by the rather pessimistic traditional literature. It is therefore pertinent to consider whether the traditional view concerning the implications of the economic challenges facing island may also be unduly pessimistic. Further, the particular problems associated with transport links for islands, including transport costs, reliability and imbalances between on- and off-island freight flows, are beginning to be challenged. There is evidence from Europe that the impact of transport barriers may well have been exaggerated in the research literature (see, for example, Armstrong et al., 1993). Moreover, international unit transport costs have been falling consistently for many years as a result of improvements in transport infrastructure, scale economies and innovation in both transport and within manufacturing, all of which have reduced costs.

The impact of islandness on growth is investigated as part of the authors' research on the economic performance of small states in Western Europe (Armstrong and Read, 1995) and at a global level (Armstrong and Read, 2000), utilising simple binary variables. These empirical results begin to shed some light on the impact of islandness on the performance of small island states, which form a substantial subset of all small states. This subset of small states includes many islands that are very remote from the main regional and global markets such that this analytical approach probably tends to over-estimate the impact of 'islandness'. Unlike the case of Western Europe where they are effectively inshore, the global set of small island states is dominated by islands that are distinctly offshore.

The empirical studies of small states, both in Western Europe and at the global level, tend to confirm the *a priori* view that islandness is negatively associated with economic growth although the relationship appears to be quite weak. The discriminant analysis results for Western Europe and the global data set show that the island variable is generally negative and has a low significance, appearing very late in the step-wise model. In two specific cases using the World Bank global data set, however, the relationship is found to be weakly positive regardless of whether autonomous regions are included or excluded (Armstrong and Read, 2000). In the censored regression results, the island variable is found to have a consistently negative sign although the *t*-ratios show that it never attains a 10 percent level of significance and is significant at the 15 percent level only once. When overseas aid flows are included in the model, the coefficient of the island variable becomes positive but is not significant at either the 5 or 10 percent levels. These results are also confirmed by an investigation of the impact of vulnerability on the economic performance of small states (Armstrong and Read, 2002c).

These empirical results therefore suggest that island status does appear to be negatively related to economic performance but that its adverse impact is considerably weaker than is generally presumed in the literature. This is the case in spite of the small states data set including a large number of some of the world's most geographically isolated island states and dependent territories, particularly those in the Pacific. One possible explanation for this unexpected result is that the data set only includes small states such that the advantages of being a small state generally outweigh the disadvantages associated with island status. While this explanation has a certain appeal, it would also suggest that the advantages of small states must be very substantial indeed to overcome the challenges faced by many of the remote small islands in the data set. A more logical and compelling alternative explanation is that the challenges of small size per se tend to dominate those of small islands such that the latter should be regarded as a special subset of small states generally rather than as a separate and discrete set of entities.

More recent empirical work focuses on the role of island status in economic performance with respect to European regions using the REGIO database which has harmonised statistics for both the present EU and the acceding Central and Eastern European states (Armstrong and Read, 2003). Further, some of these acceding countries are themselves islands and/or small states – Cyprus, Malta, Estonia, Latvia, Lithuania and Slovenia. Using a similar analytical methodology to Armstrong and Read (1995), 11 small states out of 16 are found to have higher levels of GDP per capita and lower unemployment than adjacent EU regions while the remaining 5 have lower levels of per capita GDP but also lower rates of unemployment. None of these small states therefore have lower GDP per capita and higher unemployment than their adjacent neighbouring regions. Of the 25 EU islands with no special autonomy, 11 are found to have lower GDP per capita levels and higher rates of unemployment than the adjacent EU regions and a further six have lower GDP per capita but relatively low unemployment rates. The remaining eight islands resemble the majority of small states in that they have both higher GDP per capita and lower unemployment than their adjacent regional counterparts. The highly autonomous regions, including for example the Faroe Islands, more closely resemble the small states group than the islands group in that, while only half have higher per capita GDP levels, all have lower unemployment rates than their adjacent EU regions.

These results lend further support to the view that sovereign small states and highly autonomous regions, in Europe at least, enjoy distinct economic advantages over adjacent regions that are revealed in the form of relatively high levels of GDP per capita and/or lower rates of unemployment. Island status alone does not appear to be a pre-condition for poor economic performance although the evidence suggests that there is much greater variation in their performance in terms of relative GDP per capita and unemployment. Many of the better performers in terms of unemployment are Mediterranean islands, notably those in Greece, which specialise in tourism. The greater similarity of the economic performance of autonomous regions to that of the small states group suggests that autonomy confers additional advantages.

10.5 SUMMARY AND CONCLUSIONS

This chapter has examined the economic performance of small states at the global level by summarising the principal findings of recent empirical work undertaken primarily by the authors. From this empirical review, it is possible to derive several general conclusions concerning small states and small island states.

Contrary to the *a priori* expectations of much of the traditional literature, the majority of small states – that is, those with a population below 3 million – at a global level are found to exhibit a relatively strong performance in terms of economic growth and per capita income levels.

There is certainly no empirical support for the view that small size represents a systematic barrier to growth and prosperity. On the contrary, many small states have performed exceptionally well in the light of the challenges that they face and, further, taking regional location into account, the vast majority of them perform better than larger neighbouring states.

The literature on the economic challenges facing small states and islands highlights a number of critical factors which strongly influence the structural characteristics of their economies, notably the small size of the domestic market and relative labour scarcity. This implies that growth success is likely to be based upon relatively open trade policies and, by implication, sectoral specialisation reflecting their underlying comparative advantage in niche market export-oriented services and possibly natural resources rather than scale-dependent labour-intensive activities. The empirical evidence tends to support the view that the pattern of sectoral specialisation in small states is an important factor in explaining their economic performance, with tourism, financial services and natural resources being strongly associated with growth success.

The primary focus of the traditional literature is small island states rather than small states per se. Many of the challenges faced by small states generally were therefore ascribed to small island states to the exclusion of small non-island states. The empirical analysis of the specific impact of island status on economic performance, as opposed to small size in general, finds that although the relationship is usually negative in accord with *a priori* expectations, it is rarely statistically significant. This suggests that island status is an important attribute of a distinct subset of all small states rather than being the defining characteristic of a completely separate group of states.

Research on small states and small island states highlights additional determinants of economic performance that are not so easily measurable, including sovereignty, autonomy and vulnerability. The starting point for the analysis of sovereignty and autonomy is the concept of political sovereignty; that is, national self-determination in accord with the UN Charter. Contrary to *a priori* expectations, political sovereignty is found to be inversely related to the growth performance for the global data set of small states which incorporates dependent territories and highly autonomous sub-national regions. At the European level, however, sovereignty and greater autonomy appear to confer additional benefits compared with those states, islands and other regions that lack these attributes.

The investigation of the role of economic policy autonomy as distinct from political sovereignty in small states is at an early stage, particularly in terms of robust empirical analysis. Anecdotal evidence suggests that autonomy over economic policy making in small states is a key strategic factor in their economic success through their potential to shape the domestic regulatory environment, promote niche market opportunities, and also to engage in international free riding and rent seeking.

The literature on the vulnerability of small states places particular stress on the exposure of small island states to exogenous shocks, whether economic, political or environmental in origin. Again, there has been little in the way of large-scale empirical analysis but small island states can be expected to be exceptionally vulnerable *a priori* because of their greater susceptibility to problems relating to remoteness, isolation and the impact of the dislocation of transport and communications infrastructure.

NOTE

1. This chapter represents a progress report on part of an extensive programme of ongoing research on the economic performance of small states and islands being undertaken by the authors. The authors are grateful to comments from several referees on the cited research papers as well as numerous suggestions and contributions from participants at various conferences in recent years. They are also grateful to the editor of this volume for his constructive comments and suggestions. All errors, however, remain the responsibility of the authors. The authors are grateful to the University of Chicago Press for their permission to reproduce Tables 10.4 and 10.5.

REFERENCES

Abbott, G.C. (1975), 'Small states: the paradox of their existence', in P. Selwyn (ed.), *Development Policy in Small Countries*, Beckenham: Croom Helm, pp. 105-114.

Ally, A. (1975), 'The potential for autonomous monetary policy in small developing countries', in P. Selwyn (ed.), *Development Policy in Small Countries*, Beckenham: Croom Helm, pp. 115-133.

Armstrong, H.W. and R. Read (1994), 'Micro-states, autonomous regions and the European Union', *European Urban & Regional Studies*, 1, 71-78.

Armstrong, H.W. and R. Read (1995), 'Western European micro-states and EU autonomous regions: the advantages of size and sovereignty', *World Development*, 23, 1229-1245.

Armstrong, H.W. and R. Read (1998), 'Trade and growth in small states: the impact of global trade liberalisation', *The World Economy*, 21, 563-585.

Armstrong, H.W. and R. Read (2000), 'Comparing the economic performance of dependent territories and sovereign micro-states', *Economic Development & Cultural Change*, 48, 285-306.

Armstrong, H.W. and R. Read (2001), 'Explaining differences in the economic performance of micro-states in Africa and Asia', in P. Lawrence and C. Thirtle (eds), *Africa & Asia in Comparative Development*, Basingstoke: Palgrave, pp. 128-157.

Armstrong, H.W. and R. Read (2002a), 'The determinants of economic growth in small states', *The Round Table*, forthcoming.

Armstrong, H.W. and R. Read (2002b), 'The importance of being unimportant: the political economy of trade and growth in small states', in S.M. Murshed (ed.), *Issues in Positive Political Economy*, London: Routledge, pp. 71-88.

Armstrong, H.W. and R. Read (2002c), 'The phantom of liberty: economic growth and the vulnerability of micro-states', *Journal of International Development*, 14, 1-24.

Armstrong, H.W. and R. Read (2003), 'Small states, islands and small states that are also islands', *Studies in Regional Science*, 33, 237-60.

Armstrong, H.W. and R. Read (2004), 'The implications of increasing globalisation and regionalism for the economic growth of small (island) states', *World Development*, 32, 365-378

Armstrong, H.W., Johnes, G., Johnes J. and A.I. MacBean (1993), 'The role of transport costs as a determinant of price level variations between the Isle of Man and the United Kingdom', *World Development*, 21, 311-318.

Armstrong, H.W., de Kervenoael, R.J., Li, X. and R. Read (1996), *The Economic Performance of Micro-States*, Report for the UK Overseas Development Administration, London: Overseas Development Administration.

Armstrong, H.W., de Kervenoael, R.J., Li, X. and R. Read (1998), 'A comparison of the economic performance of different micro-states and between micro-states and larger countries', *World Development*, 26, 539-556.

Ashoff, G. (1989), *Economic and Industrial Development Options for Small Third World Countries*, Occasional Paper No. 91, Berlin: German Development Institute.

Atkins, J.P., Mazzi, S. and C.D. Easter (2000), *A Commonwealth Vulnerability Index for Developing Countries: The Position of Small States*, Commonwealth Economic Paper No. 40, London: Commonwealth Secretariat.

Auty, R. (1993), *Sustaining Development in Mineral Economies: The Resource Curse Thesis*, London: Routledge.

Barro, R.J. (1991), 'Economic growth across a cross-section of countries', *Quarterly Journal of Economics*, 196, 407-433.

Barro, R.J. and X. Sala-i-Martin (1992), 'Convergence', *Journal of Political Economy*, 100, 223-251.

Barro, R.J. and X. Sala-i-Martin (1995), *Economic Growth*, Boston: McGraw-Hill.

Benedict, B. (1967), 'Introduction', in B. Benedict (ed.), *Problems of Smaller Territories*, London: Athlone Press, pp. 1-15.

Bertram, G. (1986), 'Sustainable development in Pacific micro-economies', *World Development*, 14, 809-822.

Bhaduri, A., Mukherji, A. and R. Sengupta (1982), 'Problems of long-term growth in small economies: a theoretical analysis', in B. Jalan (ed.), *Problems and Policies in Small Economies*, London: Croom Helm, pp. 49-68.

Blair, P.M. (1967), 'The ministate dilemma', *Occasional Paper No. 6*, Carnegie Endowment for Peace, New York.

Blazic-Metner, B. and H. Hughes (1982), 'Growth experience of small economies', in B. Jalan (ed.), *Problems and Policies in Small Economies*, Beckenham: Croom Helm for the Commonwealth Secretariat, pp. 85-101.

Blood, H. (1958), *The Smaller Territories*, London: Conservative & Unionist Party.

Briguglio, L. (1995), 'Small island developing states and their economic vulnerabilities', *World Development*, 23, 1615-1632.

Bune, P. (1987), 'Vulnerability', *The Courier*, 4, 85-87.

Chadha, J. (2002), 'Some observations on small state choice of exchange rate', in S.M. Murshed (ed.), *Issues in Positive Political Economy*, London: Routledge, pp. 89-102.

Chai, S.-K. (1998), 'Endogenous ideology formation and economic policy in former colonies', *Economic Development and Cultural Change*, 46, 263-290.

Chenery, H.B. and M. Syrquin (1975), *Patterns of Development: 1950–1970*, Oxford Oxford University Press.

Chenery, H.B. and L. Taylor (1968), 'Development patterns: among countries and over time', *Review of Economics and Statistics*, 50, 391-416.

Chenery, H.B., Robinson, S. and M. Syrquin (1986), *Industrialisation and Growth: A Comparative Study*, Oxford: Oxford University Press.

Clarke, C. and T. Payne (eds) (1987), *Politics, Security and Development in Small States*, London: Unwin Hyman.

Cobb, S.C. (2001), 'Globalization in a small island context: creating and marketing competitive advantage for offshore financial centres', *Geografiska Annaler*, 83 (B), 161-174.

Collier, P. and W. Gunning (1999), 'Explaining African economic performance', *Journal of Economic Literature*, 37, 64-111.

Commonwealth Consultative Group (1985), *Vulnerability: Small States in the Global Society*, London: Commonwealth Secretariat.

Commonwealth Secretariat (1996), *Small States: Economic Review & Statistics: Annual Series, 2*, London: Commonwealth Secretariat.

Corden, W.M. and P. Neary (1982), 'Booming sectors and deindustrialisation in small open economies', *Economic Journal*, 92, 825-848.

de Smith, S.A. (1970), *Microstates and Micronesia: Problems of America's Pacific Islands & Other Minute Territories*, New York: New York University Press.

Demas, W.G. (1965), *The Economics of Development in Small Countries: With Special Reference to the Caribbean*, Montreal: McGill University Press.

Easter, C. (1999), 'Small states development: a Commonwealth vulnerability index', *The Round Table*, 351, 403-422.

Erbo, G.F. and S. Schiavo-Campo (1969), 'Export stability level of development', *Bulletin of Oxford Institute of Economics and Statistics*, 31, 263-283.

Hampton, M. and J.S. Abbott (1999), *Offshore Finance Centres & Tax Havens: The Rise of Global Capitalism*, Indianapolis: Ichor Business Books.

Harden, S. (1985), *Small is Dangerous: Micro States in a Macro World*, London: Pinter.

Hein, P.L. (1985), 'The study of micro-states', in E.C. Dommen and P.L. Hein (eds), *States, Microstates and Islands*, London: Croom Helm, pp. 16-29.

Helleiner, G.K. (1982), 'Balance of payments problems and macro-economic policy', in B. Jalan (ed.), *Problems and Policies in Small Economies*, Beckenham: Croom Helm for the Commonwealth Secretariat, pp. 165-184.

Holmes, F. (1976), 'Development problems of small countries', in L.V. Castle and F. Holmes (eds), *Co-operation and Development in the Asia Pacific Region: Relations Between Large and Small Countries*, Tokyo: Japan Economic Research Centre, pp. 43-66.

Kakazu, H. (1994), *Sustainable Development of Small Island Economies*, New York: Westview Press.

Khatkhate, D.R. and B.K. Short (1980), 'Monetary and central banking problems of mini-states', *World Development*, 8, 1017-1026.

Knox, A.D. (1967), 'Some economic problems of small countries', in B. Benedict (ed.), *Problems of Smaller Territories*, London: Athlone Press, pp. 35-45.

Kuznets, S. (1960), 'The economic growth of small states', in E.A.G. Robinson (ed.), *The Economic Consequences of the Size of Nations*, London: Macmillan, pp. 14-32.

Kuznets, S. (1971), *Economic Growth of Nations: Total Output and Production Structure*, Cambridge, Mass: Belknap.

Labour Party, (1957), *Labour's Colonial Policy, Volume 3: The Smaller Territories*, London: The Labour Party.

Lal, D. (1995), 'Why growth rates differ: the political economy of social change in 21 developing countries', in B.H. Koo and D.H. Perkins (eds), *Social Capability and Long-Term Economic Growth*, Basingstoke: Macmillan, pp. 288-309.

Lewis, W.A. (1955), *The Theory of Growth and Development*, London: Allen & Unwin.

Lloyd, P.J. and R.M. Sundrum (1982), 'Characteristics of small economies', in B. Jalan (ed.), *Problems and Policies in Small Economies*, Beckenham: Croom Helm for the Commonwealth Secretariat, pp. 17-38.

MacBean, A.I. and D.T. Nguyen (1987), *Commodity Problems, Prospects & Policies*, London: Croom Helm.

Marcy, G. (1960), 'How far can foreign trade and customs agreements confer upon small nations the advantages of larger nations?', in E.A.G. Robinson (ed.), *The Economic Consequences of the Size of Nations*, London: Macmillan, pp. 265-281.

Milner, C. and A. Westaway (1993), 'Country size and the medium term growth process: some country size evidence', *World Development*, 21, 203-212.

Milner, C. and T. Weyman-Jones (1998), 'Relative economic performance and country size', paper presented at the *IESG Small States in the International Economy Conference*, University of Birmingham, mimeo.

OECD (1997), *Geographical Disbursement of Financial Flows to Aid Recipients, 1992–1996*, Paris: OECD.

Pollard, S. (1987), *The Viability and Vulnerability of a Small Island State: the Case of Kiribati*, National Centre for Development Studies, Working Paper, No. 87/14, Canberra: Australian National University.

Putnam, R.D., with R. Leonardi, and R.Y. Nanetti (1993), *Making Democracy Work: Civic Traditions in Modern Italy*, Princeton, NJ: Princeton University Press.

Read, R. (2000), 'The characteristics, vulnerability and growth performance of small economies', briefing paper for the *WTO Seminar on Small Economies*, Palais des Nations, Geneva, 21 October.

Read, R. (2002), 'Growth, economic development and structural transition in small vulnerable states', in S.M. Murshed (ed.), *Globalisation, Marginalisation and Development*, New York: Routledge, pp. 171-184.

Sachs, J.D. and A.M. Warner (1997), 'Sources of slow growth in African economies', *Journal of African Economies*, 6, 335-376.

Scitovsky, T. (1960), 'International trade and economic integration as a means of overcoming the disadvantages of a small nation', in E.A.G. Robinson (ed.), *The Economic Consequences of the Size of Nations*, London: Macmillan, pp. 282-290.

Selwyn, P. (1975), 'Industrial development in peripheral small countries', in P. Selwyn (ed.), *Development Policy in Small Countries*, Beckenham: Croom Helm, pp. 77-104.

Thirlwall, A.P. (1991), *The Performance and Prospects of the Pacific Island Economies in the World Economy*, Research Report Series, No. 14, Pacific Islands Development Program, East-West Center, University of Hawaii.

Thomas, I. (1982), 'The industrialisation experience of small countries', in B. Jalan (ed.), *Problems and Policies in Small Economies*, London: Croom Helm, pp. 103-124.

Triffin, R. (1960), 'The size of a nation and its vulnerability to economic nationalism', in E.A.G. Robinson (ed.), *The Economic Consequences of the Size of Nations*, London: Macmillan, pp. 247-264.

UNCTAD (1997), *The Vulnerability of Small Island Developing States in the Context of Globalization: Common Issues and Remedies*, Geneva: UNCTAD, SIDS.

United Nations (2000), *Committee for Development Policy's Economic Vulnerability Index: Explanatory Note*, United Nations CDP2000/PLEN/21.

Vital, D. (1967), *The Inequality of States: A Study of Small Powers in International Relations*, Westport, CT: Greenwood Press.

Wood, D.P.J. (1967), 'The small territories: some political considerations', in B. Benedict (ed.), *Problems of Smaller Territories*, London: Athlone Press, pp. 23-34.

11. Getting on to the Map of the Global Economy: The Case of Finland

Nils Bjorksten and Laura Meriluoto

11.1 INTRODUCTION

From being one of the poorest European countries at its independence in 1917, Finland now boasts a highly industrialised free market economy with an egalitarian income distribution and per capita GDP levels that are well above the OECD and European averages, in recent years surpassing even those of Sweden. Figure 11.1 compares Finland's real per capita GDP levels with OECD and EU15 averages. The current performance of the Finnish economy is exemplary in spite of devastating wars and recessions, as well as considerable handicaps in terms of remoteness, an inhospitable climate and a native language that is one of the world's more obscure. This development performance merits closer study because it is clearly more attributable to a policy strategy than to being geographically blessed.

Although the main reason for Finland's successful development has been openness to trade, such integration with the world economy would not have been possible without effective long-term management of the globalisation process through various policies. The challenge has consistently been to insulate vulnerable groups of the population from cyclical downturns while at the same time allowing the increased specialisation and narrowing of the industrial base that comes with expanded trade. This can be achieved in a variety of ways, with some of these being more growth promoting than others. Although mistakes have been made over the years, and considerable new challenges have been created by choices that were made in the past, it seems that on balance Finland has been successful in setting in motion a virtuous cycle of development which has proved surprisingly robust to serious cyclical downturns.

The policy formula that successive post-war Finnish governments adopted to secure public support for openness has undergone significant change over the past decade, coinciding with a time of particularly strong growth performance. As in much of Europe, the post-war decades witnessed the wholesale expansion of the public sector, in a bid to provide targeted payments to vulnerable groups and sheltered sector jobs to large numbers of predominantly unskilled workers. The Finnish economic crisis of the early 1990s and the 1995 accession to the EU, with its associated commitment to adhere to Maastricht Treaty restrictions on public spending, have forced a reversal of public sector expansion at exactly a time of unprecedented further opening up of the economy. The key to retaining public support for openness has been to upgrade the product mix of manufacturing and escape head-to-head competition with producers in low-wage countries. In practice, this has taken the form of a concerted push to increase the average skill level of the workforce. Whether or not this development strategy will ultimately be successful remains to be seen, but to date the signs have been promising.

Notes: OECD total excludes Czech Republic, Hungary, Poland and Slovak Republic

Source: OECD (2002b)

Figure 11.1 GDP per capita at price levels and exchange rates of 1995 (US dollars)

The remainder of the chapter looks at trade and the microeconomic policy management of Finland's economic integration with the rest of the world, drawing on insights from Edward Leamer for the trade portion (e.g., Leamer,

1987, 1996) and Dani Rodrik for the political economy portion of the study (e.g., Rodrick, 1998a, 1998b). Although there is no question that maintaining macroeconomic stability is also important, including price stability and a sound fiscal balance, these policies have played only a supporting role in putting Finland on to the map of the global economy, and they will only be touched tangentially in this chapter. Over a longer time frame, underlying microeconomic forces usually dominate macroeconomic disturbances in influencing development outcomes.

Section 11.2 provides a brief overview of the Finnish economy. Section 11.3 outlines the immediate post-war strategy of expanding the public sector to absorb unskilled labour and manage a social safety net for those affected by cyclical downturns in the metal and paper industries. Section 11.4 introduces a Heckscher–Ohlin-based framework to examine patterns of comparative advantage and specialisation among OECD countries, and argues that changes to the relative factor endowment of Finland explain a revealed comparative advantage in the electronics and telecommunications sectors.[1] Section 11.5 then devotes particular attention to the development of Nokia in Finland. Section 11.6 discusses the current performance and foreseeable challenges to Finland's new development strategy. Section 11.7 concludes.

11.2　SOME STYLISED FACTS AND HISTORICAL CONTEXT

Finland is a geographically large but sparsely populated country in a remote northern corner of Europe. Finland's area is 337,030 sq km and its population is 5.2 million, resulting in population density of 15 inhabitants per square km (similar to, for example, New Zealand).[2] Only 8 percent of Finland's land area is arable, and most of the rest (76 percent) is forests and woodland. Because of the climate, agricultural development cannot really go beyond maintaining self-sufficiency in basic products, and even that level of production has only been thanks to effective government subsidisation of the sector. Forestry, on the other hand, has traditionally been a big export earner and provides a secondary occupation for much of the rural population.

In some ways, Finland is even more remote and isolated from major export markets than geographical distance would suggest. Geographically it is on the periphery of Europe, separated from most of the continent by the Baltic Sea, large parts of which freeze over during the winter. Road connections with Norway and Sweden run through remote Lapland, above the Arctic Circle, and rail links are compatible only with Russia due to a different gauge of tracks from the rest of Europe.[3] The largest land border is with Russia, which at the moment is relatively impoverished and not a major trading partner (less than 5 percent of exports in 2000).

Economic growth has nevertheless been driven by exports, and thus by the manufacturing sector. Trade has become increasingly important for Finland. In 1990–2000, exports grew at an average annual rate of 9.5 percent, which was over seven percentage points faster than the average annual GDP growth rate during that time. This resulted in a record exports-to-GDP ratio of 43 percent in 2000 (Ministry of Finance, 2001). Main exports-are-machinery and equipment, chemicals, metals and forestry products, including pulp and paper, primarily directed towards the EU (Germany, Sweden, UK) and the United States.

For most of its post-war history, Finland has had a relatively narrow industrial base, with reliance primarily on the forestry and metals sectors. These sectors have always been subject to strong cyclical fluctuations, a fact that has consistently posed a challenge for macroeconomic stability. The electronics and telecommunications sector has developed into a third pillar supporting the economy, but this development did not take place until the 1990s. This is discussed in more detail below.

Under the circumstances prevailing until at least the mid-1990s, expanding trade therefore meant specialising in and expanding the very industries that were the most cyclical. In spite of the periodic disruptions that this would cause to the well being of the population, especially during earlier stages of industrialisation, there was strong political support for pursuing a path of increased integration into the world economy. Having fought two wars against the Soviet Union, and seen most of Central Europe absorbed into the post-war Soviet empire, Finland was particularly anxious to cement its future to Western Europe, with its traditions of rules-based democracy. Nevertheless, from a social welfare perspective, excessive cyclicality of the economy was a problem that had to be addressed.

Two main factors worked to reduce this cyclicality. First, economic factors limited the extent to which trade could develop. Distance, the smallness of the internal market and the obscurity of the national language contributed to make several sectors difficult for foreign competition to penetrate cost-effectively. Transportation between Finland and other European countries is generally costly because of the need to switch modes of transportation from road or rail to ship, across a sea that is ice-covered during the wintertime. Foreign goods marketed in Finland had to be labelled and marketed in two languages, both relatively obscure.[4] Finally, and rather importantly, a post-war 'friendship pact' with the Soviet Union also fixed a minimum proportion of Finnish international trade that had to take place with the Soviet Union. Since there were few Soviet goods that were marketable in Finland besides oil, this was at times a binding constraint to developing aggregate trade, especially at times when world oil prices were low.[5]

The second main factor ameliorating swings in the business cycle was the expansion of the state. Rodrik (1998a) has explained the risk-reducing role of government spending in economies exposed to significant external risk. In Finland, the role of state spending has expanded to well over 50 percent of the economy, and provides an effective social safety net to shield against the consequences of periodic downturns. This risk-reducing function of the state has successfully maintained social cohesion and domestic political support for ongoing trade expansion in the post-war decades.

A large role for the state creates its own set of challenges to economic development. Finnish society is very highly unionised, which makes it difficult for firms to shed unwanted labour, contributing to the wage structure being very egalitarian. Finland has one of the most centralised wage-setting systems in the OECD, involving a tripartite structure to wage bargaining between employers, wage earners and central government. While the agreements are not legally binding, they have historically been used as a lower bound for wage increases for up to 80 percent of the workforce. This contributes to making relative wages quite rigid across industries. Shifts in relative prices have to be accommodated primarily through changes in sectoral employment, which tends to happen very slowly.[6] Until relatively recently, the economy was characterised by a high level of cartelisation, which allowed more room for margins to absorb cyclical fluctuations rather than employment via firm entry/exit.[7]

To justify high wages even for unskilled labour, it helps to have relatively little unskilled labour in the first place and to employ most of that in the non-traded sector rather than in manufacturing. Public policy has helped to achieve this in two ways: by expanding education and by absorbing a lot of unskilled labour into the provision of public services. Today, 32 percent of the labour force finds employment in public services.[8]

11.3 ECONOMICS OF MANAGING INTEGRATION

The evidence is overwhelming that economic isolationism is not the way to prosperity.[9] At the same time, it is also recognised that trade cannot bring benefits without a microeconomic restructuring of the economy, or production shifting towards exportables and consumption shifting towards importables. This restructuring process is an inseparable part of globalisation. It threatens some people's livelihoods and ultimately generates understandable fear and opposition among people who believe that they bear a disproportionate share of the risks without partaking equally in the benefits.

Free trade generates net gains, so theoretically the winners from trade could be taxed and the losers compensated in a way that would make everyone better off. In practice, however, this never seems to work, and those who would on balance be made worse off with trade know better than to expect to be fully compensated after the restructuring. Moreover, the loss of jobs in import-competing sectors is not the only negative consequence that arises from globalisation. Income disparities could widen if the relative wages of unskilled labour were to be pushed down by trade. In an egalitarian society such as Finland, such a development is broadly viewed as undesirable and downright harmful to the fabric of society in the long run.

At the end of the day, successive pro-trade democratic governments have found it necessary to adopt rather complex strategies to shield those portions of the population who are made worse off by trade. In addition to the crude measure of gradualism in expanding trade, there are two more subtle, long-term measures that have systematically been pursued in Finland and elsewhere. The first measure has been to expand the role of the state by creating entitlements for persons whose jobs disappear and new employment opportunities in the sheltered, non-tradable public sector for many who would otherwise be at risk of losing their jobs. The second measure has been to invest in physical and human capital, so that the country could climb the quality ladder in output and hopefully avoid the decline in the wages of the unskilled labour. The end result has been the creation of a two-level social safety net that aims to remove the economic threat of globalisation for practically everybody and that ensures a social consensus for further expansion of trade.

11.3.1 The Post-war Social Contract

Rodrik (1998a) argues that the post-war era of sustained global integration among the OECD countries was underpinned by a particular social bargain, which necessitated a disproportionate growth of the public sector. Accordingly, he finds a positive correlation between an economy's exposure to international trade and the size of its government, with the strongest relationship holding when terms of trade risk is the highest.

Following the example of Sweden, Finland has adopted a welfare-state model of society that relies strongly on consensus building, so that no political grouping is totally left out in the cold. One underlying value of this model is that civil society is expected to take care of its weakest members, and in particular to prevent the emergence of systematically disadvantaged groups. To achieve this, the tax and transfer system has become increasingly pervasive and has resulted in a very egalitarian income distribution, with high taxes, pensions, unemployment and disability benefits.

11.4 STRUCTURAL IMMUNISATION AGAINST THE NEGATIVE ASPECTS OF GLOBALISATION

This chapter has argued that in many industrialised economies, the fear of trade boils down to the fear of economic restructuring, with the abandonment of whole industries and negative effects on the wages of primarily unskilled labour. Simply expanding the welfare system to capture all displaced workers is not a viable option in the long run, however. Government must also consider long-term structural measures to redeploy resources in a more productive fashion. The workhorse model used to analyse such questions is the Heckscher–Ohlin model, which explains interindustry trade according to patterns of comparative advantage, which in turn are determined by differences in relative factor endowments across countries.[10]

The relevant property of the Heckscher–Ohlin model is what is known as the Stolper–Samuelson theorem. In the basic case, when countries trade, the returns to the relatively abundant production factor rise and the returns to the relatively scarce production factor fall. In a simple case with two factors of production (labour and capital) and two outputs, the practical interpretation is that once trade is allowed, the relatively capital-abundant country will specialise in the capital-intensive output, and trade that for the labour-intensive output, which results in higher returns to capital and lower returns to labour.

There is one escape from this outcome, however. If both countries have sufficiently different relative endowments of inputs, so that one or both countries are fully specialised once trade is allowed, then trade will actually benefit both factors in both countries. In a practical example, as long as Finland does not produce any of the same products as Pakistan, then trade between the two countries will benefit both labour and capital owners in both countries. The countries simply continue to produce completely different products, so the inputs that go into those products are never actually in competition with each other and factor returns do not fall, even as trade improves the lot of both countries.

This escape carries a key policy implication: in high-wage countries, 'protection' from low-wage competition can be bought via sufficiently high rates of investment in physical and human capital. As long as Finland continues to invest in physical and human capital to a degree that allows it to climb the quality ladder and upgrade products, and thus remain fully specialised in a product mix that does not compete with Pakistani exports, then the rising tide of trade will simply lift all boats. By contrast, if investment is not maintained, so that the marginal unskilled worker in Finland eventually works in an industry that competes (via trade) with unskilled labour in Pakistan, then the wages of unskilled labour in Finland and in Pakistan will move to equalise.

Finland can insulate itself more fully against wage equalisation of unskilled labour by making sure that there is as little unskilled labour as possible, and that most of that factor is employed in the non-tradable sector. Imagine a few unskilled labourers in a rich neighbourhood. They would probably do very well, just by providing services to their rich neighbours. A large community of unskilled labourers next to a rich neighbourhood is another story, however; most will have to find employment elsewhere, and those that work for the rich neighbours cannot bargain for as high compensation. This is where government education policy and provision of various government services comes in. As long as the education system manages to provide good basic skills to most, and the rest are by and large absorbed into safe public sector jobs, no-one needs to feel threatened by globalisation. As a result, a consensus to integrate further is relatively easy to achieve.

However, the question then becomes: which countries are Finland's competitors in manufacturing? Which countries produce the same mix of tradables? Are they countries with relatively abundant low-skilled labour and consequently low wages, or are they capital-rich and skilled labour-rich countries with high wages, possibly even higher wages than those in Finland? It is possible to shed some light on this question with a three-factor Heckscher–Ohlin model. A necessary condition for Finland's manufacturing sector to be in competition with high-wage countries only is that Finland has a comparative advantage in capital and/or R&D-intensive products. Only then does Finland have a potential to produce a mix of products that excludes all goods that would be in direct competition with low-wage countries, making it possible for the marginal unskilled worker to be employed by the non-traded sector and therefore for the wages to be set in Helsinki and not in Islamabad.

Recall that comparative advantage in products is determined by relative abundance of inputs. Leamer (1996) has sorted two-digit SIC industries by their relative intensity of use of three distinct inputs: capital, skilled labour and unskilled labour. Figure 11.2 plots these relative intensities.[11]

Figure 11.2 can be interpreted as follows. Any straight line from the capital origin to the axis connecting the origins for skilled labour and unskilled labour consists of all points that are consistent with the same skilled labour/unskilled labour ratio, which can be read off the axis. On that line, points further away from the capital origin have relatively less capital, both in terms of skilled and unskilled labour. Any point above the line has more skilled labour for each unit of unskilled labour than points below that line. Similarly, any line from the unskilled labour origin to the axis connecting the capital and skilled labour origins consists of all points that are consistent with the same capital/skilled labour ratio and decreasing relative amount of unskilled labour. Points above the line have more skilled labour per unit of capital than points below the line. Lastly, a straight line from the skilled labour origin to the axis connecting the capital and unskilled labour origins consists of all points consistent with the same capital/labour ratio and decreasing relative amount of skilled labour. Points to the right of the line have more unskilled labour per unit of capital than points to the left of it.

One can read off Figure 11.2 that transportation, electronics and electronic instruments industries are intensive in skilled labour, using relatively little unskilled labour and capital. Petroleum is the most capital-intensive industry, and apparel and leather are the most unskilled labour-intensive industries.

The Heckscher–Ohlin model predicts that the country has a comparative advantage in the good that is intensive in its relatively abundant factor, and therefore the country specialises in, and exports, this good. It can thus be seen from Figure 11.2 that countries with factor endowments weighted towards unskilled labour will have a comparative advantage in producing apparel and leather goods. Leamer has observed that with the accumulation of more capital, they are likely to shift into producing furniture, textiles, stone- and glassware, rubber, and so on, as has happened in several Asian developing countries. With still more capital they start to gain a comparative advantage in producing chemicals. Alternatively, countries can also go the route of the Scandinavians, developing human capital and gradually shifting production into machinery, instruments and electronics that are not necessarily more capital intensive than furniture, textiles, and so on, but are much more skilled labour intensive.

Countries with similar relative factor endowments will share diversification cones; that is, they will be diversified in production so that they produce largely the same set of products. With widely different endowments, however, the mix of products produced in each country will not coincide. Thus, countries with relatively high endowments of skilled labour and capital may abandon production of commodities requiring little of each, since these goods can be imported at below local cost of production.

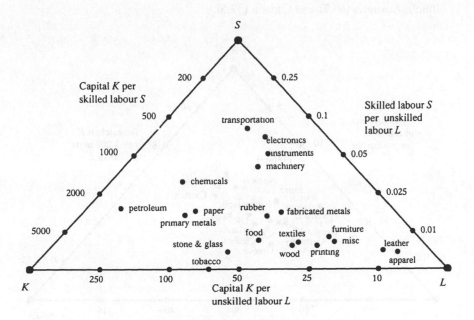

Source: The figure was constructed with a spreadsheet provided by E. Leamer using data from Datastream

Figure 11.2 Relative factor intensities of two-digit SIC industries

Figure 11.3 shows a similar triangle to Figure 11.2, but lists the endowment vectors of selected countries instead of the factor intensities of the two-digit ISIC industries. Figure 11.3 is not perfectly comparable with Figure 11.2 because of the way labour is defined: Leamer uses the variables unskilled and skilled labour in Figure 11.2, whereas the variables total labour force and researchers are used in Figure 11.3. The interpretation of this triangle is the same as that in Figure 11.2, however. For example, we can see that Finland has the most researchers per 1,000 units of labour (13.5) followed by Japan (9.6), Sweden (9.2), USA (8.8) and Norway (7.8). New Zealand is close to the bottom with 4.6 researchers per 1,000 units of labour.

Finland does not rank near the top of this group in terms of capital/labour ratio. The countries with the highest ratio of 1,000 units of capital to unit of labour are Denmark (206.7), France (196.3), Belgium (182.5) and

Switzerland (179.2). Finland is in the middle of the pack (123.1), together with New Zealand (127.9), and the countries at the bottom include the USA (68.9), Australia (60.7) and Canada (57.5).

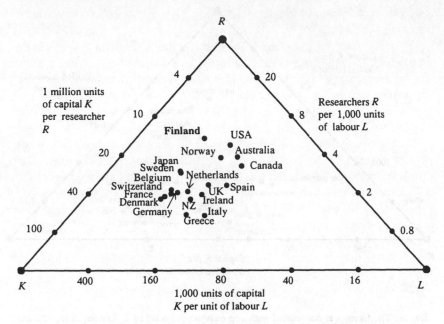

Notes: The data for researchers are for 1999 for Belgium, Canada, Denmark, Greece, Ireland, Netherlands, New Zealand, Norway, Sweden and the USA, and for 1998 for the UK

Source: The figure was constructed with a spreadsheet provided by E. Leamer using data from Datastream and OECD (2002a)

Figure 11.3 Relative factor endowments, 2000

Again, due to the relative shortage of capital and abundance of researchers, Finland ranks near the bottom for capital/researcher ratio with 9.1 million units of capital per researcher. The only countries below Finland are Australia (8.9) and the USA (7.8). The countries near the top of this listing include Greece (38.8), Italy (35.9) and Denmark (32.1). Note that Greece and Italy's high values for this index are not due to being capital rich but being researcher poor.

From this analysis, several conclusions can now be drawn with respect to comparative advantage. Most importantly for our study, we can conclude that Finland has a comparative advantage in goods that require relatively little capital but a lot of R&D. Although we lack industry-specific data on factor intensities that are perfectly consistent with Figure 11.3, it is relatively safe to assume that the telecommunications and electronics industry is R&D intensive but not necessarily capital intensive. This certainly helps to explain why the mobile phone industry and other high-tech industries have been successful in Finland.

It is also evident that Japan, Sweden, the USA and Norway are quite similar in their endowment points with Finland. These five countries top the list for researcher-to-labour ratios. However, Finland's capital–labour ratio and capital–researcher ratio are smaller than those of Sweden and Japan but greater than those of Norway and the USA. The similarity should suggest that Finland would be a close competitor with these four countries. This has been evident in the mobile phone industry, where Finland's Nokia has fought for market share with Motorola of the USA and Ericsson of Sweden. The difference should suggest that Sweden and Japan would have a comparative advantage, and therefore specialise, in R&D-intensive products that are also capital intensive and that the USA and Norway should specialise in R&D-intensive products that are also labour intensive.

It is interesting to look at how Finland's comparative advantage has evolved over time. Figure 11.4 presents the same endowment triangle as Figure 11.3 but for the year 1991.

Interestingly, Figure 11.4 shows that Finland's endowment point was much less differentiated from the rest of the OECD countries in 1991 than it is currently. Relative to these countries, Finland is now significantly more researcher abundant and less capital abundant than it was in 1991, approaching the relative endowments mix that corresponded with Japan's position in the early 1990s. Other countries seem to have had less movement in their comparative advantage.

The conclusion of this analysis is that Finland has the potential to maintain its high wage structure for unskilled labour because it is in a position to have a product mix quite dissimilar from those of low-wage countries due to its comparative advantage. However, this position is by no means sheltered. The emerging economies in Asia have witnessed huge increases in their capital and human capital stocks. If Finland does not continue to improve its human capital and R&D stocks, other countries may soon catch up. This would put pressure on the wages of unskilled labour, as lower-wage countries start competing with Finnish manufacturing, producing the same products.

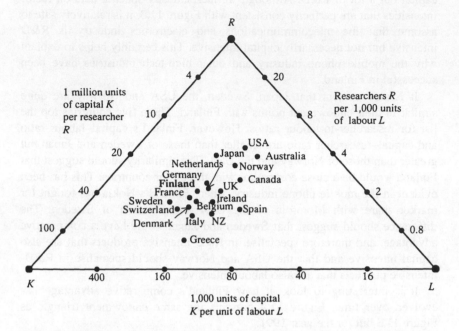

Notes: The data for researchers are for 1992 for Australia and Switzerland and 1993 for The
        Netherlands

Source: E. Leamer, Datastream, OECD (1999) and OECD (2002a)

Figure 11.4 Relative factor endowments, 1991

This analysis nevertheless abstracts from certain fairly important inputs,
such as energy, agricultural land and forest resources.[12] In the case of
Finland, which has a good endowment of forests and metal ore, plus the
possibility of transporting via waterways, a lot of available capital will easily
be tied up in the paper and primary metals industries, leaving less available
for other industries.[13] There is therefore a clear risk that unless education
levels are maintained, the marginal unskilled worker in Finland will, for
example, produce furniture in competition with Indonesians and Philippinos
instead of packaging mobile phones in competition with the Swedes. The
fewer unskilled workers available for employment in manufacturing, the
more Finland is pushed by comparative advantage to shift production into
mobile phones and other industries that are R&D intensive. Likewise,
because of specific natural resource endowments, Norway is likely to have a

great deal of capital and skilled labour tied up in extracting and refining petroleum resources, leaving less for, for example, electronics. This may explain why Norway has not had similar success in the high-tech industries as Finland, Japan and the USA, despite the similarity of its relative endowment mix with these countries.

11.5 THE SIGNIFICANCE OF NOKIA

Led by telecommunications giant Nokia, the electronic equipment industry has been a major growth engine since the mid-1990s. The output growth of the industry was around 25 percent per year in 1994–2000. The sector's output represented 4.5 percent of GDP and over 30 percent of exports in 2000 (Figure 11.5). Figure 11.6 illustrates the boost to industrial production that has resulted from growth of this sector.

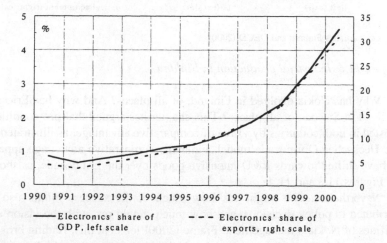

Source: Ali-Yrkkö et al., (2000)

Figure 11.5 Electronics' share of Finnish GDP and exports

About 4,000 firms are involved in ICT in Finland, including 200 companies in electronics manufacturing services and 350 first-tier suppliers to Nokia (IMF, 2001, p.9). Nokia is by far the most significant player in the sector, accounting for 2.8 percent of GDP and close to 25 percent of exports in 2001 (Ali-Yrkkö and Hermans, 2002, p.2). Furthermore, Nokia accounted for 70 percent of the Helsinki stock market capitalisation at the end of 2000 (IMF, 2001, p.10).

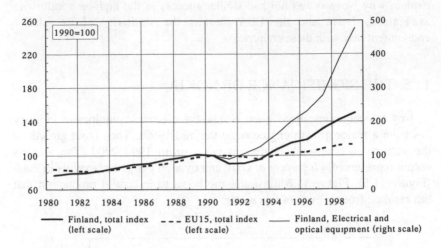

Source: Statistics Finland and OECD (2000)

Figure 11.6 Industrial production in Finland

Why has Nokia evolved in Finland, of all places? And why has Ericsson evolved in Sweden of all places? This chapter has argued that pre-conditions existed in both countries by virtue of comparative advantage, as illustrated by the Heckscher–Ohlin trade model. Finland's comparative advantage appears to have shifted towards R&D-intensive goods over the last decade, as shown by Figures 11.3 and 11.4.

Nevertheless, one might ask how much of the success might also be attributed to policy decisions, and how much should rest with the vision and abilities of Nokia's management. Frame (2000) looks at this, finding broadly that most of the business credit goes to Nokia's management, which was able to seize an opportunity that emerged thanks to long-standing sound policies that had been implemented for other reasons.

Government policy has included risk sharing in R&D projects, which has helped the R&D intensive telecommunications industry. Approximately one-third of Nokia's employees work in research and development. Nokia's R&D activity accounts for one-third of private research and development in Finland. The policy has no doubt contributed to the fact that Finland boasts one of the highest research and development intensities in the OECD (3.37

percent of GDP in 2000 (see Figure 11.7); and that Finland's factor intensity has shifted from physical capital to R&D and human capital.[14]

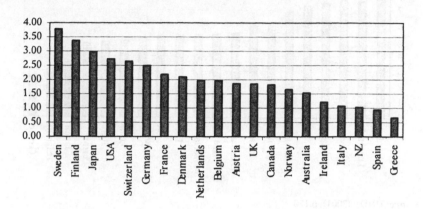

Note: The values for Belgium, Denmark, Greece, Ireland, Norway, NZ and Sweden are from 1999

Source: OECD (2002a)

Figure 11.7 Gross domestic expenditure on R&D, as percentage of GDP, 2000 (or latest available year)

The education system has helped to ensure that Nokia and other high-tech companies have a pool of well-trained engineers and other skilled labour. Finland has one of the highest public sector expenditure ratios on education among the study countries (Figure 11.8). Furthermore, the money going into education has been spent in a growth-fostering way, as evidenced by Finland's number one ranking in tertiary students studying science, maths or engineering among the study countries (Figure 11.9).

Nevertheless, growth in the electronic equipment sector is somewhat constrained by shortages of engineers and other skilled labour, in particular graduates with commercial and entrepreneurial skills. Due to this, Nokia's growth in Finland has been about half the speed of its growth abroad (IMF, 2001, p.10). Productivity is tremendously high, while total employment in the sector remains relatively small, at around 3 percent of total labour force employment (OECD, 2000, p.23).

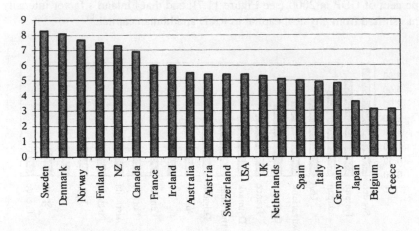

Source: UNDP (2001), p.170

Figure 11.8 Public education expenditure as percentage of GNP, 1995–1997

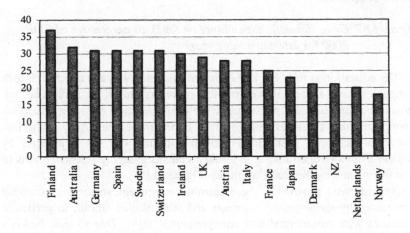

Source: UNDP (2001), p.174

Figure 11.9 Tertiary students in science, maths or engineering as percentage of all tertiary students, 1994–1997

11.6 REMAINING CHALLENGES

Since the end of the 1980s, there has been increasing concern about inefficiencies generated by a large welfare state. Perhaps the clearest manifestation of this has been in the labour markets, where European unemployment over several business cycles has consistently ratcheted up, eventually reaching levels averaging over 10 percent with particularly concerning growth in long-term unemployment. This has been widely perceived as a consequence of high tax wedges and overly generous social benefits leading to welfare traps, where incentives to seek work are too low.

In Finland, a series of coinciding shocks in the early 1990s bumped unemployment to 18 percent (with an accompanying rise in long-term unemployment), which overwhelmed the capacity of labour market institutions to effectively place persons willing to work. This development, more than anything else, caused a social outcry that galvanised policy makers to overhaul the system.

Over the past decade, there have been considerable policy efforts in Finland and elsewhere to reduce the size of the state via privatisations, reductions in social benefits and a streamlining of the tax structure. The Maastricht Treaty of 1992 enshrined such roll-backs of the state in Europe, at the same time as it set the stage for a tremendous increase in integration of European states with each other. While Finland has received good marks from the relevant European institutions for its economic performance since joining the EU in 1995, this performance has been on the back of strong bounce-back growth from the recession of the early 1990s. Once growth slows, the challenges of maintaining good performance will become much greater.

The simultaneous roll-back of the state and increase in integration are already resulting in some undesirable consequences. The smaller state is less prepared to address the tension between the benefits from trade and the consequent adjustments to the status quo of the income distribution. The Gini coefficient, which has risen from a steady 0.2 in the 1980s and early 1990s to almost 0.27 by 2000 (Statistics Finland, 2002), demonstrates that income inequality in Finland has been on the rise. This has started to undermine the political legitimacy of globalisation.

In the words of Rodrik (1998b, p.12), the post-war social bargain, whereby 'labour and other groups who feared that they would bear the risks of openness and receive few of its rewards were given reason to believe that their interests were taken on board', is being undermined. Instead, employment relationships are shifting to the disadvantage of labour, which is becoming increasingly substitutable across countries. There is also gradual deterioration in the safety net for the growing group of those who risk losing their jobs at some point during the foreseeable future.

The point is that these concerns can and should be addressed by the government, through the striking of a new social bargain to replace that which is being abandoned. In return for continued labour peace and support for further integration, the government needs to ensure sufficiently high quality domestic institutions – rule of law, quality infrastructure, macroeconomic and political stability, and a skilled labour force – so that high investment levels continue, labour can count on steadily increasing living standards and efficiently working labour market institutions can ensure a reasonable degree of job security.[15] Accomplishing this could allow for a continuation of the virtuous cycle that has been in place since the war, even as the size of the state is somewhat reduced. By contrast, if the government were to shirk its responsibilities and still insist on workers living up to theirs ('globalisation is inevitable and unstoppable, accept it because resistance is futile'), this amounts to inviting a potentially very serious backlash.

The message appears to be sinking in. Research intensity in Finland has increased by 2.5 times over the past two decades. At the moment, Finland has one of the highest research and development intensities in the OECD (as was shown earlier in Figure 11.7), with about 70 percent of it financed by the private sector (OECD, 2002a, p.24).

Finland's factor intensity has shifted from physical capital to human capital. In 2001, Finland was ranked first in global competitiveness by two studies.[16] Finland pursues an active industry policy that partially subsidises intangible investment such as research, product development, training and other non-corporeal corporate development, as opposed to physical investment or other investments that risk inhibiting competition, and strives to fund projects that would not happen without public support.[17] The education system, which is already highly regarded in international comparisons, has also been revamped to fit more closely into the enterprise and research systems, especially at the tertiary level (Frame, 2000, p.70). Mayda and Rodrik (2002) also find that pro-trade preferences are significantly and robustly correlated with an individual's level of human capital, as predicted by the factor endowments model for a country such as Finland where skilled labour is relatively abundant.

Somewhat less palatably, there appears to be increasing resistance to immigration, with the exception of highly-skilled and highly paid positions in manufacturing, especially electronics. One underlying reason for this may be economic: large-scale immigration of unskilled labour can upset the egalitarian income distribution, as the employment of the marginal unskilled worker determines the wage level for the whole group. If there are enough unskilled workers so that the marginal unskilled worker is employed in the low-tech tradables sector, foreign trade may well push wages down considerably, and this can generate widespread resistance to increased globalisation.

11.7 CONCLUSION

In the decades following World War II, Finland has grown from being one of the poorest countries in Europe to being one of the wealthiest. Growth has been largely thanks to greater trade and integration with Europe, overcoming distance and linguistic barriers. It was only during the 1990s, however, that Finland really made its mark on the world economic map due to the rapid rise of a thriving high-technology sector.

Finland's growth path has been characterised by a virtuous cycle of development, whereby trade integration with the rest of Europe has led to gains in living standards that, via effective policy intervention, have benefited the entire population. In order for the government to maintain a political consensus for greater integration, an elaborate social safety net was created to provide reasonable insurance for all groups of the population against the restructuring costs that are part and parcel of expanded trade. Without such a safety net, it is questionable whether integration would have been able to sustain enough political legitimacy to proceed as it has.

This network is therefore worth studying carefully. Portions of it have become problematic, such as the gradual expansion of the public sector to unsustainable dimensions with ensuing costs in terms of a rise in long-term unemployment. Other portions, such as investment in education and subsidies for research and development, have shifted Finland's comparative advantage to high-technology sectors and effectively shielded unskilled labour from competition in low-wage emerging markets.

The lessons to be drawn are as follows. First, obstacles of distance, linguistic uniqueness, rigid labour markets and high taxes can be overcome. Second, policy has an important role to play in sustaining political support for integration, which in turn is the engine of growth for most small countries. Nevertheless, it must be acknowledged that assigning such a role to government places considerable requirements on the administrative effectiveness of the national and local bureaucracy, and as a development strategy it is very far from being a quick fix.

NOTES

1. We gratefully acknowledge statistical assistance from Wesley Thompson, Monica Shin and Graham Howard.
2. These basic facts are drawn from CIA (2002).
3. This is because Finland was an autonomous part of Russia from 1809 to 1917, during which time the railway network was put into place. For national security reasons, Russia deliberately chose a different gauge railway from Germany.
4. The two national languages are Finnish and Swedish, spoken by 94 and 6 percent of the population respectively. The languages are completely dissimilar, and all product labelling must be in both languages.
5. Laakso (2001) has suggested that the Russian trade also helped to alleviate cyclicality through a second channel. The trade basically involved high-level negotiated exchanges of Russian oil for Finnish capital goods and construction services, via a clearing system managed through the Finnish central bank. Because Finnish contact was with Russian central planners rather than with final customers, this trade became an outlet for some large Finnish conglomerates to unload uncompetitive merchandise on the Soviet economy, particularly during downturns.
6. The exception to this is the crisis of the early 1990s, when unemployment skyrocketed from 3.5 to 18 percent. The subsequent recovery saw the rapid emergence of the electronics and telecommunications sectors.
7. This is not an unusual feature in small economies with few players in each sector. It does not preclude high living standards, although price levels will tend to look steep in international comparisons.
8. According to CIA (2002), the remainder of employment is distributed as follows: industry 22 percent, commerce 14 percent, finance, insurance and business services 10 percent, agriculture and forestry 8 percent, transport and communications 8 percent, and construction 6 percent.
9. Openness to trade is probably best thought of as a necessary but not sufficient condition for achieving prosperity. Much work exists which tries to show that lower barriers to trade correlate with faster economic progress. Rodriguez and Rodrik (2000, p.1) cite work by the IMF, the OECD and the World Bank, as well as by Fischer, Krueger and Stiglitz as examples.
10. Intraindustry trade, which makes up the bulk of trade between developed countries, is generally not identified as a major concern in this regard. Rodrik (1998a) argues that it should be, because it weakens the bargaining power of the domestic workforce. This point is returned to later.
11. The logic of this figure was first presented in Leamer (1987). The relevant data are available from the authors upon request.
12. The two-digit breakdown of industries is also fairly crude. Some two-digit or even three-digit industries may contain high-end and low-end components that differ greatly in relative intensity of, for example, skilled labour. Production and exports have become increasingly intensive in capital and skilled labour (pulp and paper, associated forestry and paper machinery/engineering, specialty metal alloys and niche shipbuilding, such as luxury cruise liners and icebreakers).
13. Figure 11.2 shows that these industries are very capital intensive.
14. See OECD (2000, p.23). This argument is similar to that made in Section 11.4 of this chapter.

15. It should be pointed out that countries have considerable leeway in designing labour market institutions that are suited for local conditions, even if path dependency means that institutional changes in this area are particularly slow.
16. World Economic Forum current competitiveness index 2001 and growth competitiveness index 2001. In addition, the IMD World Competitiveness Yearbook ranked Finland third in 2001 (after the USA and Singapore), marking the fifth year in a row that Finland has notched up a place.
17. It is noteworthy that Finnish policy makers explicitly chose not to try to anticipate which sectors would succeed.

REFERENCES

Ali-Yrkkö, J. and R. Hermans (2002), 'Nokia in the Finnish innovation system', ETLA Discussion paper, 811.
Ali-Yrkkö, J., L. Paija, C. Reilly and P. Ylä-Anttila (2000), *Nokia – A Big Company in a Small Country*, Helsinki: Taloustieto OY (ETLA B 162).
CIA (2002), *The World Factbook*, http://www.odci.gov/cia/publications/factbook.
Frame, D. (2000), 'Finland and New Zealand: a cross-country comparison of economic performance', NZ Treasury Working Paper, 00/1.
IMF (2001), 'Finland: selected issues', Country Report No. 01/215.
Laakso, A.-P. (2001), 'Finnish industry – a modern day Cinderella story', Confederation of Finnish Industry and Employers, mimeo.
Leamer, E. (1987), 'Paths of development in the three-factor n-good general equilibrium model', *Journal of Political Economy*, 95, 961-999.
Leamer, E. (1996), 'In search of Stolper–Samuelson effects on US wages', NBER working paper 5427.
Mayda, A.M. and D. Rodrik (2002), 'Why are some people (and countries) more protectionist than others?', mimeo, http://ksghome.harvard.edu/~.drodrik. academic ksg/TradePref.pdf.
Ministry of Finance (Finland) (2001), *Economic Survey*, Helsinki: Ministry of Finance.
OECD (1999), *Main Science and Technology Indicators*, vol. 1, Paris: OECD.
OECD (2000), *Economic Survey of Finland*, Paris: OECD.
OECD (2002a), *Main Science and Technology Indicators*, vol. 2, Paris: OECD.
OECD (2002b), *National Accounts of OECD Countries – Main Aggregates*, vol. 1, Paris: OECD.
Rodriguez, F. and D. Rodrik (2000), 'Trade policy and economic growth: a skeptic's guide to the cross-national evidence', in B. Bernanke and K.S. Rogoff (eds), *Macroeconomics Annual 2000*, Cambridge, Mass.: MIT Press.
Rodrik, D. (1998a), 'Why do more open economies have bigger governments?', *Journal of Political Economy*,106, 997-1032.
Rodrik, D. (1998b), 'The debate over globalisation: how to move forward by looking backward' http://ksghome.harvard.edu/~.drodrik.academic.ksg/papers.html
Statistics Finland (2002), http://www.stat.fi/tk/el/tulo/gini.html.
UNDP (2001), *Human Development Report 2001 – Making New Technologies Work for Human Development*, New York: Oxford University Press.

12. From the Periphery to the New Economy: Paths and Roadblocks for Resource Regions

Lee Huskey

12.1 INTRODUCTION

Some of the poorest parts of the United States lie in the remote rural regions of the country. The economic potential of rural America's traditional resource and manufacturing industries has been reduced by international competition, changes in technology and changes in government policy (Stauber, 2001). New economic growth in these regions is limited by their remoteness from markets and centres of economic activity. This chapter investigates the possibility that recent technological advances associated with the 'New Economy' offer remote, rural regions new opportunities for economic progress.

The business literature is full of claims about the 'death of distance' (Cairncross, 1997) and the creation of a weightless world (Coyle, 1998). These changes will limit the disadvantages of remote locations. Whether distance has died or just been abolished (Evans and Wurster, 2000), the new technologies reduce the cost of moving and communicating across space and increase the potential for increased economic activity away from population centres. The death of distance provides regional elected officials and policy makers in peripheral regions with a new path for promoting the economies of their regions.

Throughout history new technologies have been accompanied by changes in the economic relations between regions. The changes associated with the New Economy have a similar potential. The new technologies allow greater separation of consumption from the location of manufacturing and service provision. Technology would seem to make place less important in the location of economic activity and every place a potential business centre.

Kotkin (2000) disagrees, and argues that the freedom of location in the New Economy may make place matter more. In the New Economy the distinctions between communities may become more important in determining their economic success. This chapter pursues this idea by focusing on the relative importance of two place characteristics, the agglomeration of economic activity and the quality of life, in the location of employment in the high tech sector of the economy. The high-tech sector is innovative and the scale economies associated with concentrated economic activity support the creation of both new ideas and new firms. Quality of life is also important for these firms because of the human capital-intensive nature of their production.

The importance of agglomeration and quality of life creates a potential tension in the location decisions of high tech firms. Economies of scope and scale are more likely to be available in metropolitan regions. The more important they are to high tech industry, the more these firms are drawn to metropolitan areas. However, quality of life may be positively affected by the residential and recreational amenities available in rural America (Nord and Cromartie, 1997). The more important quality of life is to high tech industry, the greater will be the pull of high tech development towards rural areas.

This chapter examines the relative importance of agglomeration and quality of life in the location of high-technology employment across US states. The empirical analysis focuses on one part of the high tech sector, namely the computer and electronics industries. The next sections examine the current 'digital divide' in high tech employment and the possible policy options available to state and local governments. The chapter then looks at the literature on the role of agglomeration and quality of life in the location of economic activity. A regression model of high tech location is presented and estimated. The results suggest that while quality of life does matter, the importance of agglomeration economies may have constrained the recent growth in high tech industries in rural areas. The final section offers some policy suggestions based on these findings.

12.2 THE DIGITAL DIVIDE AMONG US REGIONS

Income, education, tastes and infrastructure limit access for certain population groups to the Internet, the highway of the New Economy (Dunham, 1999; Crockett, 2000). This limited access has been called a 'digital divide' that separates one group of Americans from the New Economy. A similar type of digital divide occurs in the location of employment in the electronics and computer industries. High tech jobs are concentrated in the more metropolitan states and are less likely to be found in rural states.

According to the American Electronics Association every state has some employment in the high tech computer and electronics industries (Platzer, 2001). However, employment in these industries is concentrated outside the rural parts of the country. The high tech industry concentration is similar to the concentration found for invention in the USA (Ceh, 2001). A few states represent a large share of both inventions and high tech employment. Almost 20 percent of total computer and electronics employment was located in California in 1999.

Table 12.1 illustrates the digital divide in employment. The table compares the high tech employment in the most urban states with that of the most rural states. An urban state in Table 12.1 was, rather arbitrarily, assumed to have 80 percent or more of its population in metropolitan areas. A rural state was defined as one with less than 50 percent of its population in metropolitan areas. There were 18 urban and 13 rural states under these definitions.

Table 12.1 The 'digital divide' in employment among US states, 2000

	Share of national population	Share of national high tech employment	Communications services share of high tech employment
Urban states	63.3%	69.3%	24.2%
Rural states	7.4%	4.3%	31.3%
US total			25.6%

Note: Urban states: Arizona, California, Colorado, Connecticut, Delaware, Florida, Illinois, Maryland, Massachusetts, Michigan, Nevada, New Jersey, New York, Ohio, Pennsylvania, Rhode Island, Texas, Washington
Rural states: Alaska, Arkansas, Idaho, Iowa, Kentucky, Maine, Mississippi, Montana, North Dakota, South Dakota, Vermont, West Virginia, Wyoming

High tech employment is relatively more concentrated in urban states than population. The urban states had 63 percent of the US population but almost 70 percent of the employment in the high tech sector. The rural states had 7 percent of the US population and 4.3 percent of high tech employment.

The distribution of employment may not tell the complete story of the digital divide. Rural states' high tech employment was concentrated in communications services. 'Communications services' refers to the industry composed of suppliers of local services such as telephone and cable. Employment in this industry is relatively evenly distributed across states. Employment in communications services accounted for almost one-third of the high tech employment in rural states in 2000. In five states (Montana, Wyoming, Mississippi, West Virginia and Alaska), this industry accounted for over one-half of the high tech employment (Platzer, 2001). The employment 'digital divide' suggests that it is not a foregone conclusion that footloose New Economy firms will bring economic prosperity to rural parts of the USA.

12.3 POLICY OPTIONS

How do rural states and communities make the most of the growth potential provided by the new technology? This is a question that policy makers in Alaska and other remote/rural places are asking. The policy options for a rural place range between two extremes. On the one hand, policy makers can simply 'get ready' for high tech industry and if a location offers the right attributes, market forces will encourage high tech firms to invest there. On the other hand, if policy makers choose not to fully rely on market forces, they could do something to encourage high tech development. This section examines some of the policy options available to rural places that want to encourage high tech employment.

One popular approach to promoting community high tech development in the United States is by means of a name or slogan to attract the attention of the industry. Many places have attempted to draw attention to their region as a high tech location by emulating the public recognition of Silicon Valley. Rural regions have christened themselves the Silicon Prairie in Nebraska, the Silicorn Valley in Iowa, the Silicon Orchard in Washington and the Silicon Mesa in New Mexico (Sterlicchi, 2001).

This approach is similar to local development campaigns that emphasise the welcoming business climate ('Alaska is open for business') or the strategic location ('Alaska: the crossroads of the world'). Such marketing through slogans has little real effect on attracting business because there are too many 'Silicons' for any one place to stand out (Sterlicchi, 2001). However, the slogan strategy has one advantage, namely that it is a relatively cheap way to promote a region.

A second policy approach to attract high tech industries is similar to what is traditionally used to promote local economic development: the use of government spending and subsidies. An example of the use of this strategy to attract high tech firms is Oakland in California, which offered land and infrastructure development as well as tax breaks to attract new high technology firms (Rogers, 2001).

The Progressive Policy Institute (Atkinson et al., 1999) has suggested a set of more active policies to create a state economy that could take advantage of the New Economy opportunities. These strategies include economic reform and investment in education and training for skill development. They also include investing in tertiary education, supporting infrastructure growth and subsidising industry R&D. In addition the Progressive Policy Institute calls for changes to the way in which local government operates, changes in local legal systems and the development of a culture of civic collaboration.

There are two problems with the government spending and subsidy-based schemes. First, they are costly. Bartik has estimated that the traditional tax breaks and subsidies in the USA may cost state and local governments $4,000 annually per job created (Bartik, 1994). The success and potential benefits of these options must be measured against their opportunity costs. The second problem is that they may not work. In their study of the determinants of metropolitan economic growth between 1977 and 1984, O'hUallachain and Satterthwaite (1992) found little evidence that tax breaks and subsidies affected the growth of industries, including high technology manufacturing. Moreover, these programmes tend to be risky. The returns from investments in high tech education, Internet infrastructure and R&D, or offers of tax and finance subsidies, are uncertain.

The final type of strategy is concerned with promoting a region's quality of life. For example, Ft. Collins Co. has used promotion of its quality of life as a tool to attract high tech firms (Gavin, 2001). A good quality of life has also been suggested as an important reason for the growth of the high tech sectors in Boise, Denver, San Diego and Tulsa (Rogers, 2001). This policy strategy differs from the old 'industry chasing' approaches because it offers residents benefits even if no businesses respond.

The difficulty of implementing this type of strategy is to determine what aspects of the quality of life should be promoted. Quality of life is a subjective concept. Peaceful small towns might provide a high-quality living environment for some and yet be rather unattractive to others.

State or local policy makers must understand the determinants of regional economic growth in order to choose the best approach. However, our knowledge of the determinants of the location of high tech employment is limited. Efforts to gain a better understanding of what influences the location of these industries must be a high priority for the formulation of policy in this area.

12.4 HIGH TECH LOCATION

With the 'death of distance' high tech firms no longer need to seek locations near their markets. Cairncross (1997) offers the growth of call centres and telemarketing operations in the upper Midwest states of the USA as an example of this freedom of location. This new footloose character of firms does not imply, however, that every place can be a potential business centre. According to Kotkin (2000), the freedom to move anywhere makes place matter more and the distinction between communities is more important in determining the relative economic success of communities. This section identifies some of the important place characteristics that may matter to high tech industries.

A survey of business opinion as reported in the popular press provides some general factors that may contribute to successfully attracting high tech firms (see Rogers, 2001; Rogers and Jastrow, 2000; Levy and Stone, 1998). These influential factors fit into four groups: agglomeration or scale, quality of life, cost of production, and 'attitude' or 'style' of businesses and policy makers in the region. The first three of these are familiar factors in theories of the location of economic activity.

Agglomeration economies reflect an economy's history and size. Concentrations of economic activity lower the cost of production. This is especially true for new firms, and the innovative nature of the high tech sector makes these economies of scope and scale significant. Regions with industry concentrations have the support of a web of suppliers, potential partners, and legal and technical specialists that new firms require. The historic location of research universities and other institutions provides the stream of ideas for new ventures plus the manpower to start and staff these businesses. Finally, the large concentration of activity provides a potential customer base for new businesses.

However, high tech firms will also be affected by access and the cost of inputs. While the cost of labour may be the most important cost, other costs also matter. High tech firms will be affected by the cost of space as well as the taxes and other public costs associated with a location. Finally, distance may not be entirely unimportant for high tech firms. These firms do need access to suppliers and customers, and face-to-face contacts remain important (see also Part A of this book).

In addition, the quality of life is also an important factor because it may affect labour costs and the potential to attract in-migrants and discourage outward migration. The quality of educational opportunities, the climate, and recreational and cultural amenities can differ greatly across space. Based on the theory of compensating differentials in competitive labour markets, the wage that a firm has to pay in more attractive places will be lower, all else being equal. With recruitment being easier, the costs associated with worker turnover may also be lower in these places.

The final identified factor can be referred to as 'attitude' or 'style'. This might simply mean the existence of a welcoming business climate, but it means more than that in the case of high tech industry. For example, there needs to be an abundance of venture capitalists, not just conventional sources of finance, for high tech industry to be nurtured. Venture capitalists with a high-risk/high-reward attitude are more willing to invest in new high tech ventures. Attitude may reflect agglomeration or local economies of scale, since the historic development of the economy will have been driven by attitudes in the past.

Newsweek identified ten new high tech cities in the USA (Rogers, 2001). They illustrate the role of these four factors. The ten cities are Oakland, California; Omaha, Nebraska; Tulsa, Oklahoma; Dallas, Texas; Huntsville, Alabama; Akron, Ohio; Ventura, California; Washington DC; Denver, Colorado; and San Diego, California. Agglomeration, quality of life, production costs and attitude play a role in all these cases. Oakland, Omaha and Dallas all had a low-cost advantage, primarily in real estate and through government tax incentives. Dallas and Denver had an access advantage because of their central location and major airports. San Diego, Denver and Tulsa all grew partly because of their good quality of life. Omaha, Huntsville, Ventura and Washington DC received the agglomerative effects from a history of military and government-funded research and production activity. Denver, Dallas and Akron had historical experience with technology industries. Finally, Omaha and Tulsa had the advantage of the existence of high tech physical infrastructure.

12.5 AGGLOMERATION AND THE QUALITY OF LIFE

This section examines the economics literature on the importance of agglomeration (scale and density) and the quality of life in location decisions. The literature indicates that both factors influence the location of economic activity. The literature also provides some insight into the relative importance of the two factors.

Research on the concentration of industries has witnessed a revival (Krugman, 1993). This is partly a result of the research that was triggered by trying to explain the growth of Silicon Valley (Kenney and von Burg, 1999; Saxenian, 1996). There is also a renewed interest in explaining the general concentration of industries (Ellison and Glaeser, 1997). While this interest is new, the explanations of the economic consequences of concentration go back to Alfred Marshall (see O'Sullivan, 2003 or Krugman, 1993 for a summary of Marshall).

Agglomeration economies are economies of scope and scale that cause production costs to be lower in places of economic concentration. Such economies also make it easier for new firms to enter. Agglomeration economies can occur at the industry level (localisation economies) or at the level of the place (urbanisation economies). While localisation economies are specific to firms in an industry, urbanisation economies are more generally available to all firms at a location. Marshall identified three reasons for this positive externality: labour market pooling, scale economies in inputs and knowledge spillovers.

Labour market pooling and a concentration of labour with industry-specific skills lower the cost of hiring workers. Firms face lower search costs because there is a skilled pool of workers from which to hire. Workers with experience in an industry also possess the skills and talents the industry requires, as well as an understanding of the way in which the industry works.

Marshall suggested that clustering of firms allows producers of inputs to achieve economies of scale by expanding the size of the local market. The clustering of customers and suppliers also lowers the transport cost and the cost of face-to-face negotiations. Finally, clustering of suppliers may result in greater competition and specialisation among suppliers, which lowers the costs of inputs to firms. The concentration of specialists with industry-specific knowledge provides support for new innovative firms.

Knowledge spillovers are the third source of agglomeration economies according to Marshall. Being close to competitors offers the opportunity to exchange information and ideas, and pass on new technology. This is especially important in industries with significant and rapid innovation, such as the high tech sector. The exchange of ideas may come through a variety of channels, such as through suppliers of intermediate inputs. It may also come through formal and informal interaction between workers and managers of different firms.

Saxenian (1996) examined the role of structure and industry spillovers in her study of the contrasts between Silicon Valley and the Route 128 high tech corridor in Massachusetts. Agglomeration economies may depend as much on the internal structure of companies and their relations with other firms as on scale. Social structure and local institutions create networks that may provide advantages in a place. The ability of ideas and people to move through local firms and for firms to develop cooperative as well as competitive relations with one another creates local networks. These networks or industrial clusters develop a localisation of 'know-how' that creates a place-specific competitive advantage. These types of relational economies provide a strong pull for existing areas and foster an agglomeration force that may be difficult to overcome in remote areas, even when the latter offer a greater quality of life.

However, a region's economic growth potential is influenced not just by the size of its economy but also by the structure of this activity as well. Chinitz (1961) showed that the cost of doing business and the potential for new business differed between entrepreneurial New York and corporate Pittsburgh. The acceptance of entrepreneurs, the existence of supporting suppliers and differences in lending patterns of banks were affected by the economic 'culture' of the place. These types of locational attributes are available to firms in general, not just to firms within an industry. Access to such attributes may be one reason why innovative high tech firms are often attracted to metropolitan areas.

Large places may also be attractive for innovative firms because these places offer advantages for research and development. The inventive process (Usher, 1954) has five steps: perceiving the problem, assembling data on potential solutions, insight, perfecting of the invention and standardised use of the invention. The scale of problems, the diversity of experiences, the interaction with others and the great variety of supporting activities make invention and innovation easier in an economy of large scale. Only insight and standardised production are not limited by being located away from a centre of activity.

O'hUallachain and Satterthwaite (1992) tested for the relative importance of agglomeration economies in the local growth of industrial employment. They examined employment growth in 37 industrial sectors across US metropolitan areas between 1977 and 1984. They found that localisation and urbanisation economies were some of the strongest determinants of metropolitan industrial growth. Localisation economies were significant in over 86 percent of the sectors, while urbanisation economies were significant in about one-third of the industries they examined. Localisation economies were significant in explaining the growth of service industries as well as manufacturing. Variables describing labour costs were the other set of significant factors affecting location. They found little significance of amenity or quality of life variables at the metropolitan level.

However, a region's quality of life may have an effect on local wage rates. A number of studies have shown that wage rates reflect differences in regional amenities (e.g., Rosen, 1974; Gyourko, 1991). Migrants are attracted to nicer regions. This increases the supply of workers in such regions and reduces the wages paid, all else being equal. Workers migrate until their utility cannot be improved. In equilibrium, they are paid lower wage rates in the nicer region and compensated by increased amenities. The lower wages in attractive regions provide an incentive for the location of labour-intensive firms.

Kohler (1997) developed a theoretical model of the interaction between migration decisions, regional amenities and industrial location. He showed that human capital-intensive firms in emerging industries would tend to follow workers to high-amenity locations. However, the precise pattern of location would be fairly sensitive to utility functions of workers and production functions of firms. The tradeoffs between amenities, compensation and other costs may result in firms locating on the periphery of a region with attractive amenities rather than following workers completely to the most attractive places.

Kohler's work reminds us that firms' location choices involve a tradeoff between a reduction in wages and increases in other costs. This tradeoff places a limit on the use of quality of life as an industrial attraction strategy. Not every nice place can spawn a high tech economy.

A number of studies have found that, once they account for agglomeration, amenities matter. Granger and Blomquist (1999) tested the importance of amenities for the location of manufacturing industries. They found that, after controlling for urban scale, amenities influenced the location of manufacturing establishments. The more labour-intensive industries were more strongly attracted to high-amenity areas.

Gottlieb (1995) examined the effects of amenities on the location of high tech employment in New Jersey. He concluded that firms consider certain amenities in places where their employees would be likely to live when they selected a location for the firm. He found that while agglomeration economies influenced the absolute number of employees at a location, amenities influenced the occupational composition of employment.

Rural regions do not have the scale and density of economic activity that have been shown to be important. Rural regions, however, can provide high levels of outdoor recreation and land-based amenities that are limited in more developed regions. The quality of life advantage of rural residential and recreational amenities has been shown to be important in the recent growth of rural America (Nord and Cromartie, 1997). A number of studies have looked specifically at the role of quality of life in attracting businesses to rural areas.

Deller et al. (2001) examine the importance of amenities in the population, employment and per capita income growth of rural counties. They describe the amenity inventory of rural counties in great detail. They use principal components to reduce this information into five measures (climate, developed recreational infrastructure, land, water and winter recreation), which describe a county's developed recreational areas and natural attributes. Looking at growth across rural counties they found that an increase in each of the five county amenity measures was positively associated with the economic growth of rural counties.

Barkley and Keith (1991) looked specifically at the location decisions of high tech industry in the rural USA at the county level. They did not find significant direct effects of amenity differences. They did find that the pattern and strength of the determinants vary for branch plants and unit plants. The county population, proximity to metropolitan areas and net migration rates positively affect branch plant location. Branch plants tend to stay out of rural counties with significant agriculture or manufacturing employment. The positive effect of net migration and the negative effect of other types of employment were considered proxies for the importance of quality of life in high tech location decisions.

In conclusion, there is both theoretical and empirical evidence that amenities matter in determining the location of high tech firms. The literature also suggests that agglomeration matters to the location of economic activity. What does this mean for rural regions? The ability of rural regions to attract these industries depends, as Kohler (1997) has suggested, on the importance of the tradeoff between these factors.

12.6 THE DETERMINANTS OF THE LOCATION OF HIGH TECH EMPLOYMENT

This section describes the regression model that was estimated to investigate the relative roles of agglomeration and quality of life on the location of high tech firms. High tech firms are assumed to be footloose, and the characteristics of a place are expected to be important factors influencing firm location (more so than distance to other markets and the suppliers of inputs).

Three broad sets of factors are hypothesised to affect a firm's location decision by directly or indirectly lowering the costs of production or the costs of acquiring new information. The estimated regressions describe the density of high tech activity at the state level in 1999. State per capita high tech employment is assumed to be a function of three types of factors in each state: production costs, agglomeration and the quality of life.[1]

The regressions examine the electronics and computer component of the US high tech sector. Per capita employment is a measure of location density of high tech industries. Per capita employment would be similar in each state if high tech employment were distributed proportionally to market sizes as measured by state populations.

Separate regressions were estimated for the manufacturing and service industries.[2] It is expected that the location decisions of the two sectors differ. Manufacturing industries might be expected to be more like those of firms in the 'old economy'. The cost of transporting inputs and goods to market may be important in those industries. Manufacturing includes branch plants with little innovation, so agglomeration economies may be less important.

High tech employment by state is assumed to be a good proxy for the location of firms. Employment is likely to be an important policy variable for rural regions. However, employment may underestimate the importance of scale. The supporting aspects of larger economies may be more important for smaller firms. Relative to employment, the number of firms may be more heavily concentrated in larger places.

Factors affecting production costs will affect firm location and employment. Higher unit production costs will make a location less attractive to a high tech firm. One factor that may influence production costs is the level of business taxes. This factor is included in the regression model in the form of corporate income and property tax relative to personal income tax. A higher business tax burden is expected to lower per capita high tech employment.

Labour market conditions are proxied by the state unemployment rate. However, the sign of this variable cannot be theoretically ascertained. On the one hand, a higher unemployment rate may reflect a more abundant labour supply and lower wages. In this case the unemployment rate would have a positive effect on the dependent variable. Alternatively, a high unemployment rate may signal structural problems in the state that could have a detrimental impact on business prospects and lead to increased uncertainty. When this effect dominates, the unemployment rate will have a negative coefficient.

Agglomeration economies reduce the cost of production and the cost of acquiring information, and encourage innovation. We hypothesise that agglomeration will be positively related to per capita high tech employment. The share of the state's population living in metropolitan areas is the measure of agglomeration used in the regressions.

A state's distance from the dominant high tech states (California, Texas, New York, Massachusetts, Florida and Illinois) is a second measure of the importance of agglomeration. Distance is hypothesised to have a negative effect on high tech employment. It is here assumed that location does matter and that the benefits of agglomeration economies may be available to firms in the vicinity of the high tech activity. Closer states may also be more likely candidates for branch plant locations for the more traditional reasons of lower transportation and communication costs.

As noted earlier in this chapter, a firm's wage and labour turnover costs may be lower in places with a higher quality of life. Consequently, we hypothesise that higher quality of life will be positively related to per capita high tech employment. Two measures of the state's quality of life are used. The state's open space density measures the acres of parks, public forests\ and wilderness per square mile in each state.

The score of the state's highest-ranked city in the Places Rated Almanac (Savageau, 1999) is another measure of quality of life. This score is based on a city's ranking in nine categories, comprising cost of living, transportation, jobs, education, climate, crime, arts, health care and recreation. A higher score indicates a better place across these categories. This quality of life variable is also likely to be positively related to high tech employment.

A 'small state' dummy variable is included in the regressions to account for possible border effects. For smaller states both quality of life and scale in neighbouring states may matter. States of limited area would benefit from scale and quality of life dimensions in adjacent states, so that the expected sign on this variable is positive.

The results of the regressions are presented in Table 12.2. Quality of life matters for both manufacturing and service industries. The signs on the Places Rated score and open space density are positive and significant in both high tech manufacturing and high tech services. Thus, the regression results suggest that high tech employment is more likely to be found in states which offer a higher quality of life. The positive coefficient on the small state variable also supports the hypothesis that these factors in neighbouring states matter.

The negative coefficient on the unemployment rate suggests that the 'labour surplus and low wage' effect is dominated by the 'business prospects and uncertainty' effect. High tech employment is less in states with a higher unemployment rate.

The coefficients on the agglomeration variable 'metropolitan population' tell a mixed story about the role of agglomeration economies. The result for the service industry is as predicted. Scale and density matter for the location of these firms. Moreover, the coefficient on the distance variable has also the expected sign, although it is not significant.

The regression for the high tech manufacturing sector tells a different story. The distance variable has a negative and significant coefficient, as we would expect for manufacturing firms. However, the negative coefficient on the metropolitan population variable was not expected. This sign suggests that the urbanisation economies, which are important to the service industries, are not so important for manufacturing. In fact, the regressions suggest that high tech manufacturing firms locate away from the states that are highly metropolitan in nature.

This result may reflect the importance of the product cycle in the manufacturing sector. There may be less innovation per employee in manufacturing which would reduce the importance of agglomeration. When production becomes standardised, production costs become relatively more important. Lower land prices outside of metropolitan areas may be as much of a draw for manufacturing in the high tech sector as they have been for other manufacturing.

Table 12.2 Per capita high tech employment, regression results

	High tech manufacturing	High tech services
Constant	2.590	0.715
	(0.317)	(0.139)
Metropolitan population	−0.094	0.062
	(−2.293)**	(2.404)**
Distance	−0.005	−0.001
	(−3.051)***	(−0.806)
Open space	0.123	0.042
	(3.917)***	(2.124)**
Places Rated score	0.245	0.012
	(2.319)**	(1.745)*
Unemployment rate	−1.540	−1.510
	(−2.875)***	(−4.500)***
Tax burden	−0.008	0.028
	(−0.083)	(0.467)
Small state	4.957	1.708
	(2.673)**	(1.466)
Adjusted R^2	0.348	0.465

Notes: The *t*-statistics are in parentheses and *, ** and *** indicate that the variable is significant at the level of 10 percent, 5 percent and 1 percent respectively.
For ease of interpretation, the coefficients have been multiplied by 1,000 and therefore measure the effect of the variable on high tech employment per 1,000 of the population

The tax burden has the right sign but is insignificant in both regressions. This variable represents the relative importance of taxes on business in the tax structure of the state. However, it can be argued that inter-state differences in state spending on business services should be taken into account. Personal taxes and public spending are captured in the Places Rated scores.

These equations offer some hope for state development strategies that emphasise quality of life. The results suggest that states with high quality of life that are close to major high tech areas have a chance of attracting high tech firms. However, agglomeration economies also matter. The urbanisation economies available in large metro areas appear to matter more for the service industries. The results also suggest that rural areas can attract high tech firms but should expect to be more attractive to firms in the standardisation phase of the product cycle.

Future work on the location of firms in the high tech sector needs to confront a series of fundamental research questions. First, the high tech sector is made up of a number of industries. As this chapter has suggested, different factors will determine the location of these specific industries. Future work should be done at a more detailed industry level. The related second question concerns the appropriate regional level. Areas within a state may vary in both agglomeration economies and quality of life. This variety is difficult to capture at the state level. The county may be the better geographic unit for examining the location of high tech employment.

A more important concern is the specification of both agglomeration economies and quality of life. These two explanatory variables have many dimensions, and the importance of each of these may vary across types of industries. Using only metropolitan population to represent agglomeration economies has drawbacks. It measures directly only urbanisation economies. A more detailed set of factors would also be helpful for policy makers. Quality of life measures present similar problems. The problems with using quality of life rankings are well known (Stover and Leven, 1991). The robust nature of the open space variable suggests that more specific definitions of other dimensions of quality of life may pay off.

12.7 FINAL THOUGHTS ON POLICY

The growth of the US high tech sector and its labour-intensive businesses provides a potential path for low-income rural resource-based regions to move closer to income parity with urban centres. The footloose nature of these firms and the absence of a need for an existing manufacturing base or a large labour force suggest that rural regions possess no obvious disadvantage. In fact, if quality of life amenities are sufficiently important to New Economy workers, rural location might even be an advantage. The primary roadblock on this path is the attractiveness of agglomeration economies to high tech firms. The regression results above illustrate this dilemma. They show that while quality of life matters, there is also evidence that the scale and density of activity matter equally. The lack of agglomeration economies in rural areas provides a major roadblock to this development path.

The positive effect of quality of life still offers a development strategy for rural areas. Focusing investment and policy on improving a region's quality of life may increase the quantity of high tech business in a region. These investments may eventually increase economic growth and even if they do not, they will at the very least improve the lives of people in the region.

Pursuing a quality of life strategy may, however, be constrained by resource considerations. Investing in quality of life improvement is not free and there are opportunity costs. In addition, nature has not endowed all rural areas with quality of life aspects that people are attracted to.

There may be two other avenues to rural high tech growth. First, a region may possess some cost advantage that would attract high tech firms. One example may be inexpensive land and housing. Energy might provide another resource advantage. The high tech sector involves a variety of activities and some use significant amounts of energy. For example, one firm investigated the use of the natural gas resources currently trapped on Alaska's North Slope to run a major Internet server farm. Such activities are high-energy users and the location would provide low-cost production, since it is easier to move information from the North Slope than natural gas (Clark, 2001).

A second source of high tech industry growth might come from serving the resource industries that dominate these regions, such as mining and agriculture. If industry activity in a region generates significant scale economies and if the resource industry relies on high tech applications, high tech businesses might be attracted. While such firms might be established initially to serve the natural resource industry, they might serve a broader market at a later stage. The region's natural resource base would provide the foundation for this growth.

Reliance on a homegrown competitive advantage seems consistent with the pattern of high tech specialisation found by Cortright and Mayer (2001). They found that high tech concentrations tended to specialise in relatively few products. Specialisation was found in production, patents and venture capital. The natural resource base of a rural region may give direction to high tech specialisation.

States may attempt to spend their way to induce agglomeration economies by investing in research, venture capital or university development. The connection to the region's local industries is also important in these strategies. Experience with R&D investments in rural regions of Europe suggests that they have a limited impact on economic growth. Rural regions may not have the industrial structure and infrastructure to incorporate new ideas found in these programmes (Rodriguez-Pose, 2001). Investing in the high tech component of homegrown industries means that the region is more likely to have the internal businesses, skills and infrastructure to make the most out of new ideas.

This study adds to the literature that seeks to understand the role that quality of life and agglomeration play in determining the location of high tech employment. Both quality of life and agglomeration affect the location of high tech employment. These results offer both hope and caution for rural policy makers. Unfortunately, the regression results are not specific enough to provide definitive policy answers. Developing a policy-relevant understanding of the importance of these two dimensions will require greater in-depth identification of the various dimensions of both agglomeration advantages and quality of life.

NOTES

1. Definitions and sources of the regression variables: *Per capita high tech employment*: 1999 manufacturing and services high tech employment in each state divided by state population (Platzer, 2001). *Metropolitan population*: Share of the state's population in metropolitan areas in 1990 (US Bureau of the Census, 2000, Table 33). *Distance*: The distance from a state's major city to the major city in one of the top six high tech employment states. These states are California, Texas, New York, Florida, Massachusetts and Illinois. *Open space*: A state's open space density is measured as acres in state and national parks, public forests and wilderness areas divided by state square miles (Vesterby and Krupa, 2001). *Places Rated score*: The score of each state's highest-ranked city in 1999 based on rankings in nine categories: cost of living, transportation, jobs, education, climate, crime, arts, health care and recreation (Savageau, 1999). *Unemployment rate*: State unemployment rate in 1994 (US Bureau of the Census, 2000, Table 680). *Tax burden*: Corporate income tax and property taxes per $1,000 of state personal income tax in 1990 (Tannerwald, 1996). *Small state*: A dummy variable that equalled one for the smallest US states: Connecticut, Delaware, Hawaii, Maryland, Massachusetts, New Hampshire, New Jersey, Rhode Island and Vermont.
2. Industry definitions have been derived from Platzer (2001). High tech service does not include Communication services (SIC 4812, 4813, 4822, 4841 and 4899). The High Tech Manufacturing Sector includes: Computer and office equipment (3571, 3572, 3575, 3577, 3578, 3579); Consumer electronics (3651, 3652); Communication equipment (3661, 3663, 3669); Electronic components & accessories (3671, 3672, 3675, 3676, 3677, 3678, 3679); Semiconductors (3674); Industrial electronics (3821, 3822, 3823, 3824, 3825, 3826, 3829); Photonics (3827, 3861); Defence electronics (3812); and Electro-medical equipment (3844, 3845). The High Tech Service Sector includes: Software services (7371, 7372, 7373); Data processing and information services (7374, 7375, 7376); and Computer rental, maintenance and related services (7377, 7378, 7379).

REFERENCES

Atkinson, R., Court, R. and J. Ward (1999), *Economic Development Strategies for the New Economy*, Washington, DC: Progressive Policy Institute.

Barkley, D. and J. Keith (1991), 'The locational determinants of western nonmetro high tech manufacturers: an econometric analysis', *Western Journal of Agricultural Economics*, 16, 331-344.

Bartik, T. (1994), 'Jobs, productivity, and local economic development: what implications does economic research have for the role of government?', *National Tax Journal*, 46, 847-861.

Cairncross, F. (1997), *The Death of Distance*, Boston, Mass.: Harvard Business School Press.

Ceh, B. (2001), 'Regional innovation potential in the United States: evidence of spatial transformation', *Papers in Regional Science*, 80, 297-316.

Chinitz, B. (1961), 'Contrast in agglomeration: New York and Pittsburgh', *American Economic Review*, 51, 279-289.

Clark, M. (2001), 'Server firm eyes the slope', *Anchorage Daily News*, 14 May.

Cortright, J. and H. Mayer (2001), 'High tech specialization: a comparison of high technology centers', *The Brookings Institution Survey Series*, Washington, DC, January.

Coyle, D. (1998), *The Weightless World*, Cambridge, Mass.: The MIT Press.

Crockett, R. (2000), 'Commentary: how to bridge America's digital divide', *Business Week*, 8 May.

Deller, S., Tsai, T., Marcouiller D. and D. English (2001), 'The role of amenities and quality of life in rural economic growth', *American Journal of Agricultural Economics*, 83, 352-365.

Dunham, R. (1999), 'Commentary: across America a troubling digital divide', *Business Week*, 2 August.

Ellison, G. and E. Glaeser (1997), 'Geographic concentration in US manufacturing industries: a dartboard approach', *Journal of Political Economy*, 105, 889-927.

Evans, P. and Wurster T.S. (2000), *Blown to Bits*, Boston, Mass.: Harvard Business School Press.

Gavin, R. (2001), 'The Rockies emerge as pocket of prosperity in a slowing economy', *Wall Street Journal*, 10 June.

Gold, R. (2001), 'Cities pursue benefits of clusters', *Wall Street Journal*, 6 June.

Gottlieb, P. (1995), 'Residential amenities, firm location, and economic development', *Urban Studies*, 32, 1413-1436.

Granger, M. and G. Blomquist (1999), 'Evaluating the influence of amenities on the location of manufacturing establishments in urban areas', *Urban Studies*, 36, 1859-1873.

Gyourko, J. (1991), 'How accurate are quality of life rankings across cities?', *Business Review of the Federal Reserve Bank of Philadelphia*, March/April.

Kenney, M. and U. von Burg (1999), 'Technology, entrepreneurship, and path dependence: industrial clustering in Silicon Valley', *Industrial and Corporate Change*, 8, 67-103.

Kohler, H.-P. (1997), 'The effect of hedonic migration decisions and region-specific amenities on industrial location: could Silicon Valley be in South Dakota?', *Journal of Regional Science*, 37, 379-394.

Kotkin, J. (2000), *The New Geography*, New York: Random House.

Krugman, P. (1993), *Geography and Trade*, Cambridge, Mass.: MIT Press.

Levy, S. and B. Stone (1998), 'The hot new tech cities', *Newsweek*, 9 November.

New Mexico Business Journal (1999), 'Where high tech counts', November.

Nord, M. and J. Cromartie (1997), 'Migration: the increasing importance of rural natural amenities', *Choices: The Magazine of Food, Farm, and Resource Issues*, 12, Third quarter.

O'hUallachain, B. and M.A. Satterthwaite (1992), 'Sectoral growth patterns at the metropolitan level: an evaluation of economic development incentives', *Journal of Urban Economics*, 31, 25-58.

O'Sullivan, A. (2003), *Urban Economics*, Boston, Mass.: McGraw-Hill.

Platzer, M. (2001), *Cyberstates 2001*, Washington, DC: American Electronics Association.

Rodriguez-Pose, A. (2001), 'Is R&D investment in lagging areas of Europe worthwhile? Theory and empirical evidence', *Papers in Regional Science*, 80, 275-296.

Rogers, A. (2001), 'A new brand of tech cities', *Newsweek*, 30 April.

Rogers, A. and D. Jastrow (2000), 'From the valley to the alley', *Computer Resellers News*, 905, 31 July.

Rosen, S. (1974), 'Wage based indexes of urban quality of life', in P. Mieszkowski and M. Straszheim (eds), *Current Issues in Urban Economics*, Baltimore, Maryland: Johns Hopkins University Press.

Savageau, D. (1999), *Places Rated Almanac, Special Millennium Editon*, New York: Wiley.

Saxenian, A. (1996), *Regional Advantage: Culture and Competition in Silicon Valley and Route 128*, Cambridge, Mass.: Harvard University Press.

Stauber, K. (2001), 'Why invest in rural America and how? A critical public policy question for the 21st century', *Federal Reserve of Kansas City Economic Review*, 86, 57-87.

Sterlicchi, J. (2001), 'Saturation is near as more of world's cities fall for lure of Siliconia', *Evening Standard*, 4 April.

Stover, M. and C. Leven (1991), 'Methodological issues in the determination of the quality of life', *Urban Studies*, 29, 737-754.

Tannerwald, R. (1996), 'State business tax climate: how should it be measured and how important is it?', *New England Economic Review*, Jan./Feb., 23-38.

US Bureau of the Census (2000), *Statistical Abstract of the United States*, Washington, DC: US Department of Commerce.

Usher, A.P. (1954), *A History of Mechanical Invention*, Cambridge, Mass.: Harvard University Press.

Vesterby, M. and K. Krupa (2001), *The Major Uses of Land in the US, 1997*, Statistical Bulletin No. 973, Resource Economic Division, Economic Research Unit, US Department of Agriculture.

13. Ireland's Economic Renaissance: The Success of a 'Peripheral' Economy

Brendan Walsh

13.1 INTRODUCTION

This chapter focuses on the miracle years of the 'Celtic Tiger' or 'Irish Hare' and asks what happened and why and what lessons can be drawn for Ireland and other countries.[1] The period covered is the 1990s, defined (correctly) to end on 31 December, 2000. The world, and Ireland with it, began to move in the months after this towards a period of slower growth.

Between 1993 and 2001 the annual real growth rate of the Irish economy had been more than double the average recorded over the previous three decades – 8 percent compared with 3.5 percent. Figure 13.1 shows the Irish and EU average growth rates. Ireland has out-performed the EU average since 1987. After 1993 the country went through a phase of a very rapid catching up to the wealthier EU economies. The Irish boom of the 1990s was exceptional not just by historical Irish standards but also in an international perspective. Apart from the 'Asian Tigers' between 1960 and 1990 and China since 1978, no other country has sustained such rapid growth for any length of time.

The performance of the labour market was even more remarkable. The number at work rose by over 50 percent – representing an annual average increase of 3.4 percent a year. In contrast, over the same period there was little net employment growth in the EU overall and employment in the USA increased by 'only' about 1 percent a year (Figure 13.2). The Irish unemployment rate fell from a peak of 17 percent in the mid-1980s to under 4 percent in 2001, moving it from close to the top to the bottom of the EU league table (Figure 13.3).

Figure 13.1 Real GDP growth in Ireland and the EU, 1987–2001

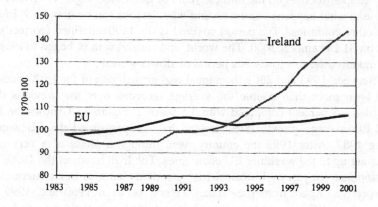

Figure 13.2 Employment in Ireland and the EU, 1985–2001

The boom in employment and output accomplished many things:

* The proportion of the total population employed outside agriculture rose from 25 percent to 40 percent. Women's labour force participation rate rose from a low initial level to close to the EU average. The traditional high net emigration rate was replaced by the highest net immigration rate in the EU.[2]

- As a result of the decreased burden of dependency and growth in output per worker, Ireland moved up in the international living standards league table. Having long endured a standard of living that was only two-thirds of the EU average, the country rose to the European average in terms of GDP per person adjusted for the purchasing power of currencies (Figure 13.4). On a global basis, Ireland moved from 24th among the nations to 22nd in 1993 and 9th in 1999.

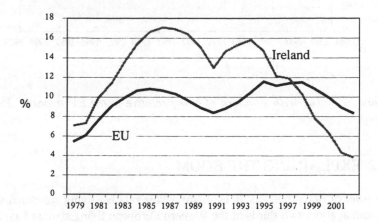

Figure 13.3 Irish and EU unemployment rates, 1979–2001

However, some caution is required in the interpretation of the Irish macroeconomic data. There is an exceptionally large and growing gap between GNP and GDP. This reflects (i) interest on national debt paid to non-residents and (ii) the profits and related payments remitted abroad by the Irish affiliates of multinational corporations. The first component declined steadily after the fiscal correction of the 1980s, but the second increased in line with the inflow of FDI during the 1990s. Real GDP growth exceeded GNP growth by 1.2 percentage points a year over the period 1995–2000 and the GDP–GNP gap widened from 11.3 percent to 15.8 percent.

We can allow for these caveats by comparing the growth of Ireland's Gross National Disposable Income, 8.0 percent a year, with the EU's GDP growth rate of 2.6 percent.[3] Clearly, even when the caveats are taken into account, the Irish boom remains an impressive reality.

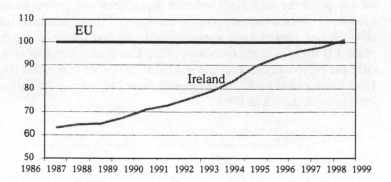

*Figure 13.4 The Irish standard of living relative to the EU average, 1986–
1999*

13.2 EXPLAINING THE BOOM

The point of departure was an economy where relative living standards were
stagnant at about two-thirds of the Western European living standard average
and the total population and labour force had changed little since Irish
Independence in 1922. This stagnation was often attributed to, among other
factors, its relative remoteness as an island offshore Great Britain, which in
turn was offshore the more dynamic European mainland. While geographical
factors are immutable, one of the hoped-for benefits of joining the European
Economic Community in 1973 was to lessen the dependence on the slow-
growing UK economy. Moreover, liberalisation of air and sea transport in the
1980s helped to reduce the economic burden of Ireland's remote location.
Nonetheless 'peripherality' was emphasised in the negotiations for
'Objective One' status in the European Union, which entitled the country to
favourable treatment in the share-out of EU regional, social and cohesion
funds in the 1990s.

Viewed from a wider perspective, Ireland's location may not be too great
an economic penalty. Ireland's location between the USA and Europe,
combined with the use of the English language, is in fact often cited as an
attraction to inward investment.

13.2.1 Belated Convergence

The reason why 'Irish Hare' rather than 'Celtic Tiger' might be a more appropriate soubriquet for the Irish boom – apart from its greater zoological realism – is that as late as the 1980s there was so much ground to be made up to bring Ireland up to the average of the EU. Economists puzzled over Ireland's failure to grow as rapidly as several poorer European economies, such as Italy for example, over the immediate post-war period. Many economic growth models predict that countries that are open to trade and investment and have similar educational levels should experience real convergence. Ireland's performance was below that predicted by these models up to the mid-1980s, but significantly above thereafter (Leddin and Walsh, 1998; O Grada and O'Rourke, 2000). An obvious explanation for the improvement is that bad economic policies, such as the continuation of protectionist trade policies into the late 1950s, an excessive role for the state in the productive sectors of the economy and irresponsible fiscal experimentation in the late 1970s, delayed Ireland's entry to the European 'convergence club'. Once the country had rectified its fiscal imbalances in the first half of the 1980s, moved towards more market-friendly policies and copper-fastened its access to EU markets by implementing the Single European Act in the early 1990s, it was well positioned to attract FDI from the booming US economy and to catch up quickly – if belatedly – with the world's richest countries.

But this interpretation does not explain why Ireland caught up so rapidly during the 1990s and why some other EU member states – Spain, Portugal and Greece – failed to do so. Further afield, New Zealand and Canada were once close to the top of the international living standards league table but have fallen behind in recent decades, while Argentina fell behind earlier. It is obvious that there is nothing automatic about catching up or staying at the top.

To what can the sudden invigoration of the Irish economy that began in the second half of the 1980s and that has continued to the present then be attributed? The consensus view is that the timing of the boom was the product of a number of interacting factors, a mixture of good domestic economic policies and favourable external developments. While it is difficult to quantify the individual contributions of these factors, there is general agreement about what should be included in the list. These are discussed under two sub-headings – favourable external developments and sound domestic policies.

13.2.2 Favourable External Developments

The improvement in Irish economic performance in the late 1980s and during the 1990s owes a lot to the following favourable external developments:

- The so-called 'Lawson boom' in the UK in the late 1980s and the sustained US boom in the 1990s.
- The impact of new IT technologies on productivity and Ireland's success in attracting FDI in the associated industries.
- Low energy prices.
- Reductions in the cost of access to Ireland.
- Significant additional EU transfers for infrastructure and training.
- A soft exchange rate against sterling and the US dollar.

Only the last two require elaboration here.

EU aid

The increased inflow of EU assistance to Ireland in the late 1980s coincided with the start of the Irish economic boom. The importance of this factor is, however, often exaggerated by outside commentators. Ireland had benefited disproportionately from the Common Agricultural Policy since joining the EU in the 1970s. The country received additional aid on joining the European Monetary System (EMS) in 1979 and more aid flowed from the cohesion, regional, and social funds to help the country cope with the completion of the implementation of the single European market and the adoption of the euro. These inflows were counter-cyclical and helped to offset the effects of the global recession of the early 1990s on the economy. The EU aid peaked at about 7 percent of GDP in the early 1990s and had declined to less than 4 percent by the end of the decade. 'Structural funds' – aid designed to help a country overcome specific infrastructure deficits and the adverse effects of a country's peripheral European location – approached 4 percent of GDP in the early 1990s and declined from then. As Ireland is now above the EU average GDP per person, the country will not be eligible for aid under these headings when the next round is allocated in 2004 and will become a net contributor to the EU budget. The increase in aid during the late 1980s created leeway for tax concessions in the 1990s even as spending on infrastructure was increased. Moreover, the aid was used effectively and the process of applying for funding and prioritising projects led to a marked improvement in the overall planning of Irish public spending.

The exchange rate

The launch of the EMS in 1979 forced Ireland to choose between maintaining the peg with sterling and throwing its lot in with the continental European currencies. The decision to end the 57-year-old sterling link began the process that culminated in the adoption of the euro in 1999 and the consequential elimination of exchange rate uncertainty *vis-à-vis* the continental economies. The most important influences on this decision were the perceived political benefits, the promise of additional EU subsidies and a desire to shift the currency's nominal anchor from sterling, then considered to be inflation prone, to the new 'zone of monetary stability' centred on the German mark.[4] But despite these possible advantages, many Irish economists believed that it was inappropriate to join a currency zone that accounted for only about one-third of international trade. In fact sterling continued to influence Irish policy long after the formal link was broken, as may be judged from the fact that on the three occasions when the Irish pound was devalued in the Exchange Rate Mechanism (ERM) – in 1983, 1986 and 1993 – the action was taken defensively as sterling weakened relative to the continental currencies. It is striking that the Irish boom really got underway shortly after the 10 percent devaluation of the Irish pound in January 1993. Furthermore, when the euro was launched in 1999 the trade-weighted value of the Irish pound was low and over the following year and a half the value of the euro fell by about 25 percent. This competitive boost was reinforced by the convergence of Eurozone nominal interest rates, which led to a significant fall in Irish real interest rates.

Some have argued that the use of a common currency is a major stimulus to trade.[5] If this were the case, Ireland's decision to break the link with sterling in 1979 before adopting the euro in 1999 could be expected to have checked the growth of the openness of the economy – trade with Britain falling without any offsetting increase in trade with continental Europe. However, this does not appear to have been the case (Thom and Walsh, 2002). Diversification of trade from the UK had been occurring for some time and accelerated with Ireland's entry to the EEC in 1973 but seems to have been relatively unaffected by the change of exchange rate regime. There are some interesting parallels with New Zealand's experience: the decision to break with sterling in the 1930s was beneficial, while the UK's application for EEC membership in the 1960s was very detrimental to the expansion of the New Zealand economy (Gould, 1982).

13.2.3 Sound Domestic Policies

The domestic policies and developments that can be invoked to explain the timing of Ireland's economic renaissance include:

*   Fiscal stabilisation leading to healthy public finances, nominal convergence *à la* Maastricht and qualification for membership of the Eurozone.
*   An elastic supply of good quality and relatively inexpensive labour.
*   Flexible labour market practices and industrial peace.
*   A welcoming environment for FDI, including low corporate tax rates.

Fiscal stabilisation
In the course of the 1980s Ireland struggled to correct the imbalance in the public finances inherited from the failed fiscal expansion of the late 1970s. At the start of the decade the fiscal and the current account deficits were both close to 15 percent of GDP and external indebtedness was rising at an unsustainable rate. Initial attempts to correct these imbalances by increasing taxes were frustrated by – and contributed to – the economy's slow recovery. High taxes contributed to capital flight, smuggling from Northern Ireland to the Republic and emigration. In 1988 a prominent American economist referred to Ireland's 'failed stabilisation' and advocated a default on the country's mountain of debt (Dornbush, 1988). However, the switch to cuts in current and especially capital spending in 1987 met with more success. A major shift from domestic absorption to net exports was required and as a consequence there was a considerable delay before the revival of growth became evident in rising living standards (Walsh, 1996). The painful adjustment was helped by the agreement of the largest opposition party not to make political capital from the austerity measures introduced by the governing coalition.

The Irish record supports the belief that fiscal adjustment based on the 'shock therapy' of sharp expenditure cuts is likely to be more successful than a gradualist approach relying on tax increases. By the early 1990s the government budget and the current account had both moved into surplus and the debt/GDP ratio was falling rapidly (Figure 13.5).

The fiscal adjustment began as the 'Lawson boom' (1985–1990) gathered pace in Britain; Ireland was well positioned to take advantage of this boom due to the devaluation of the Irish pound in 1986. The resurgence of external demand is a more plausible explanation of the recovery than the 'expansionary fiscal contraction' hypothesis proposed by Giavazzi and Pagano (1990).

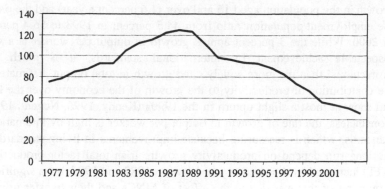

Figure 13.5 National debt as a percentage of GDP

Productivity

Only a rise in the rate of productivity growth would justify applying the label 'miracle' to the transformation of the Irish economy after the 1980s. Between 1993 and 2000 real GNP grew by 8 percent and employment grew by 5 percent a year, so output per person employed grew by 3 percent a year. Figure 13.6 shows the relative contribution of (i) productivity growth, (ii) the growth of the population of working age and (iii) the rising employment rate to the boom of the 1990s.

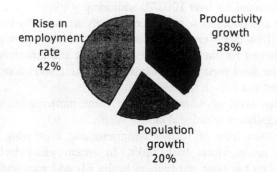

Figure 13.6 Sources of growth, 1993–2001

Increased productivity accounted for 38 percent of the total growth of output, population growth for 20 percent, and the remaining 42 percent was due to the rise in the employment rate. Thus, over 60 percent of the growth in output was due to the growth in employment, which reflected the rapid growth in the population aged 15 and over (1.6 percent a year) and the rise in the employment/population ratio from 44.5 percent in 1993 to 56.4 percent in 2000. While the 3 percent annual growth in output per worker is a very respectable achievement by international standards, it is much less 'miraculous' than the more widely cited growth in total output. Estimates of the contribution of productivity to the growth of the economy over the long run show at most a slight upturn in the 1990s (Kenny, 1996; Nugent, 1998). Nonetheless, the rate of growth in output per worker is high by international standards, which is reassuring because improvements in living standards in the long run depend on productivity growth. Irish total factor productivity (TFP) increased by 4 percent a year between 1987 and 1997, but a significant proportion of this was due to the effect of MNCs and their transfer pricing, so that the underlying rate of productivity growth in the economy has been less remarkable, or not remarkable at all, by some measures (Honohan and Walsh, 2002).

Elastic labour supply
Ireland's exceptional rate of employment growth was facilitated by a relatively elastic supply of labour that allowed employment to grow at an exceptional pace without – until 1999–2000 – much evidence of labour market overheating. The factors contributing to the elastic supply of labour were:

* The large initial pool of unemployment. The fall in the unemployment rate alone accounted for over 100,000 additional workers.
* The working age population grew very rapidly as the baby boom of the 1960s and 1970s came on the labour market. Initially this population bulge was blamed for the rise in unemployment and emigration, but as the growth rate quickened the availability of a young and educated labour force was cited as a reason for the boom.
* The low initial level of women's labour force participation rates gave scope for a significant additional labour supply.
* A sizeable return flow of former emigrants and a growing inflow of people with no previous Irish links. In recent years Ireland's net immigration rate has been the highest in the EU and accounts for about half of the growth of the labour force.

Falling unemployment, rising labour force participation rates and the drop in the proportion of young dependants in the population all contributed to the rising employment/population rate. As we have seen, without any improvement in productivity or increase in the working age population, the higher employment rate would have accounted for 40 percent of the growth of output that was recorded after 1993. But a rising employment/population ratio is a transitional phenomenon and Ireland is now close to the European average on this measure, so this factor will contribute little to future gains in average living standards.

The average educational attainment of the employed labour force grew steadily from the mid-1960s to the mid-1990s. By the 1980s the majority of those leaving the educational system were well-qualified young people with second and third level qualifications. A recent estimate suggests that the rising stock of human capital accounts for about 20 percent of total output growth during the boom (Durkan et al., 1999). Much of this reflected a belated catch-up of Irish educational levels to the European average.

Industrial policy
The contribution of foreign direct investment to Irish economic growth has been significant since the 1960s. By the late 1990s foreign-owned firms accounted for about 47 percent of Ireland's industrial employment, 77 percent of net industrial output and 83 percent of merchandise exports. Foreign firms also predominate in the International Financial Services Centre (IFSC), where over 7,000 people are now employed in back-office and higher value-added activities in a designated area of Dublin. Several of the larger overseas companies employ over 3,000 people in Ireland. Most of the global microelectronics, computer and pharmaceutical firms now have Irish plants. The computer industry is the most striking industrial policy success story. The sector was targeted by the industrial promotion agencies. Foreign companies were attracted to Ireland by the low corporation tax (CT) rate and the availability of a well-educated English-speaking labour force. It now accounts for one-quarter of industrial employment and there have been notable spin-offs and start-ups of strong indigenous firms, especially in software development. Clearly, any disadvantages attributable to Ireland's 'peripherality' have been more than offset by the fiscal incentives to FDI (discussed in the next section) and the availability of a skilled English-speaking labour force at competitive wage levels.

13.3 IRELAND'S ATTRACTIVENESS AS A LOCATION FOR FDI

In view of the crucial role of FDI in Ireland's economic development, it is important to try to account for Ireland's attractiveness as an industrial location.

13.3.1   A European Export Platform

Although Ireland emerged from its protectionist cocoon only in the 1960s, by the 1990s it was fully integrated into the EU and global economies. An eagerness to attract inward investment replaced hostility to foreign ownership of Irish firms. Tax breaks and grants for exporting firms replaced the emphasis on catering to the domestic market. With the completion of the EU single market in the early 1990s, Ireland offered US firms a convenient platform from which to supply their European customers. While its peripheral island location added to transport costs, this disadvantage was not significant for the high-value/low-weight products of the electronics, pharmaceutical, and financial services sectors where inward investment has been concentrated. Moreover, the sea and air transport routes to the country were liberalised during the 1980s. Lower access costs also played an important role in the growth of tourism. The pattern of growth of the Irish economy fits well with the thesis that moving from a closed economy to an open trade-oriented one can significantly raise a country's growth rate. Ireland has been a super-trader by any standards and there was a dramatic increase in the openness of the economy that accelerated as the boom gathered pace (Figure 13.7). By the end of the 1990s Ireland was exceptionally open to trade: merchandise trade (imports plus exports) was about twice as high relative to GDP as in Denmark, Portugal and New Zealand.

While economists may believe that trade is something of which we cannot have too much, the growth of exports and imports relative to production in Ireland prompts the question: has the structure of the Irish economy been distorted towards trade by the type of export-oriented industries attracted by its low tax regime and the opportunities the country offers for transfer pricing? Figure 13.8 is a first cut at answering this question by looking at the association between trade and size. While Ireland lies above the regression line, it is less of an outlier than such obvious entrepôt economies as Singapore, Hong Kong and Belgium. Interestingly, Ireland is about as far above the line as New Zealand is below it. Clearly Ireland has pursued a very trade-oriented policy but one that is judged to have paid off in terms of employment and wealth creation.

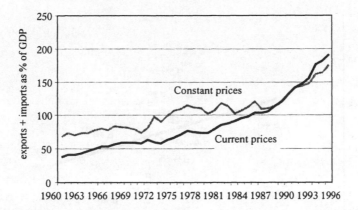

Figure 13.7 Openness of the Irish economy

13.3.2 Favourable Climate for FDI

Ireland has shown a consistently favourable attitude towards overseas investment since the early 1960s. The low rate of CT and liberal grants for fixed assets and training have been paramount among the inducements to firms to choose Ireland as their European location. Ireland has the lowest statutory and effective CT rates in the EU. But even though its importance in the economy's longer-term success is not disputed, there were no changes in the tax system in the late 1980s that could be given credit for triggering the boom. Indeed, the effective CT rate actually increased in the 1990s and Ireland's advantage relative to other European countries has been eroded as those countries have cut their tax rates in recent years. The broader point is that there was no sudden policy initiative in the 1990s that accounts for the sudden leap in the growth rate. A more detailed discussion of the role of CT in the Irish economy is contained in the next section.

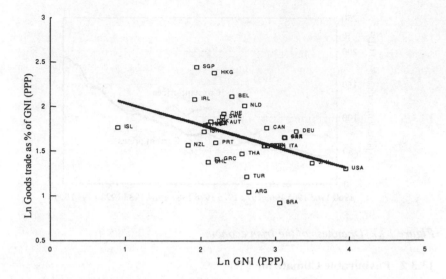

Figure 13.8   Openness and size

Note: GNI (PPP) is Gross National Income measured at purchasing power parity exchange
rates

13.3.3   Industrial Promotion

The main Irish industrial promotion agency – the Industrial Development
Authority – has long experience of trying to attract inward FDI to the
country. It has learned through a process of trial and error to identify the
industries most likely to be attracted by the advantages that Ireland has to
offer and now targets the electronic engineering, pharmaceuticals, medical
instrumentation, computer software and biotechnology sectors. When the
former insistence on regional decentralisation was tacitly relaxed, cities such
as Dublin, Cork and Galway attracted significant clusters of firms in these
industries. The firms that come to Ireland share a need for a supply of well-
educated flexible workers and an ability to extract the maximum benefit from
the low CT rate applied to the manufacturing industry (see Section 13.4).

13.3.4   Low Cost Labour Supply

When asked about the key attraction of locating in Ireland, we would expect
an industrialist to stress the importance of Ireland's plentiful supply of
English-speaking, skilled labour. The contribution of the elastic labour

supply to the exceptional growth of the economy in the 1990s was noted earlier. The qualified young people leaving the educational system in the 1990s were eager to work in Ireland at wage rates that were relatively low by comparison with those prevailing on the European mainland. Subsidiaries of multinationals employing these young people in Ireland achieved high productivity levels.

13.3.5 Wage Bargaining and 'Corporatism'

The impetus behind the bargaining approach came from the desire to improve Ireland's poor industrial relations record, which had periodically caused severe economic disruption. The early agreements dealt with the nitty-gritty of percentage pay increases, the treatment of lower-paid workers, cost of living adjustments and mechanisms for resolving disputes, but in 1976 the government sought an integrated pay agreement linked to changes in social welfare benefits and accepted some responsibility for job creation in return for pay moderation. This model was influenced by the experience of countries such as the Netherlands, Austria, Norway and Sweden.

In 1979 the first 'National Understanding for Economic and Social Development' was negotiated against a backdrop of disastrous industrial strife (Durkan, 1992). While this agreement achieved a reduction in the level of strikes, a second agreement collapsed in 1982 and a five-year period of decentralised collective bargaining followed. It was not until 1987 that a new National Agreement was negotiated. This was the first of several whose ambition and scope grew exponentially, as did the list of NGOs involved in the negotiations. The range of objectives has been extended far beyond the basic goal of promoting industrial peace and keeping the economy competitive to include objectives such as 'bringing about a fairer and more inclusive Ireland' and 'promoting an entrepreneurial culture'. The broad tax-based incomes policy has been given much credit for the exceptional growth in employment that accompanied the boom of the 1990s, but many economists view its effects with scepticism, pointing rather to the high initial level of unemployment as the key factor behind both the willingness to enter into these agreements and the resultant wage moderation.

A comparison of the Irish and British industrial disputes records is instructive. The Irish strike rate was similar to the British in the 1970s. There was a dramatic spike in 1979 related to a national postal strike. This concentrated minds on the need to promote industrial peace. The strike rate fell to a much lower level after the new wage bargaining system was launched in 1987 and during the 1990s strikes ceased to be a general problem. The UK experience was broadly similar, with a dramatic fall in strike activity after the 1984 miners' strike and virtually no strike activity in the 1990s. Thus the Irish and British records might be viewed as separate paths to the same destination, but a caveat should be noted due to the evidence of an increase in Irish trade union militancy in recent years. A number of disruptive strikes, mostly in the public sector and state-owned industries, have occurred. This underscores the fact that the less confrontational Irish approach to the industrial strife of the 1970s and 1980s did not dislodge the trade union movement from a central role in pay bargaining or reduce its legal prerogatives.

13.3.6   Reducing the Burden of Taxation

Ireland went from being a relatively highly taxed country in the mid-1980s to one of the least heavily taxed countries in the EU by the end of the 1990s (Figure 13.9). In addition to their contribution to moderating pay demands, income tax reductions concentrated on situations where high marginal tax rates prevailed and lowering tax rates was expected to encourage increased participation in paid employment. In particular, the income tax code was restructured to increase the rewards to two-earner households and encourage labour force participation of married women. The falling tax burden may also have played some part in attracting former emigrants back to work in Ireland.

13.3.7   A Competitive Economy

The combination of (i) moderate nominal wage increases, (ii) rapid productivity growth and (iii) a moderately weak exchange rate spells a steady gain in competitiveness. This was indeed the Irish story during the 1990s. The best measure of the economy's improved international competitiveness is shown by a 40 percent decline between 1990 and 2001 in an index of 'relative unit wage costs in a common currency'.[6] Although confined to manufacturing industry, where productivity gains due to inflows of FDI have been greatest, this is an important indicator of the economy's ability to compete internationally. The steady decline in the index coincided with a steady increase in the country's current account balance in the course of the 1980s and 1990s and the rise in the openness of the economy depicted above. The export boom has been a central driver of the overall boom.

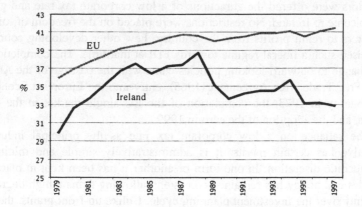

Figure 13.9 Tax revenues as percentage of GDP

13.4 IRELAND'S CORPORATION TAX POLICY

From the 1930s to the 1960s Ireland relied heavily on protectionist measures to promote industrial development. The result was some net employment gains in small inefficient firms oriented almost exclusively towards the tiny domestic market. During the 1950s it became evident that this policy offered little prospect of solving the age-old problems of emigration and high unemployment, while the prospect of economic integration in Europe could open up other routes to industrialisation. The Irish response was to move to attracting FDI with a zero rate of corporation tax on manufacturing exports and a generous system of fixed asset grants. Initially foreign investment was encouraged only in areas where it would not represent a threat to established domestic firms. However, this consideration declined in importance as tariffs were dismantled and employment in 'infant industries' shrank. The hope that employment in new, outward-oriented firms would offset the loss of employment in the older firms was realised in the 1990s.

The switch to outward orientation could be traced back to the establishment of a customs-free zone that was created at Shannon Airport in 1947. The Industrial Development Authority was established in 1949 and during the 1950s it was given increased powers and resources to aid manufacturing industry. In 1956 a 100 percent tax remission – known as Export Profit Tax Relief (EPTR) – was applied to profits from manufacturing exports. Any remaining restrictions on inward foreign investment were removed by the repeal of the Control of Manufactures Act in 1958. Foreign investors were offered the attractions of a low corporate tax rate and grant-aid to come to Ireland. No restrictions were placed on the freedom of foreign investors to remit profits from the country. Few other developing countries exercised such a liberal regime towards FDI at that time. The completion of the change to outward-looking policies came with the passage of the Anglo-Irish Free Trade Area Agreement (1965), entry into the European Economic Community in 1973, the completion of the EU single market in the early 1990s, and the adoption of the euro in 1999.

The reliance on a low corporate tax rate as the principal industrial incentive has certain merits. It is administratively simple and minimises bureaucratic discretion. In one form or another it has been kept in place for decades and policy has remained consistent, allowing firms a high degree of certainty over the investment planning cycle. Unlike up-front grants, the low tax rate is only effective when firms become profitable, and the more profitable the firm, the greater the value of the incentive. Firms that fail to achieve profitability are likely to close rather than to come looking for bailouts, as might be the case under a grants scheme.

But inevitably the EEC/EU questioned the compatibility of the Irish corporate tax structure with the country's obligations under the Treaty of Rome. The EPTR was deemed discriminatory – between domestic and export sales – and was phased out over the period 1981 to 1990. In its place a 10 percent 'preferential' corporate tax rate was applied to profits from manufacturing industry and internationally traded services.[7] In the late 1980s the 10 percent preferential corporate tax was extended to activities located in the IFSC in Dublin. But the success in attracting FDI in the 'high tech' and financial sectors provoked claims of 'unfair tax competition' from countries such as Germany and Belgium that were not pleased to see some relocation of activity to Ireland.

A problem with the Irish corporate tax system was that it was dualistic, with low rates applicable to export sales (up to 1981) or manufacturing and internationally traded services (post-1981), on the one hand, and a high 'standard' rate applicable to the remainder of the corporate sector, on the other. In the early 1980s the standard rate was 50 percent. This had been reduced to 20 percent by 2001 (see below). Such has been the growth of manufacturing in the 1980s and 1990s that tax payments at the 'preferential' rate quickly grew to more than half of the total take from corporate tax. However, the only major taxpayers that paid the 'standard' corporate tax rate were the non-IFSC banks. The anomalous situation in which the lowest rate of profit tax in the EU applied to one set of businesses and one of the highest rates applied to all the rest was not acceptable to the EU. The preferential rate was originally introduced as a temporary measure, to be phased out in 1990, but it was subsequently extended to 2010 (2005 in the IFSC). As a result of negotiations between the Irish government and the EU Commission a compromise was approved and the 1999 Finance Act set out a schedule for implementing a single corporate tax rate of 12.5 percent by 2003.

These changes in the Irish tax regime should be viewed in the context of a general tendency towards lower tax rates across the EU. To the degree that these cuts reflect a desire to attract foreign firms at the expense of other countries, they are part of a non-cooperative game. Bearing in mind that corporation taxes account for a relatively small proportion of total government revenue, there are grounds for fearing that a 'race to the bottom' will develop as countries use lower tax rates to try to raise domestic employment as long as FDI is highly sensitive to tax differentials.

It is important to try to assess the sensitivity of FDI to tax differentials. While firms may be attracted to, and anchored in, locations by agglomeration economies – that is, the advantages of operating in an area where a concentration of similar firms has created deep labour, capital and sub-supply markets – and may be reluctant to relocate, flows of FDI are nonetheless sensitive to tax differentials, and perhaps have become more so as markets become increasingly integrated. A recent study concluded that taxes appear to be an important consideration for firms decisions whether or not to invest abroad, as well as where to invest abroad (Gropp and Kostial, 2000).

In the late 1990s, as Ireland announced an increase in its statutory rate from 10 percent to 12.5 percent, Germany, Denmark, France, the United Kingdom and Italy implemented or announced corporate tax rate cuts. As the movement to reduce corporate tax rates gathers momentum in Europe, Ireland's competitive advantage in this area is being eroded. However, this is not necessarily a zero sum game. Is it too much to hope that the aggregate performance of the European economy could be improved by the example of Ireland's success?

13.5 FUTURE PROSPECTS

Sound domestic policies, favourable external developments and good luck all played a part in Ireland's economic boom. The result was a very rapidly growing economy in which real living standards converged on the EU average and the age-old problems of high unemployment and emigration were solved. But as the boom lengthened there was growing evidence of 'overheating'. Rising wage inflation, increased congestion and soaring house prices were cited as symptoms of an economy careening out of control whose fate exercised little influence on the policies of the European Central Bank in Frankfurt. In light of the sharp reversal of the boom in Asia in the late 1990s, and the subsequent uneven recovery, it is understandable that some commentators warned of a 'hard landing' in tones that sometimes suggested it would be only appropriate retribution for the hubris of the boom years.[8] But there are profound differences between Ireland and the Asian 'Tiger' countries – Ireland benefited from an inflow of FDI that has proved less footloose than the portfolio investment that dominated the capital flows to the Asian economies; the Irish pound floated smoothly after the currency crisis of 1992/93; the Irish banking system is well regulated and although credit expanded very rapidly as the boom gathered pace, asset price inflation was never on the scale of the Asian bubbles.

In the run-up to the adoption of the euro it was generally expected that inflation rates in the common currency zone would be very similar, but soon after the launch of the new currency Irish inflation surged significantly above the Eurozone average (Figure 13.10). This gave rise to much soul searching in Ireland and in Frankfurt. The high Irish inflation rate was blamed on the weak euro (which mattered more to Ireland – still dependent on imports denominated in sterling – than to the continental countries) and the fall in nominal interest rates, as well as on the so-called Balassa–Samuelson effect, which suggests that an export-led boom tends to raise the internal terms of trade and leads to relatively high inflation.[9] However, the differential between Irish and Eurozone inflation peaked in late 2000 and convergence has re-emerged.

In the course of 2001 worries about overheating quickly gave way to concerns that the Irish economy will prove very vulnerable to the global recession. The pessimists now switched their concern to 'excessive dependence' on foreign-owned firms (especially US ones) and on the information technology/computer and financial sectors. Of course, they have a point. Greater geographical and sectoral diversification of Ireland's economic base would be desirable, although not easily achieved. Although a number of Irish firms have gained global status and are investing heavily outside the country,[10] it would be desirable to see more indigenous Irish firms developing world-renowned brand names, like Finland's Nokia.

The real test of how radically the Irish economy was transformed in the course of the 1990s will be how rapidly it adjusts to the recession at the beginning of the 21st century. Above all, will the labour market exhibit greater flexibility than it did in the first half of the 1980s and can the economy retain its competitive edge in the Eurozone? But regardless of how the economy evolves in the years ahead, Ireland's dramatic economic catch-up during the 1990s shows that a small offshore island can overcome significant locational disadvantages through a combination of good domestic policies, a favourable external environment and some good luck.

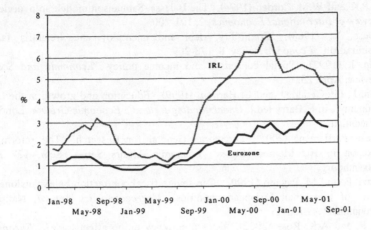

Figure 13.10 Irish and Eurozone inflation rates

NOTES

1. See Honohan and Walsh (2002) for a more extended analysis.
2. In 1999 the net immigration rate to Ireland was 4.9 per 1,000 population, which is more than twice the EU average and surpassed only by Luxembourg.
3. This subtracts out net factor payments abroad, adds in current transfers from abroad and, in constant prices, allows for changes in the terms of trade.
4. However, as a result of the unexpected strength of sterling, the Irish pound had fallen to Stg £0.73 by 1981.
5. See Glick and Rose (2002) and also the review of this issue by Christie Smith in Chapter 8 of this book.
6. The impact of transfer pricing on this measure of productivity leads to an exaggeration.
7. A plethora of additional tax incentives were also introduced, such as accelerated depreciation allowances and tax breaks linked to preference share financing and leasing.
8. They tended to overlook the fact that after the crash these economies remained prosperous and successful, and several countries – Malaysia, for example – recovered quickly.
9. See, for example, Asea and Corden (1994) for a survey of research on the Balassa– Samuelson effect.
10. Examples are the Jefferson Smurfit Corporation, Waterford–Wedgeworth, Cement Roadstone Holdings and Kerry Foods. Several new Irish firms have been quoted on NASDAQ in recent years, notably Iona Technologies and Baltimore Technology, and their valuations have suffered from the telecommunications, media and technology sector crash.

REFERENCES

Asea, P.K. and W.M. Corden (1994), 'The Balassa–Samuelson model: an overview', *Review of International Economics*, 2, 191-200.

Dornbush, R. (1988), 'Credibility, debt and unemployment: Ireland's failed stabilisation', *Economic Policy*, 8, 173-209.

Durkan, J. (1992), 'Social consensus and income policy', *Economic and Social Review*, April 23.

Durkan, J., FitzGerald, J. and C. Harmon (1999), 'Education and growth in the Irish economy', in F. Barry (ed.), *Understanding Ireland's Economic Growth*, London: Macmillan.

European Parliament (2001), Directorate-General for Research, 'The reform of taxation in EU Member States', Economic Affairs Series, Econ 127 EN, Luxembourg.

Giavazzi, F. and M. Pagano (1990), 'Can severe fiscal contraction be expansionary? Tales of two small European countries', *Macroeconomics Annual*, National Economic Research.

Glick, R. and A.K. Rose (2002), 'Does a currency union affect trade?', *European Economic Review*, 46, 1125-1151.

Gould, J. (1982), *The Rake's Progress? The New Zealand Economy Since 1945*, Auckland: Hodder and Stoughton.

Gropp, R. and K. Kostial (2000), 'The disappearing tax base: is foreign direct investment eroding corporate income taxes?', Working Paper No. 31, European Central Bank.

Honohan, P. and B. Walsh (2002), 'Catching up with the leaders: the Irish hare', *Brookings Papers on Economic Activity*, 0(1), 1-57.

Kenny, G. (1996), 'Economic growth in Ireland: sources, potential and inflation', *Central Bank of Ireland Bulletin*, Autumn, 43-54.

Leddin, A. and B. Walsh (1998), *The Macroeconomy of Ireland*, 4th edn, Dublin: Gill and Macmillan.

Nugent, J. (1998), 'Corporate profitability in Ireland: overview and determinants', Central Bank of Ireland, *Quarterly Bulletin*, Winter, 51-80.

O Gráda, C. and K. O'Rourke (2000), 'Living standards and growth', in J. O'Hagan (ed.), *The Economy of Ireland*, Dublin: Gill and Macmillan, pp. 178-204.

Thom, R. and B. Walsh (2002), 'The effect of a currency union on trade: lessons from the Irish experience', *European Economic Review*, 46, 1111-1124.

Walsh, B. (1996), 'Stabilisation and adjustment in a small, open economy: Ireland, 1979–1995', *Oxford Review of Economic Policy*, 12, 74-86.

14. The State of E-Commerce in New Zealand

Bronwyn Howell and Lisa Marriott

14.1 INTRODUCTION

During the 1970s and 1980s, New Zealand saw its relative economic performance (in terms of GDP per capita and economic growth per annum) slip relative to others against which it has regularly benchmarked itself – its major trading partners such as Australia and the United States, and the other member countries of the OECD. An improvement in growth during the 1990s did not yield a significant catching up. As a consequence, a national strategic objective of returning New Zealand to the top half of the OECD has become a government policy imperative. If a small country such as New Zealand – geographically isolated from its main trading partners – is to implement such a policy and move towards greater prosperity, then new technologies such as the Internet and electronic commerce may provide vehicles via which this can be achieved.

If use of these new technologies offers increased economic advantage, New Zealand and other peripheral countries must gain an even greater benefit from the use of these technologies than the comparison countries in order to achieve an improvement in their relative standing. That is, such countries must utilise the new technologies either more, or more effectively, than their trading partners.

While the advent of the Internet and electronic commerce generated much promise for higher economic growth, there are inherent difficulties in defining and measuring the impact of electronic commerce on economic potential. Electronic commerce cannot be neatly separated from other aspects of the economy. Suitable proxies have to be developed to measure a country's e-commerce utilisation and potential both in absolute terms and relative to the rest of the world. In order to develop policies and encourage practices that will improve performance, it is also necessary to identify who is utilising electronic commerce, where the benefits (if any) are being accrued and where potential benefits may be in the future.[1]

The relative youth of the Internet as an infrastructure, and electronic commerce as an economic activity that takes advantage of the facilities that the Internet offers, makes measurement and benchmarking problematic. Lengthy data series are as yet not available to track relative performance, and even where metrics have been developed their relevance is constantly changing as new uses for the technologies are invented, and new statistics for monitoring new activities are required. Furthermore, achieving international consistency in data collection is fraught with the difficulties of both identifying which new activities are (or will be) significant and establishing data collection standards. Nonetheless, some measures must be developed in order to assess relative performance by means of the best national and international data available. This chapter relies primarily on international data collected by the OECD and population-based New Zealand data. However, only survey data, which may be less reliable and not directly comparable internationally, are available for many key indicators. We have endeavoured to focus as much as possible upon New Zealand's relative position and the change therein in our analysis, in order to determine whether New Zealand does in fact have a realistic opportunity to leverage better relative economic performance by means of Internet use and electronic commerce.

14.2   ISCR RESEARCH

Since June 2000, the New Zealand Institute for the Study of Competition and Regulation (ISCR) has produced a number of analyses of New Zealand's level of uptake of, and potential to capitalise upon the benefits offered by, electronic commerce.[2] Using a variety of publicly available data, we adopted the working hypothesis that, unless there are any indicators to the contrary, New Zealand's level of uptake of telecommunications and communications infrastructures can be taken as a benchmarking indicator of the level of uptake of electronic commerce applications. Presuming that high levels of uptake of new technology infrastructures occur as a result of productivity advantages accruing to the adopters, then infrastructure uptake is the best internationally consistent proxy currently available to estimate relative economic performance and potential improvement.

ISCR analysis in 2000 (Boles de Boer et al. 2000b) showed that New Zealand had not only by international standards high uptake levels of the telecommunications infrastructures that underpin successful electronic commerce, but also that there was a consistent picture across practically all of these indicators. Twelve months later, New Zealand's position was re-examined (Howell and Marriott, 2001), adding further analytic criteria and statistics. In particular, we used the framework developed in Howell (2001c) to examine more closely the elements of connectivity to and uptake of the underpinning computer and telecommunications infrastructures. These elements are seen as core measures of both accessibility and utilisation of the fundamental components underpinning electronic commerce – the creation, transmission, storage, utilisation and communication of information. Enhanced connectivity and uptake should in future lead to improvements in the key performance indicators – productivity, GDP per capita and economic growth.

The results continue to reinforce New Zealand's consistent position within the top ten OECD countries. Not only is New Zealand among the world leaders in all Internet-related indicators but it also continues to lead Australia – its main trading partner and competitor in world export markets – in most statistics. In particular, significant pricing and productivity advantages exist for New Zealand in the core telecommunications and Internet Service Provider (ISP) products that form the backbone of information exchange in a 'wired' and 'wireless' economy.

New Zealand is thus well placed to participate in and benefit from international electronic commerce, and potentially 'close the gap' between its economic and social performance indicators and those of its major partners. There is significant evidence of uptake of specific technologies on the basis of business need. Most businesses are using e-mail routinely, and over 60 percent have a website. While there are as yet few data on actual usage of Internet applications such as supply chain management and B2B exchanges, the level of comfort apparent in the use of electronic technologies for communicating fundamental business information (at a level of sophistication compatible with the use and value of that information) is reassuring, as it is perhaps a better indicator of business usage and relevance than dollars of sales exchanged (Howell, 2001c).

The hypothesis that we maintain is that if New Zealand is performing at the international forefront of infrastructure indicators, then there is every reason to believe that it is also performing well in those areas where no reliable indicators of performance are available. Additionally, we draw attention to the need to interpret the available indicators in the light of the particular characteristics of New Zealand's economy. Differences in the ways in which business environments utilise the core product of electronic technologies – that is, information – are crucial to understanding the benefits (or detriments) arising from the use of these technologies.

14.3 METHODOLOGY

In all of our analyses, we have taken as our basis the OECD definition of electronic commerce:

> Electronic commerce refers generally to all forms of transactions relating to commercial activities, including both organisations and individuals, which are based upon the processing and transmission of digitised data, including text, sound and visual images, (OECD, 1997, p.6).

This definition presumes that the electronic infrastructures underpinning electronic transactions are fundamental components of the ability of any economy to participate in electronic exchange, as illustrated in Figure 14.1.

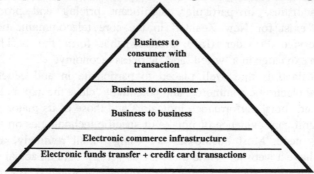

Business to consumer with transaction

Business to consumer

Business to business

Electronic commerce infrastructure

Electronic funds transfer + credit card transactions

Source: OECD (1997 p. 19)

Figure 14.1 Typology of electronic commerce definitions

Howell (2001c) argues that the fundamental component of electronic commerce is not the electronic technologies (e.g., telephones, computers, modems) that underpin the exchange processes but the creation, storage, transmission and utilisation of actual information that these technologies facilitate. Technologies (e.g., telephony and the Internet) are necessary, but not sufficient, for gains from electronic commerce to accrue. Technologies are like the pipes that carry gas or the wires that convey electricity: they are conduits that enable exchange of information. However, the commodity utilised in actual value-creation is the commodity that these conduits convey – information. Indeed, it is information exchange that is the necessary and sufficient condition for all economic activity to occur (Evans, 2001; Shapiro and Varian, 1999). Hence, while electronic commerce infrastructure utilisation gives a measure of 'connectivity', it does not inform on what information is being exchanged or the purpose of its exchange. Neither do these figures indicate the ability of the entities at either end of the 'pipe' to effectively or efficiently utilise the information they transmit or receive.

A series of additional measures is required to provide a more comprehensive assessment of electronic commerce performance. These include 'capability' measures (assessing the ability of the generators and users of information to both create and utilise information as well as the technologies that transmit, store and process it); 'uptake' measures (assessing the utilisation of processes and applications that use electronic forms of information as an input or create, process and transmit it), and 'performance' measures (that provide an assessment of the economic and social impacts of the utilisation of electronically created, stored, processed and transmitted information). Thus, we revise Figure 14.1 to a multi-dimensional framework recognising the role of information in this analysis, as in Figure 14.2.

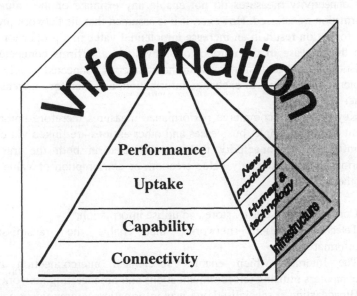

Figure 14.2 Electronic commerce performance measurement framework

This framework allows us to extend our analysis to test whether there is any evidence that infrastructure leadership is leading to improved social and economic performance. However, the methodological foundations for linking e-commerce with measures of productivity may be inadequate due to their inability to capture the economic consequences of the use of intangible, and as yet unmeasured, aspects of information (Howell, 2001a; Howell, 2001c).

Each of these elements is analysed separately in the balance of this chapter. We focus specifically on New Zealand's performance across time and its comparative position with Australia, as summarised in Table 14.1.

14.4 CONNECTIVITY

Connectivity provides linkages between individuals and firms. These linkages are achieved via a number of media, extending from purely human to purely electronic. The existence of electronic mechanisms of connectivity has enabled the development of new methods of capturing and measuring the extent to which individuals and firms share information (Howell, 2001c, p.68).

Connectivity measures do not enable any estimate of the value of the information transferred. However, if it is assumed that the network properties of information result in an increase in potential value in a proportion greater than the increase in the number of individuals and firms connected, then statistics that indicate an increase in the number of connected people suggest an increased potential to exchange information, and therefore increased total value.

Key electronic commerce performance measures therefore embrace the extent to which people, businesses and other entities are linked via channels of information connectivity that can be used in both the transfer of information and ultimately value creation, or consumption of value created by others:

• Computers, that create, store and utilise information;
• Telecommunications networks, that enable the transmission of information;
• The Internet, which enables specialised interconnection between computers utilising telecommunications and broadcasting networks; and
• Broadcasting, a specialised one-way information communication system.

ISCR studies show that New Zealand is among the world leaders in all of these indicators, and enjoys significant advantages over its trans-Tasman neighbour Australia in many of them. This bodes well for future benefits to be gained from Internet access and e-commerce utilisation, and for New Zealand's relative economic and social position *vis-à-vis* its neighbour.

14.4.1 Computers

New Zealand demonstrates strong uptake of computers for both personal and business use. The reported percentages vary across different sources, but this is primarily due to sampling variability in the surveys.

Personal use of computers in the home
New Zealand is ranked seventh in the world, with 58 percent of households having at least one Personal Computer (PC) (Ministry of Economic Development, 2001). Australia is ranked second, with 65 percent. New Zealand is eighth in the world with respect to households with more than one PC (22 percent), with Australia being one of four nations leading the world with 26 percent. These statistics and others quoted below can be found in Table 14.1.

Business use of computers
Over 92 percent of New Zealand businesses employing more than 10 people were using computers as of March 2001 (Clark et al., 2001), compared with 95 percent of similar Australian businesses (NOIE, 2001). This compares with the Ministry of Economic Development (2000) finding of 93 percent of all New Zealand businesses using computers, and 92 percent of firms with five or fewer employees using computers.

Very few New Zealand businesses do not use computers in their daily operations. Even very small businesses not owning or leasing a computer can, by selective outsourcing, utilise specialist computer functions for tasks that benefit from computerisation (e.g., accounts management), even though the production process does not justify the firm owning a computer (Howell, 2001c, p.109). Hence, it is unlikely that business ownership of computers will reach 100 percent, especially in the small (fewer than five employees) category that comprises over 90 percent of New Zealand's producing entities (see also Chapter 7 in this book).

Table 14.1 *E-commerce key indicators – Australia and New Zealand compared*

		2001				2000				Comment
		Australia	Rank	NZ	Rank	Australia	Rank	NZ	Rank	
	Households with a computer	65%	2	58%	7					
	Households with more than 1 PC	26%	1=	22%	8					
	No. of computers per 100 full-time students	18	5	24	4					
	Businesses with more than 10 people using computers	95%		92%						OECD ave 12
	Telecom channels per 100 people (standard + mobile)	100.2		81.0						OECD ave 2001 84.1
	Internet subscription per 100 people					12.7	9	14.0	8	OECD ave 2001 10.9
Connectivity	Internet sessions per month	12		14						
	Unique sites visited per session	16		18						
	Time per site (minutes)	27		20						
	Total time online per month (hours)	7		6						
	Time per session (minutes)	34		26						
	Computers connected to Internet per user	17%		24%						
	Internet hosts per 1,000 people	88	10	105	8	75	9	93	7	OECD ave 100 (2001)
	Websites per 1,000 people					7.5	13	11.4	12	Both below OECD ave.
	Domain names per 1,000	17.6		23.4			16		11	NZ half that of UK (top)
	Cost of registering domain name($US PPP)	52.88		41.61						OECD ave 58.40
	Secure servers per 100,000 people	19.7	5	20.3	3	14.9	3	12.7	4	OECD ave 11.9 (2001)
Capability	Telecommunications revenue as % of GDP					4.18	3	3.97	6	=1999 figures
Uptake	EFTPOS transactions per annum per person	62		121						
	No. of persons (over 16 yr) with Internet access	65%		69%						

14.4.2 Telecommunications

International figures show that New Zealand is extremely well placed in relation to the rest of the world to capitalise on electronic connectivity.[3] In particular, given the disadvantages of low population density and physical distance from the rest of the world, New Zealand's telecommunications infrastructure and environment appear to be comparable with, or even outperforming, similar environments such as in Sweden and the UK (Alger and Leung, 1999; Office of Telecommunications, 2002).

Access: land-based and mobile telephony connections

New Zealand ranks slightly lower than the OECD average for telecommunications channels (the sum of standard and mobile connections) per 100 inhabitants, with 81.0 connections per 100 inhabitants in New Zealand and an OECD average of 84.1. This compares with Australia with 100.2, the USA with 101.4, Ireland with 89.1 and Canada with 88.1. The Nordic countries have the highest number of access channels (Norway 132, Sweden 131.3, Finland 120.2), while Mexico (19.1) and Poland (34.8) have the lowest.

New Zealand has both a lower number of standard access lines and fewer mobile connections than Australia. While Australia maintained a cumulative 3.3 percent average growth rate in standard access lines over the 1990s, New Zealand's growth rate started the 1990s at a similar level but tailed off to 0.4 percent between 1995 and 1999. This appears to be due to two factors:

- New Zealand's standard network was completely digitised by 1997, so that it was more likely to have had a stable number of standard lines, while Australia did not achieve this target until 1999; and
- New Zealand showed slower initial uptake of mobile telephony, with 32.9 subscribers per 100 inhabitants in 1999 as opposed to Australia's 39.5 (compared with an OECD average of 32.4).

However, New Zealand's cumulative average growth rate for mobile subscribers over the period 1997–1999 (58.7 percent) has outstripped Australia's (23.3 percent), indicating that the gap in the paths of total access rates is closing.

The OECD attributes New Zealand's high mobile telephony increase to growth in subscribers using prepaid services (52 percent of Telecom's mobile subscribers in New Zealand used prepaid services in 1999, compared with none of Telstra's in Australia). Australia's high rate of standard line growth is attributed to growth in second lines for Internet access (OECD,

2001, p.70). However, anecdotal New Zealand evidence suggests that substitution of prepaid mobile telephones for second lines is stronger, as no rental charge is incurred if the prepaid mobile is retained for voice telephony and incoming callers pay the call charge, thereby reducing the cost to the Internet user and call recipient (Boles de Boer et al., 2000b). This is consistent with New Zealanders traditionally facing a zero marginal call cost for the use of land-based calls. Prepaid mobiles purchased predominantly for receiving calls offer a zero marginal cost option (capped purchase cost and no commitment to a monthly line rental), compared with the positive marginal cost of using a second line. Hence, second lines are less common in New Zealand but prepaid mobiles are more common than in Australia and the United States.

Prices

Telecommunications pricing policies are acknowledged as one of the key factors enabling growth of electronic information exchange. In particular, unmetered charging of local telephone access has been a key determinant of the high levels of Internet access recorded in countries where these policies apply, namely the United States, Canada, New Zealand and Australia. Unmetered charging has encouraged 'always on' use, and hence prompted high dial-up Internet access uptake (Boles de Boer et al., 2000b; OECD, 2000).

New Zealand domestic subscribers have benefited from unmetered pricing.[4] However, business subscribers are liable for per minute charging, which may have had some impact upon usage patterns of Internet-based business telephony. Connection charges have decreased in markets where the alternative network infrastructure is mature (e.g., wireless; see OECD, 2001), and there is evidence of significant substitution of broadband ADSL connections for time-metered ISDN and dial-up Internet connections by business users (Howell and Obren, 2002).

Using the OECD's composite basket of calls, New Zealand residential prices in 2000 were below the OECD average, despite New Zealand residential and business charges being primarily determined by Telecom New Zealand – a near-monopoly lines provider. Prices were less than those of both Australia and the United States. However, using baskets of consumer and business mobile charges (which are determined in a competitive market), New Zealand prices are slightly higher than the OECD average.

New Zealand does not perform as well in the basket of charges for leased lines. The charges for higher capacity (64 kbit/s and 1.5/2 Mbit/s) lines are particularly important for dedicated data transfer functions and high-speed Internet access. Charges for all capacities are higher than the OECD average, with the charges for 64k lines in particular about 66 percent higher than the OECD average, and twice that of Australia. However, 1.5/2 M lines, although still above the OECD average, are slightly less expensive than those of Australia.

It is noted, however, that the OECD figures capture only traditional telecommunications company provision of these lines. Furthermore, other utility providers (such as gas and electricity utilities) are entering leased line provision, and this may be expected to place pressure on the prices charged by telecommunications companies for leased line services. New Zealand has had local competitive provision of broadband services since 1996, with CityLink providing fibre optic LAN-based connectivity in the central business district of the capital city.

14.4.3   Internet Indicators

Internet subscribers
New Zealand continues to display strong growth in Internet subscribers, being among the top ten OECD countries for Internet subscription rates per 100 inhabitants, with 14.0 subscribers per 100 inhabitants in January 2000, compared with 12.7 subscribers in Australia.

Internet usage
New Zealanders participate in more Internet sessions per month than Australians – 14, as compared to 12 (*NeilsenNet*, September 2001). While online, they visit more unique sites (18 versus 16) but spend less time at each site (20 minutes versus 27), spend less total time online (6 hours per month versus 7 hours and less time per session (26 minutes versus 34). By comparison, the US figures are an average of 10 sessions per month per user, visiting 40 unique sites for an average total time of 10 hours and duration per session of 54 minutes.[5]

More sites visited and less average time per site spent by New Zealanders may indicate that New Zealand users are more 'efficient' in their use of the web, as they are (on average) more familiar with the sites they visit and revisit them repeatedly for extraction of specific information, thereby needing a shorter visit on each occasion.

Internet hosts per 1,000 inhabitants
This statistic reflects the number of hosts (computers) connected to the Internet (via full- or part-time, direct or dial-up connections) (OECD, 1998, p.8). New Zealand has more computers connected to the Internet per user than Australia (24 percent versus 17 percent), consistent with the higher

number of Internet subscribers. As of October 2000, New Zealand was seventh among the OECD countries for Internet hosts per 1,000 inhabitants (with 93 hosts per 1,000), while Australia was ninth (75 hosts per 1,000).

Websites

The number of websites recorded per country reveals information about the amount of content produced in each country for distribution over the Internet. New Zealand's relative leadership over Australia per head of population in content created is evident, with 11.4 sites per 1,000 compared with Australia's 7.5 per 1,000 in 2000. New Zealand's growth rate in this statistic also outstrips Australia's (223 percent as opposed to 156 percent), indicating that this dominance will continue. However, both countries trail the OECD average for these figures, with the United States, Canada, Germany and the Nordic countries being the clear leaders.

Domain name registrations

A count of New Zealand's registered domain names (e.g., iscr.org.nz) provides a measure of organisational penetration of the Internet. New Zealand has a higher proportion of domain names per 1,000 inhabitants, with 23.4 compared with Australia's 17.6. The New Zealand rate is approximately half that of the world leader, the United Kingdom, which is probably a reflection of the large number of multi-national companies operating in New Zealand with websites registered in overseas domains.

Domain name registration pricing can influence the ability of an entity to exchange information over the Internet. The cost of registering a domain name (under licence from the International Corporation for the Assignment of Names) is in New Zealand at $41.61 US PPP substantially below the OECD average of $58.40 US PPP and some 20 percent lower than the comparable price in Australia (Boles de Boer et al., 2000a).

Secure web servers per 100,000 inhabitants

Traditionally, strong commercial (as opposed to recreational) uptake of Internet usage has been assumed to result in higher secure socket layer server utilisation for encrypted transmission over TCP/IP networks. This presumes that commercial transactions have a greater requirement to protect sensitive data from scrambling, loss and hacking than recreational transactions. The most common usage of secure servers is thus to provide a secure link for e-commerce transactions, such as encryption of credit cards and restriction of access to private information.

In July 2001 both New Zealand and Australia were above the OECD average of 11.9 secure servers per 100,000 inhabitants with 20.3 (ranked third) and 19.7 (ranked fifth) respectively. This was an improvement for New Zealand, which was fourth in July 2000 with 12.7, while Australia was ahead at that point with 14.9 (ranked third) (OECD, 2002).

It should be noted that the nature of trade patterns in New Zealand (single desk exporters, a high level of imports, trading in a volatile fringe currency, etc.) may encourage New Zealand firms to conduct a higher proportion of their electronic commerce transactions on foreign-based servers (Boles de Boer et al., 2000b, pp.17-18) or through single, centralised servers rather than with each individual producer. Figure 14.3 provides evidence of New Zealand's world leadership in potential to utilise e-commerce activities based upon its combination of hosts and secure servers connected to the Internet.

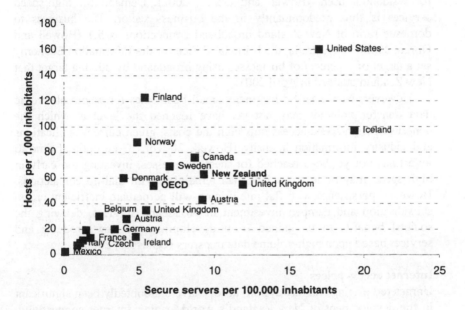

Sources: Netcraft (www.netcraft.com), Netsizer (www.netsizer.com), OECD

Figure 14.3   Hosts and secure servers per capita

High-speed Internet access uptake
Much emphasis has been given recently to high-speed Internet connection access (cable modem and broadband services such as Digital Subscriber Lines). Worldwide, uptake of such services has been variable. Korea leads the OECD with the number of connections per 100 inhabitants. New Zealand has slightly more than half the connections of Australia.[6]

While regulation and infrastructure investment have influenced broadband connectivity in other countries, dial-up pricing has been significant in New Zealand. Flat rate dial-up pricing has biased usage of these services to the extent that the heaviest users use disproportionately more of the resource than the lighter users (Howell, 2001c, pp.81-83; Varaiya et al., 1999). Charging broadband services per Megabyte downloaded biases heavy users towards continued use of dial-up services, especially if the information they are downloading is neither time nor mission-critical (Lehr and McKnight, 2000). If heavy users are predominantly recreational users (e.g., teenagers downloading MP3 music files and video clips – see Howell, 2001c), then the time–cost trade-off may not yet justify the substitution of dial-up by high-speed pay-per-use services for residential users (Howell and Obren, 2002). Demand for high-speed services is thus predominantly in the business sector. The business to domestic ratio of New Zealand broadband connections is 5:1 (Howell and Obren, 2002). In Australia, the National Office for the Information Economy set a target of 3 percent of businesses using broadband by 2003, a target that New Zealand attained in April 2001.

However, New Zealand has many small businesses for whom electronic data transfer volumes may not yet have reached the level at which the benefits of high-speed access outweigh the costs, given current applications and industry information intensity (Howell, 2001b). If the optimal time to invest has not yet been reached for these businesses, investing too early in high speed may be less efficient than remaining with dial-up connections. However, persistence with flat rate pricing will perpetuate inefficient cross-subsidisation and dampen investment in broadband services, delaying the societal benefits to be gained from development of new products and services based upon high-volume data transfers (Goolsbee, 2000).

Internet access prices
Unmetered pricing and 'always on' access have undoubtedly been significant in the development of New Zealand's world-leading Internet connectivity. Further, the relative pricing advantages in ISP prices have demonstrably contributed to the higher ranking of New Zealand over Australia in terms of the numbers of Internet hosts, Internet users and hours of use (Boles de Boer et al., 2000c).

Using the OECD basket of Internet access prices, Australian ISP prices are between 38 and 75 percent higher than New Zealand prices, although New Zealand exhibits higher prices for the fixed line telephony component of Internet access. New Zealand also has a clear pricing advantage over Australia in total price (including both telephony and ISP) for higher levels of use (40 hours). Total prices for higher usage are also significantly below the OECD average, as well as total prices for lower hours of usage at peak times. New Zealand prices exceed the OECD average only for 20 hours peak time usage.

Summary
New Zealand continues to show high levels of connectivity to Internet services with the exception of broadband services. Figure 14.4 illustrates its position among the leading players. New Zealand demonstrates not only significant levels of Internet connectivity capacity, but also significant levels of utilisation of that capacity for the exchange of information.

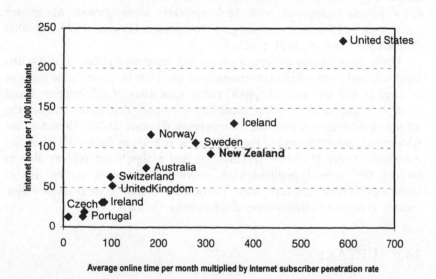

Source: OECD; Netsizer (www.netsizer.com), April 2001

Figure 14.4   Online time and Internet hosts

14.5   CAPABILITY

Capability measures reflect the quantity and quality of resources available to an economy or society to be applied to productive and welfare-enhancing endeavours (Howell, 2001a). These measures include levels of investment in human and organisational capital, as well as investment in telecommunications and computer equipment and software.

New Zealand leads the OECD in the percentage of GDP spent on telecommunications and computer hardware, software and services – 10.6 percent in 1999 – and has done so consistently for the last five years (OECD, 2002), reflecting the relative importance of computer and telecommunications-based information use in this country. Software spending constitutes nearly 10 percent of computer-related expenditure. Investment in training has been proportionately the strongest growth area in the nation's information technology spending, although it still comprises only 2.4 percent of sales (Ministry of Economic Development, 2000). Growth of persons employed in information technology occupations outpaced growth of the workforce between the 1991 and 1996 censuses (21.4 percent compared with 16.5 percent), while growth of tertiary enrolments in IT-related courses grew 260 percent between 1994 and 2000 (Howell and Marriott, 2001, p.62).

While these figures indicate a strong and increasing ability to utilise the electronic and technological components of the 'New Economy', the focus of research is still on users of 'pipes' rather than users of information. More work is required to develop capability measures that better reflect the information utilisation potential of a country (Howell, 2002). However, the widespread use of Electronic Funds Transfer at Point of Sale (EFTPOS) and Automatic Teller Machines (ATMs) has had a significant role to play in training the general population in essential skills such as the use of keyboards, visual display units, passwords, secure central information transfer systems and substitution of information for cash.

14.6 UPTAKE

While statistics of connectivity and capability offer measures of potential benefit, the process of converting potential into subsequent benefits requires the linking of these through the uptake of technologies. Like connectivity and capability statistics, uptake statistics track utilisation of specific skills and technologies. However, these measure only utilisation and not the consequent benefits (or detriments) that arise from their use.

This section surveys measures of applications utilising information and electronic technologies to create, process, store, transmit and utilise information, as distinct from the infrastructure measures identified in the section on connectivity. The key factors underpinning the effects yielded by applications uptake are the changes in the prices, speed, medium and method of utilisation of information. However, uptake measures alone are merely 'tracking signals' of what individuals and businesses are using connectivity and capability for. Interpretation of the consequences requires detailed understanding of how uptake impacts upon wider performance measurements (Howell, 2001c, pp.89-90).

14.6.1 Electronic Banking

Boles de Boer et al. (2000b) demonstrate the near-ubiquitous state of electronic banking in New Zealand. The centralised clearance system for trading banks has nurtured the development of ATMs and EFTPOS, which in turn offer benefits to banks (reduced transaction and branch operating costs), retailers (cash handling and security benefits) and customers (time savings, convenience, 24/7 banking), to the extent that New Zealand has world-leading uptake figures for each of these technologies. The role of these technologies in preparing people culturally, and equipping them with skills relevant to the use of other electronic technologies where information substitutes for other 'hard' products such as coinage, is significant.

New Zealand's dominance in the world in the number of EFTPOS terminals per head continues, indicating a greater facility of New Zealanders to substitute information for cash. New Zealand EFTPOS terminals are each used to process 45 percent more transactions than Australian terminals. The average New Zealander processes nearly twice as many EFTPOS transactions in a year than the average Australian (121 as opposed to 62).[7]

14.6.2 Telephony Uptake

Household telephone use in New Zealand is strong, with over 96 percent of households having access to a telephone (Statistics New Zealand, 2001). Mobile penetration is also extensive, standing at nearly 60 percent of the population in 2001 (Ministry of Economic Development, 2002).

Discrepancies between rural and urban telephony access have been cited in some studies as inhibitors to electronic commerce development (Howell, 2001c). While telephone access is slightly less in rural areas than urban, there is some evidence that mobile telephony, and prepaid mobile in particular, provides a cost-effective and more flexible method of communication in rural areas and that there may be some substitution of mobile phones for land lines as a consequence (Boles de Boer et al., 2000b). With the growth of mobile telephone access to the Internet (e.g., Wireless Area Protocol, DoCoMo in Japan), rural areas will be less dependent in the future on wire-based telecommunications, in particular for small-volume personal data communications. Further research is required to explore the extent of this substitution.

14.6.3   Internet and E-Commerce Applications

Boles de Boer et al. (2000b) highlight the need to identify business application usage by the type of firms participating – by ownership (public or private), firm size (large, medium or small) and geography – in addition to connectivity and capability measures. Various studies of New Zealand usage demonstrate a consistent theme – high levels of awareness and utilisation of electronic technologies, and the Internet in particular, for a variety of business and personal purposes.

A significant omission in these studies is information pertaining to business-to-business electronic interconnection that does not rely upon the Internet. Galbi (2000) found that 98 percent of data transferred via telecommunications networks in the United States is not Internet related. Instead, such data transfer primarily takes place through private direct connections, either within or between businesses. No comparable New Zealand data are available. However, given the high prices for 64k leased lines, the geography of New Zealand and the concomitant patterns of laying telecommunications trunks and branches, the small number of large-scale businesses and the large number of small-scale businesses, it is expected that the proportions of businesses utilising alternative methods of data interconnection would be larger than in the USA. Indeed, this scenario is consistent with the high levels of Internet connectivity discussed in Section 14.4. Clear differences appear to be emerging between business and personal use in what this Internet connectivity is being used for.

Internet uptake for personal use

The number of New Zealanders over 16 years of age with Internet access from any location was fifth highest in the world in the fourth quarter of 2000 (at 69 percent), ahead of Australia (at 65 percent) but trailing the Scandinavian countries.[8] The percentage accessing the Internet via a home PC is equal to that in Australia (NOIE, 2001), indicating that access via other avenues, such as work, school, libraries, and so on, is higher than in Australia. This is consistent with the slightly lower New Zealand levels of domestic PC ownership compared with Australia.

Metropolitan users demonstrate a higher uptake than provincial urban and rural users. However, there are marked regional differences. The highest use is recorded in Otago (74 percent) and Canterbury (71 percent), with Gisborne (28 percent) trailing (Te Puni Kokiri, 2001). The distinct South to North trend for personal uptake of Internet usage mimics that for business use found in Howell (2001b) and is most probably a function of the higher costs of communication and access to information via other sources (telephone, library visits) in smaller, more remote but more prosperous South Island locations. Rural and remote users facing higher communication costs appear to be investing (time and capital) sooner as the net benefit of adopting new communication technologies becomes positive earlier. It is also significant that use of the Internet at sites such as libraries and Internet cafes is much more significant in Canterbury (32 percent use the Internet at libraries, 20 percent at Internet cafes) and Otago (22 percent and 19 percent respectively) than in Auckland (5 percent and 2 percent) and Wellington (3 percent and 2 percent).

Demographically, there is a slightly higher uptake among males (64 percent) than females (60 percent), with males also more likely to have access to the Internet at work. Europeans have greater levels of access (65 percent) than Maori (46 percent) and Pacific islanders (35 percent), but the highest level of access can be found among the 'other ethnicities' group (primarily skilled Asian immigrants). The highest level of access (81 percent) is recorded among young people aged 10 to 19 years, decreasing steadily as age increases and reaching 31 percent for people aged 60 years and over. Access percentages for all groups exceed Australian percentages (NOIE, 2001) but most significantly in the oldest group.

Personal usage statistics show that European and 'other' ethnic groups use computers most for word processing (38 percent and 36 percent), Internet access (31 percent and 42 percent), games and entertainment (30 percent and 28 percent) and education/work (20 percent and 27 percent). Computers in Maori households are used predominantly for games (40 percent), followed by word processing (35 percent), Internet access (29 percent) and education/work (27 percent). Pacific island household computers are most extensively used for word processing (43 percent), followed by games (40 percent), education/work (35 percent) and Internet access (30 percent). Internet usage is equally spread between e-mail and web browsing for Europeans and 'other' ethnicities. For Maori respondents, web browsing exceeds e-mail usage.

Internet uptake for business use

Using population-based business e-mail and website listings, Howell (2001b) finds that businesses in the South Island use proportionately more e-mail than their North Island counterparts. Further, affluent provincial areas (e.g., Nelson and Marlborough) have higher e-mail use than their metropolitan counterparts (e.g., Auckland, Wellington). However, this does not carry through to website listings. This is consistent with higher costs of rural communications leading to earlier substitution of other methods of communication (e.g., phone, fax, physical mail, face to face) by e-mail, which has similar functionality (Madden et al., 2000). This is not true for websites, as the constrained format of website exchanges does not allow perfect substitution of other communication methods. While some components are substituted, websites cannot replicate the free form of exchange of a fax, physical mail, e-mail or phone call.

The Ministry of Economic Development (2000) reports high levels of New Zealand business Internet uptake, in many cases higher than comparable businesses (by size and sector) in Australia. Clark et al. (2001) focus more specifically on business applications using the Internet. Both studies find that e-mail is the most frequently used application (99.6 percent of businesses), followed by searching for information (98.4 percent) and sending and receiving files (95 percent). There is evidence of significant inter-firm transactions, with 55.6 percent purchasing supplies online and 47.7 percent using the Internet for competitor intelligence. Marketing is the next most predominant application (e.g., promotion 42.2 percent and market research 54.8 percent). Online training (19.8 percent) is the least-used application, probably due to greater effectiveness of face-to-face in-house training in smaller New Zealand businesses. Online sales to customers (23.5 percent) and businesses (24.1 percent) are also little used at present. However, as argued in Howell (2001c), the low level of online sales may be affected by both the small scale of New Zealand businesses, leading to a much later optimal time to invest in new technologies, and the degree of sophistication and maturity of the centralised bank clearing system, which provides a very cost-effective and efficient substitute for direct exchange between many companies.

The emphasis of these studies is predominantly upon the use of the Internet for online buying and selling. Yet, the overwhelming message of these statistics is that businesses already see the exchange of information to support all aspects of the operation of the business as the primary use of the connectivity offered by this technology. While streamlined, customised and standardised transactions online may offer further benefits (e.g., further savings of transaction costs), these should not overshadow the very real benefits that have already accrued from the extensive use of e-mail and websites. That New Zealand's use of these applications for business purposes exceeds that of Australia implies that the benefit to New Zealand has been commensurately greater on a per business basis.

14.7 PERFORMANCE

Howell (2001a) notes that information is both an input into production processes, leading directly to productivity gains, and a direct output of those processes, of which the consumption impacts should be measured. The economic properties of information – including its intangibility, non-rivalry, non-excludability and network effects – pose significant problems to determining reliable performance measures. Hence, traditional measures such as GDP per capita and GDP growth are not very helpful in deriving inter-country comparisons. Thus, it is more helpful to assess performance by the hypothesis that in the absence of any indication to the contrary, high levels of infrastructure uptake imply high levels of utilisation of electronic commerce applications in New Zealand.

New Zealand does provide evidence of high relative levels of electronic infrastructure connectivity, capability and uptake. Computer and Internet use is widespread. A sound telecommunications base, offering a variety of technologies (land based and wireless) at low prices (by OECD standards) and based upon unmetered tariffs, provides a foundation for the electronic communications required in a vibrant information-based economy. The strong telecommunications infrastructure supports levels of Internet connectivity that are among the highest in the world. Practically all measures of connectivity examined in this chapter lead those of Australia – New Zealand's closest neighbour and the country with a similar trading profile.

Strong levels of connectivity are supported by an equally high uptake of specific applications. Demand-driven uptake of applications such as EFTPOS and e-mail can be expected to result in a more efficient application of investment in technologies than if the availability of such applications, rather than user need and benefit, drives the uptake.

This is a consistent story. New Zealand has lower per person domestic usage of the Internet than Australia, but higher levels of individual access at work and other locations. If work-based access is utilised more in New Zealand, this rationalises the higher number of Internet hosts and domain names compared with Australia and promises higher business-related benefits. Uptake of specific business applications is dependent on the scale and scope of New Zealand businesses. The high levels of uptake compared to larger countries are even more remarkable given the disadvantages of scale and scope faced by businesses in a small, geographically isolated open economy. That New Zealand can provide services such as ISP connectivity at world-leading prices, and telephony services at competitive prices *vis-à-vis* other countries, despite these disadvantages, is to be applauded.

14.8   POLICY AND MANAGEMENT IMPLICATIONS

Just like its small rural South Island communities, New Zealand faces high communication costs due to being a small and distant economy. Hence New Zealand firms are expected to be early adopters of technologies that offer cheaper and more effective substitutes for communication. These should have already led to improved performance measures. However, to yield ongoing performance advantages, these levels of connectivity, capability and uptake must continue to exceed those of New Zealand's main trading partners. While the advantage over Australia appears to have been sustained over the period considered in this chapter, this advantage must also be sustained in relation to other trading partners.

Infrastructure is an important part of this sustained advantage. One challenge is to continue to build upon the infrastructure that has led to this world-leading state, and to continue to develop and utilise technologies and applications that support the use of information in creating value in businesses and in private lives. There is as yet little documented evidence that greater levels of telephony-based Internet access will lead to greater levels of Internet connectivity than New Zealand already enjoys (Howell, 2002).

However, infrastructure provides only the 'pipes' for carrying information, and as such provides only a temporary competitive advantage (Barney, 1995). Information remains the key. Sustainable competitive advantage comes from value created from the uptake of applications that use that information for producing the goods and services that will ultimately, through their sale and consumption, determine relative well being in a global economy. The main challenges facing businesses relate to choosing the optimal time to invest in new electronic and business system infrastructures that utilise and create information more efficiently. Substitution of new information content for old remains the key element in determining this investment strategy.

Policy makers face the challenge of maintaining and improving the infrastructure environment that has enabled New Zealand's current high ranking and relative advantage over Australia. Moreover, policy makers should also encourage efficient infrastructure use and efficient substitution of new methods of information processing for old. However, a focus on infrastructure policy alone is insufficient in addressing this challenge. Technology is an enabler, but economic value is ultimately added by the productive use of information. Learning to use the applications that take advantage of the new technology may be as important in stimulating economic advantage as availability of the technology itself (Howell and

Obren, 2002; Howell and Marriott, 2001). Moreover, attention to the environment in which information products (designs, biotechnology, etc.) are exchanged is also important. Policy emphasis should thus also concentrate upon competition law, property rights (copyright, trademarks and patents) and human information-processing capability (e.g., via the education system), rather than merely upon the 'pipes' that convey the information. For information alone is both necessary and sufficient for economic and social benefit creation.

NOTES

1. This chapter summarises a portfolio of work undertaken by various staff at ISCR since June 2000. The authors acknowledge the contributions of David Boles de Boer, Christina Enright Lewis Evans, Melinda Malloch, Matthew Morrison and Mark Obren to the development of this portfolio. Neil Quigley has provided helpful comments throughout this work, and Bob Stephens provided comments on an earlier version of this chapter. The authors also thank Jacques Poot for his editorial assistance, and an anonymous referee for comments, in the preparation of this chapter.
2. For a full list of works, see papers authored by David Boles de Boer, Christina Enright, Lewis Evans, Bronwyn Howell, Melinda Malloch, Lisa Marriott and Mark Obren in the References. All of these papers are available on the ISCR website, http://www.iscr.org.nz.
3. The source of these figures is OECD (2001) unless stated otherwise.
4. This is due in part to price regulation of domestic line rentals introduced upon the privatisation of Telecom in 1991, which specified a zero marginal cost of local calls.
5. The figures are obtained from surveys and reflect domestic usage patterns of 'surfing' by individuals, rather than targeted, specific usage of the Internet for business-related purposes.
6. A full analysis of the OECD broadband application uptake is contained in Howell (2002).
7. In terms of both the number of transactions and the number of terminals, EFTPOS usage in New Zealand is 'levelling off'. This implies that the technology is now quite mature and the ease of substitution of information for cash in retail purchasing is now ubiquitous.
8. These figures are based on sample survey data. Population counts can be obtained from the 2001 census.

REFERENCES

Alger, D. and J. Leung (1999), *The Relative Costs of Local Telephony Across Five Countries*, Wellington: ISCR. http://www.iscr.org.nz.

Barney, J. (1995), 'Looking inside for competitive advantage', *The Academy of Management Executive*, November.

Boles de Boer, D., Evans, L. and B. Howell (2000a) *Governance of the Internet: Emerging Issues*. Wellington: ISCR. http://www.iscr.org.nz.

Boles de Boer, D., Enright, C. and L. Evans (2000c), 'The performance of Internet service provider (ISP) markets of Australia and New Zealand', *Info*, 2, 487-495.

Boles de Boer, D., Evans, L. and B. Howell (2000b), *The State of e-New Zealand*, Wellington: ISCR. http://www.iscr.org.nz.

Clark, D., Bowden, S., Corner, P., Gibb, J., Kearins, K. and K. Pavlovich (2001), *Adoption and Implementation of E-Business in New Zealand: Empirical Results, 2001*, Hamilton: Department of Strategic Management & Leadership, University of Waikato Management School.

Evans, L. (2001), 'The New Economy: a force for competition or market power?', Paper presented to the PAFTAD Conference, Canberra, October.

Galbi, D. (2000), *Growth in the New Economy: U.S. Bandwidth Use and Pricing Across the 1990s*, Washington: Federation Communications Commission.

Goolsbee, A. (2000), 'The value of broadband and the deadweight loss of taxing new technology', Graduate School of Business Working Paper, University of Chicago.

Howell, B. (2001a), 'Information, technology and the productivity paradox', Paper presented at the PhD Conference in Economics and Business, Perth, Australia, November 7-9.

Howell, B. (2001b), 'The rural–urban digital divide in New Zealand: fact or fable?', *Prometheus*, 19, 231-251.

Howell, B. (2001c), *Scoping Report: e-Commerce Performance Measurement for New Zealand*, Wellington: ISCR. www.iscr.org.nz.

Howell, B. (2002), 'Broadband uptake and infrastructure regulation: evidence from the OECD countries', Wellington: ISCR. www.iscr.org.nz.

Howell, B. and L. Marriott (2001), *The State of e-New Zealand: 12 Months On,* Wellington: ISCR. http://www.iscr.org.nz.

Howell, B. and M. Obren (2002), 'Broadband diffusion', Paper for presentation at the 20th Annual International Communications Forecasting Conference, San Francisco, June 25-28.

Lehr, W. and L. McKnight (2000), 'A broadband access market framework: towards consumer level agreements', Paper presented at the 28th Annual Telecommunications Policy Research Conference, Alexandria, Virginia, September.

Madden, G., Savage, S., Coble-Neal, G. and P. Bloxham (2000), 'Advanced communications policy and adoption in rural Western Australia', *Telecommunications Policy*, 24, 291-304.

Ministry of Economic Development (2001), *Statistics on Information Technology in New Zealand 2001*, Wellington.

Ministry of Economic Development (2000), *Electronic Commerce in New Zealand: A Survey of Businesses on the Internet,* Wellington: Information Technology Policy Group, Competition and Enterprise Branch.

National Office for the Information Economy (NOIE) (2001), *The Current State of Play May 2001*, Canberra. http://noie.gov.au/.

Ministry of Economic Development (2002), 'Current statistics', Wellington. http://med.govt.nz/pbt/infotech/currentstats.

OECD Committee for Information, Computer and Communications Policy (1997), *Measuring Electronic Commerce*, OCDE/GD(97)185'. Paris: OECD. http://www.oecd.org/.

OECD Directorate for Science, Technology and Industry (2001), *Scoreboard 2001: Towards a Knowledge-Based Economy.* Paris: OECD. http://www.oecd.org/

OECD Directorate for Science, Technology and Industry Committee for Information (2000), *Local Access Pricing and E-Commerce*, Computer and Communications Policy Working Party on Telecommunications and Information Services Policies, Paris: OECD. http://www.oecd.org/.

OECD Information Society (2001), *Communications Outlook*, Paris: OECD. http://www.oecd.org/.

OECD Working Party on Telecommunications and Information Services Policies (1998), *Internet Infrastructure Indicators*, DSTI/ICCP/TISP(98)7. Paris: OECD. http://www.oecd.org/.

OECD Working Party on the Information Economy (2002), *OECD Information Technology Outlook: ICT's and the Information Economy*, Paris: OECD.

Office of Telecommunications (Oftel) (2002), *International Benchmarking Study of Fixed Line Services*, London: Director General of Telecommunications.

Statistics New Zealand (2001) *Census of Population and Dwellings 2001*, Wellington: Statistics New Zealand.

Shapiro, C. and H. Varian (1999), *Information Rules: A Strategic Guide to the Network Economy,* Boston, Mass.: Harvard Business School Press.

Te Puni Kokiri (2001), *Maori Access to Information Technology*, Wellington: Te Puni Kokiri.

Varaiya, P., Varian, H., Edell, R., Chu K. and W. Beckert (1999), 'INDEX: a status report,' Berkeley: EECS, SIMS at University of California.

Index